Designing
A Digital World

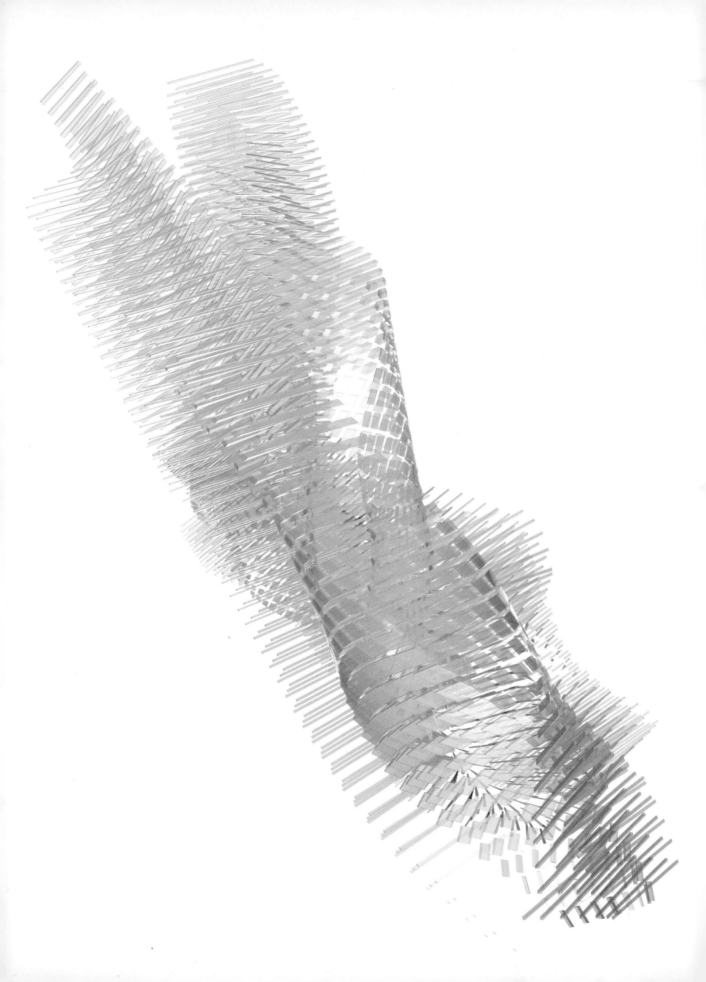

Designing For
A Digital World

Edited by Neil Leach

WILEY-ACADEMY

Produced in association
with RIBA Future Studies

Acknowledgements

This volume is based on the conference E-Futures:
Designing for a Digital World, held at the RIBA, London,
on 4 June 2001. The conference was organized under
the auspices of RIBA Future Studies, an interdisciplinary
think-tank whose task is to target concerns likely to
affect the future of the profession of architecture,
and to provide a forum for informed predictions about
those concerns. I am extremely grateful to all those
who helped to organize this event, but special thanks
must go to Claire McCoy, Secretary of RIBA Future
Studies, for her energetic and highly professional support,
and to Russell Brown, Chairman of RIBA Future Studies,
for his unwavering enthusiasm for the project.
All images are reproduced courtesy of their originators,
noted in the captions.

Cover Illustration and Section Dividers: 'Upgraded
Landscape' by Alisa Andrasek in collaboration with
Gernot Riether.

Photographs on pages 16, 50, 65, 117, 127 and 142-4 are by David Purdie,
reproduced with permission.

First published in Great Britain in 2002 by
WILEY-ACADEMY

A division of
JOHN WILEY & SONS
Baffins Lane
Chichester
West Sussex PO19 1UD

ISBN: 0-470-84419-1

Design: Neil Pereira
Printed and bound in Italy.

Produced in association with RIBA Future Studies
www.riba-futurestudies.com

CONTENTS

INTRODUCTION
Neil Leach

This volume attempts to address a new paradigm, a condition in which digital technologies have started to have a significant impact on the ways in which we live and work. For so long much debate about the potential of these technologies has operated within the realms of visionary speculation, as though it were a branch of science fiction. Recent developments, however, have caused us to rethink that outlook. The demise of various hi-tech shares on the stock exchange has taught us that operations within the digital realm – however seemingly novel and exciting – will have no value unless they impact directly upon the material world. At the same time, the ways in which digital technologies are actually influencing that world are becoming increasingly recognisable. Working practices, social interaction and many other facets of contemporary life have been radically changed. The world is becoming digitalised. But how is this changing the discipline of architecture? And what are the lessons for the future?

This volume brings together some of the world's leading voices from cultural theory, technology and design. It offers a snapshot of informed opinion at a crucial juncture in the history of the interface between the discipline of architecture and digital technologies. In so doing it also provides a glimpse of some of the emerging ideas and cutting edge practices that are likely to be setting the pace for the future. But although the volume offers a preview of a possible future world, it is grounded in actual practices which are already taking place. It addresses the concrete impact that digital technologies are already having on our everyday lives. In this sense, the volume is as much about the present as it is about the future; as much about the e-present, as it is about e-futures.

Below: Spela Videcnik and Rok Oman, housing project, Graz, Austria

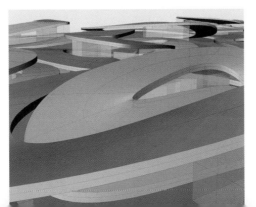

Digital Culture

Bill Gates has predicted that the present decade will be known as 'The Digital Decade' in that, by the time that it comes to an end, the impact of the digital realm will have been so far-reaching that scarcely any facet of human existence will remain untouched by it. There will have been a digital revolution. Douglas Rushkoff prefers to describe this development in terms of a 'renaissance'. Less nihilistic than a 'revolution', according to Rushkoff, this process reconfigures the ways in which we experience our realities. Throughout history there have been many such paradigm shifts – 'renaissance moments' – when the narratives by which we relate to the world enter a state of flux and indeterminacy, as we adapt to new technological conditions. These are moments when, as Rushkoff puts it, 'we pull out of a particular story long enough to consider the way in which it is being told'. The potential of any such moments is that they can be enabling and lead to an 'open source reality'. Rather than simply eulogising the potential impact of digital technologies, we must take charge of them. What needs to be negotiated, according to Rushkoff, is a way of engaging with that new paradigm so as to make it work for human beings, instead of allowing it to be co-opted to serve the vested interests of big business.

This state of fluidity and flux has colonised even the realm of identity. The development of online *personae*, as Sherry Turkle has argued, has led to a condition that enhances the performativity at the heart of cultural life today, and encourages a fluid and dynamic play of identity that ascribes to the emerging culture of theming and role-playing.[1] Interactions in cyberspace may serve as a tool for thinking about how identity is constituted today. 'When [people] log on,' Turkle notes, 'they may find themselves playing multiple roles, they may find themselves playing characters of the opposite sex. In this way they are swept up by experiences that enable them to explore previously unexamined aspects of their sexuality or that challenge their ideas about a unitary self.'[2] These technologies do not merely reflect prevailing conditions. They act as a catalyst in promoting them. New technologies breed new ways of thinking. Our lives are being changed. As Mark Goulthorpe puts it: 'The digital revolution… marks a profound realignment of our base categories of thought, our relation to memory, our *cultural* aptitude.' Digital technologies are spawning a Digital Culture.

But this Digital Culture has not been universally welcomed, especially by the older generation. Significantly, as Rushkoff points out, it is kids who have the greatest capacity to assimilate and adapt to it, and to grasp its potential.[3] On the whole, the younger generation is perfectly at ease with these new technologies, and − as is no doubt obvious to most parents − has come to treat them as a kind of prosthesis to the human body, and to absorb them into their operational methods like some second nature. All this should lead us to rethink the relationship between humankind and technology, and to challenge the antipathy towards the computer still evident in certain schools of architecture. What has become obvious is that nothing is alienating for ever. Human beings adapt. They are chameleon-like creatures, seemingly programmed to survive, who can assimilate to ever new conditions. As I argue in my own contribution, we therefore need to move beyond the old suspicion, emanating from a Heideggerian way of thinking, that technology − and more especially *digital* technology − is and always will be the perpetual source of alienation.

This sense of adaptation to new conditions is what informs Sarah Chaplin's exploration of cybervisuality. Here she argues that the dominant Western condition of ocularcentrism has mutated into a computer-mediated cybervisuality. Just as Walter Benjamin had argued that in an age of the camera human beings had come to view the world *in terms of* the camera − hence the various photographic allusions, such as the 'snapshot', that pepper his own writing − Chaplin argues that in an age of the computer we have come to view our world *in terms of* the computer. This has caused a fundamental shift in the ways in which we see the world. Thus, not only do we find operations within the digital realm mimicking those in the analogue, but the whole world of the analogue is mediated through − and enhanced by − our experience of

the digital realm. As an example of this, Chaplin offers the evocative illustration of the simulated trip to the top of the Empire State Building in New York, which is packaged together with the actual trip, so that it 'heightens the experience of the real city'.

It is important, however, to maintain a critical attitude towards the digital domain, and not to descend into some empty panegyric. Richard Coyne questions the more extravagant claims made for its potentialities. Often viewed in an abstract, reductivist or totalising fashion, some unreasonable expectations have been projected on to it. Seen in this light, it is bound to fail. Still worse, far from improving the world, it may even exacerbate existing deficiencies. Nonetheless, the digital domain does hold out the promise of the 'not yet' − of a better future. But rather than trying to justify that potential in instrumental terms or positing it as a utopian ideal, gasping at it 'in breathless wonder', a more effective strategy might be to focus on its *suggestive* potential. Like science fiction, speculative digital work can provoke us to rethink the possibilities of the future by challenging the givenness of the present.

Digital Cities

While much business and social interaction will soon have been displaced to the *digital* realm, it will have a reciprocal effect upon the *physical* realm, and will have a concrete impact on the material fabric of our cities. For example, we need only consider the fleets of vans delivering online purchases now beginning to proliferate everywhere, especially in places like LA, to realise that e-commerce is leading to shifts in traffic patterns, the establishment of new warehousing facilities, and changing shopping habits. Yet, equally, the qualified survival of physical shops points to the very complex interaction that exists between the digital and the material domain. Human beings will always want to have recourse to materiality. Indeed, it could be argued that the more immaterial our lives become, the greater our corresponding desire for a material world. In some sense, far from undermining our interest in material reality, e-commerce − and indeed the whole domain of

Above: Oliver Bertran, Jan Henrik Mansen, Reinhard Prikoszovich and Thomas von Pufendorf in association with Greg Lynn and Marcelyn Gow, *Stripes* project ('Machinic Processes in Architectural Design')

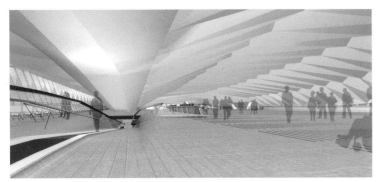

Above: Foreign Office Architects, Port Terminal, Yokohama, Japan

Below right: Lars Spuybroek, installation, Nantes, France

the digital – can be seen to be enhancing it. To borrow one of the conclusions from a recent conference, it is not a question of 'bricks *versus* clicks', so much as 'bricks *and* clicks'.[4]

These concerns are precisely those which ground Bill Mitchell's investigations into the impact of digital technologies on the urban realm – 'urban life, Jim, but not as we know it'. Mitchell offers a helpful overview of this complex interaction. The advent of the digital revolution, he notes, does not lead to a complete liberation from material constraints. Rather, the selective 'loosening' of spatial and temporal restrictions engenders a 'fragmentation and recombination' of existing patterns of land use. The relations between home and the work space can be reconfigured, while there will be a 'revenge of place', as choice of location takes precedence over physical accessibility. And in specific circumstances the precise requirements of industry to cluster around enhanced electronic communications centres will lead to a 'tunnel effect' – such as that between the post-production film facilities in Soho, London, and film studios in Hollywood – whereby certain key locations are hooked up on some information superhighway to other communications 'hot-spots' around the globe.

The experimental digital artists Yvonne Wilhelm, Christian Huebler and Andreas Broeckmann, who comprise Knowbotic Research, show how the digital domain can open up and reveal the potentialities of the material city. Their experimental reappropriation of the city comes across as a form of updated Situationism of the digital age, subverting hegemonic conditions, and opening up new terrains of participation. Their *10_dencies* projects focus on interactive user participation, not as a way of modifying the physical form of the city, but in order 'to create events through which it becomes possible to rethink urban planning and construction.[5] They see the city in

Deleuzian terms as a 'field', a network of processes, 'a complex machine, consisting of multidirectional processes of connection and separation, of layering, enmeshing and cutting, which leads to ever different formations.'[6] Through their work, Knowbotic Research investigates how the extension of the urban environment into 'electronic spaces' might allow for 'changed qualities of urbanity', that serves to highlight differentiation, and counter the homogenising shift towards the Generic City.

Digital technologies can be an important catalyst for social revolutions within the urban realm. This is not limited to First World cultures. As Sadie Plant describes, the internet and other hi-tech systems of communication have had a major impact on even the most traditional of cultures, often in a very liberating way. Plant analyses how the advent of the internet in the city of Peshawar, Pakistan, has opened up access to educational and political information in a society still otherwise constrained by repressive social customs. The mobile phone has also had a significant impact on social life, just as the static phone had in the past. In providing instantaneous communication, not bound by physical location, it has opened up new ways of operating within the public realm. The recent example in the Philippines, where protesters used text messaging in order to mobilise a political demonstration almost instantaneously, illustrates how the mobile phone opens up a new spatial dynamic to political life in the city.

However, as Andrew Gillespie argues, the effect of digital technologies on the urban realm has not always been positive. Rather than contributing – as environmentalists might hope – to a more sustainable city, or leading –

as planners might hope – to an urban renaissance, they often serve merely to exacerbate existing trends, and further to polarise social imbalances. Gillespie offers a dystopian vision of a proliferation of suburban call-centres developed to service these technologies, which only reinforce the already dominant shift in social life from the city centre towards the periphery, and do little to reduce traffic. Gillespie's thorough research into the actualities of the digital city serves to challenge much of the euphoric utopianism that so characterised early writing within the digital domain. He also draws attention to the failure of the planning profession to address the advent of digital technologies in any meaningful way. 'Planners,' he argues, 'have yet to develop the awareness, let alone the expertise or appropriate policy intervention mechanisms, that would enable them to influence the spatial development of a digital society.'

David Turnbull picks up on similar concerns in his portrait of the emerging 'genetically modified city'. Whereas there has been significant public concern over the development of genetically modified crops and genetically engineered animals – and even the threat of genetically engineered human beings – hi-tech modifications to the city through hi-tech advances have passed by without much critical comment. Indeed, if anything, the proliferation of 'silicon-based' conurbations is often celebrated as a mark of economic progress. But what kind of urbanism are they producing? Turnbull highlights the problems of these new patterns of urbanism, often characterised by a bland 'degree zero architecture'. These are atopias that are quite different from the fabric of the traditional urban landscape. They raise new problems that require new solutions.

Digital Tectonics

Within the discipline of architecture the impact of this new paradigm has been especially marked. For some time now various architects have been exploring the potentialities of the digital domain. This has led to some exciting visual imagery that has hitherto remained confined largely to the utopian world of the screen. Within architectural schools such as Columbia University, New York, which was one of those to lead the way in the early explorations in this field, this 'free invention' – as it

was seen by its critics – spawned a critical counter-culture of 'tectonics' that is perhaps best articulated by commentators such as Kenneth Frampton.[7] Architecture, according to this viewpoint, is a question of building, and forms generated on the screen are just utopian fantasies if they do not conform to the tectonic requirements of the real world. And indeed these critics may have a point. There is a big difference between designing a building according to the algorithmic potential of software programs and the tectonic parameters of actual building materials.

There comes a time, however, when those architects experimenting at the very forefront of digital design begin to realise their designs in a material world. Here we might point to much of the design work featured in this volume, work which seems to take its inspiration from the new territories of formal exploration opened up by the digital realm, but which is directed ultimately towards realisation in the material world. The old opposition of 'tectonics *versus* digital design' has given way to a new tectonics *of* digital design. And, of course, architects are not the only members of the construction team to benefit from advances afforded by the computer. Everyone has been affected by the possibilities of digitally modelling the performance of a building, especially structural engineers. Software programs are allowing engineers to understand

in far more detail the stresses and strains of surface tectonics. The collaboration between engineers like Cecil Balmond and various avant-garde architects is helping to generate a new language of architectural form. The whole construction team has entered a new paradigm. It is no longer a question of the digital *versus* the material, but of the digital *in the service of* the material.

Eventually the sheer volume of work produced in this mode will bring about a new way of thinking about architecture. But it is only when a building of major significance – such as

Top: Marcelyn Gow, Urbantoys project

Above: Formal Study, Mark Goulthorpe

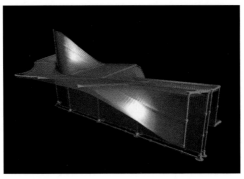

This page: Theo Lorenz and Anna Sutor, deforming partitions, Learning Environments

Jorn Utzon's Sydney Opera House or Frank Gehry's Guggenheim Museum in Bilbao, Spain – has been completed that the experimental work of the avant-garde is recognised by the general public. In this respect the construction of major projects, such as the competition-winning design for the Yokohama Ferry Terminal in Japan by Foreign Office Architects, marks a crucial moment in the interface between digital technologies and the realm of architecture. Farshid Moussavi and Alejandro Zaera Polo of Foreign Office Architects describe their rollercoaster ride in translating this project from the digital realm into a physical one. It is only through the computer's sophisticated operations that the building's complex mutating form could be effectively described. Their design for the ferry terminal folds programmatic, constructional and structural concerns into a single formal expression. Yet in order to resolve the complex interplay between these concerns, the profile of the building needed to be explored on the computer through an ever more finely calibrated series of sections. This project was not only *born of* the digital – it was also *realised through* the digital.

At the opposite end of the spectrum, we might point to the exquisitely tooled formal explorations led by Greg Lynn and Marcelyn Gow, using computer-numerically-controlled (CNC) milling processes. These rapid processing experiments demonstrate a form of modelling that is surely to be adopted more widely within the construction industry. For the computer can be used not only to calculate and 'tool' up individual building components, as happened with the Guggenheim Museum in Bilbao, but also to help fabricate individual formal studies that feed into stage one of the design process. Just as the pen and parallel motion have given way to the cursor and the VDU screen, so the scalpel and cardboard model are beginning to give way to computer-linked machinic processes.

The computer, through its capacity to clone, warp, tweak, map, rotate, distort and perform other related operations, has contributed to the emergence of new modes of formal expression. So, too, the potential to plot a design in three dimensions and generate perspective views, 'fly-throughs' and so on, has shifted the emphasis away from plan, section and elevation, towards a more cinematic and animated way of understanding a building. But perhaps the most exciting recent development afforded by the computer has been the introduction of the genetic algorithm into architectural design. This can produce extraordinary results in the hands of talented designers. As Manuel DeLanda explains, the process involves the adaptation and translation of computer simulations of evolutionary processes in biology into the domain of architecture. This allows architects to 'breed' forms, and adapt their role from being form makers to decision makers within an organisational process. Of course, such an approach needs to be integrated with an understanding of the structural properties of form, and a further component in this process must be an awareness of stresses and strains. So too, as DeLanda points out, one has to take account of 'populational, intensive and topological' thinking before any such experimentation – fascinating as it might be – approaches the definition of architecture.

In his wetGRID 'Vision Machine' gallery installation in Nantes, Lars Spuybroek uses the capacity of the computer as a 'self-choreographing machine' to introduce vortex forces in the initial part of the design process, relying on software programs used in the film industry for simulating tornadoes. In this sense his approach is quite different to the standard design procedure of working from drawing a diagram to materialising form, in that the computer is used as an animating engine, and is integral to the process of generating form. The end result is one that responds to the motility at the heart of human perception. Spuybroek describes this design strategy in terms of the liquid-crystal state of the 'wet-grid', as the structural authority of the grid gives way to the self-organising principles of the network. This is a condition controlled not by some abstract imposed order but by 'material interactions', to create a form of order 'on the edge of chaos'. Spuybroek sees this not so much as an in-between state, but as higher form of order partaking of both the structural coherence of the crystal and the fluid dynamism of liquid.

A similar approach is found in the work of Mark Goulthorpe who claims that we have entered a stage which he compares to a *smectic* state – the liquid-crystal condition between solid and fluid, where molecules begin not just to link up, but also to form patterns. For Goulthorpe this is a traumatic condition, where certainties are dissolved, and where matter is given over to 'rapid, almost convulsive fluctuation', and gripped by flickering impulses that pitch us into a sort of 'shoal-of-fish' mentality. This state of indeterminacy has engendered a new way of relating to the environment. There has been a shift, for Goulthorpe, from an *autoplastic* fixed relation between the self and the environment to an *alloplastic* one of fluidity and flux.

This has been articulated through the emergence of physical forms programmed to adapt to the presence and movement of users. One example is Goulthorpe's own *Aegis* project, which responds to sound and movement to create an animated interactive surface, controlled by pistons responding to real-time events. Another example is Hani Rashid's *FluxSpace* projects. The first of these responds to physical presence through wireframe assemblies projected on to a gallery, and the second by a pneumatically controlled air-filled envelope, whose ever-mutating form is relayed on to the Web. Both Goulthorpe and Rashid use digital technologies as a way of augmenting our experience of physical spaces.

This *alloplastic* dimension takes on a more product-oriented expression with the operational design method of *servo*'s 'Urbantoys' project. Here the design interface is brought forward to the potential user, who is able to manipulate and reconfigure the proposed furniture within a given set of spatial variables and formal parameters. Not only does this 'purveyance' system help to trigger a new set of consumer desires, but it reconfigures the relationship between consumer, designer and manufacturer into a dynamic and non-conflictual collaboration. Furthermore, by allowing the environment to be reconfigured – whether intentionally or otherwise – by the user, such design interfaces serve to break down the opposition between users and their environment.

As a further extension of this, Patrik Schumacher analyses the potential of interactive robotic forms to help facilitate the programmatic operations of corporeal organisations. Here furniture is viewed as part of the dynamic landscape of the office, which through its capacity to self-organise makes possible new spatial connectivities. It has an emancipatory role in helping to break down command and control structures into a more open and less determined environment. Schumacher proposes a series of interactive solutions ranging from dynamic spatial reconfigurations, where the boundary between furniture and architecture becomes blurred, to animated robotic creatures that mutate into workstations and other facilities, and cluster into self-organising assemblages, thus inviting various patterns of colonisation on the part of the user.

What unites all these variations is the notion, as Goulthorpe puts it, that these forms have

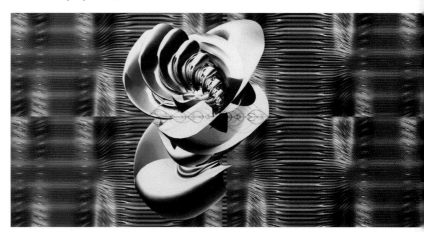

been '*born*' digitally, and not '*designed*' according to the conventional understanding of the term. We are witnessing a new generation of designers operating within the digital domain, who are not simply using these technologies as a sophisticated tool for testing out designs conceived in a more traditional paradigm, or as a technique for assisting in constructional calculations, but rather as a medium through which to pursue design itself.

Above: Karl S Chu, *X_Phylum*

Digital Realities

'For the first time in history,' notes Karl Chu, 'we are now entering into a completely artificial space, a parallel universe.' In contrast to the analogue world where architecture has always operated as a form of 'machinic *in vivo*', as a mechanism 'for territorialisation and colonisation that alters the biography of the surface culture of Earth', we are now encountering a parallel digital realm of simulation, where architecture may operate *in vitro*, 'inside the simulated glass of cyberspace or virtual reality'. Chu's own design work, utilising genetic algorithms to 'grow' forms, provides a good example of this *in vitro* experimentation.

Chu conjures up an image of what he calls the new 'Hyperzoic Paradigm' of 'demiurgic capitalism', where these two spheres of the *in vivo* and the *in vitro* begin to interact. This is a technological world that has not been severed from the biological or natural world, but rather reinvested with its potential. It is, moreover, an animated, seemingly enchanted world. On the one hand, capitalism has been exposed as a quasi-religious demiurgic force. On the other hand, the creative matrix of the universe – the origin of life – is being decoded such that biogenetics itself has come to overlap with other, more theological, explanations of the origin of the universe. The realms of computation and biogenetics have come together in a productive synthesis under the conditions of capitalism to create a new state: a cosmocapital organism.

But how are we to understand this 'parallel universe'? Chu evokes the principle of 'simulation'. Certainly, one way to figure these virtual operations would be through Jean Baudrillard's deliberations on hyperreality. The simulation of digital environments echoes the simulation of hyperreality. If, as Baudrillard claims, hyperreality marks that moment when a world of the image has become so detached from any point of reference in the 'real' world that it now constitutes an autonomous form of reality, might not virtual

reality itself also be understood as a parallel structure of reality, remote from the first order reality yet equally structuring a whole other system of ideas? For Chu, however, we need to search for a model 'infinitely more intense and variable than Baudrillard's exposition'. Moreover, far from detaching this simulation from reality, Chu sees this 'parallel universe' as the very key to our own 'reality'. 'Simulation of reality,' he notes, 'can now be understood as forming part of the search for theory concerning the Real.' In this sense, Chu provides a powerful riposte to positivistic outlooks which seek to denigrate the realm of simulation, and champion instead some supposedly 'authentic' realm of the real.

There can be no 'authentic' reality, since 'authenticity' is itself nothing more than a projection. No matter how 'real' the world may seem, all perception must remain a 'construction' – a negotiation between hard objective materialities and the 'gloss' of subjective interpretation. Virtual reality helps to expose this, no less than Disneyland helps to expose the simulated nature of tourism today.[8] Disneyfication is not limited to Disneyland. It has become a universal phenomenon.[9] As such, we might even go so far as to ask – in line with Slavoj Žižek – whether the lesson of virtual reality might not be that the 'real' has always been in some senses 'virtual', so that even traditional discourses of 'reality' are compromised, since, as Žižek observes, there is nothing that we perceive which is not already mediated – 'filtered' through the imagination. According to this argument, it is not that we have lost touch with 'reality' in our hyperreal world. Rather, we never had access to that 'reality' in the first place. But whether reality has always been virtualised (as Žižek would argue) or the virtual has begun to constitute its own variation of the 'real' (as Chu might maintain), it is clear that there has been an effacement of the distinction between 'reality' and the simulation of a digital environment. The one folds into and informs the other.

In this context it is worth reflecting upon another aspect to the digital realm, one which remains decidedly immaterial, and yet which is also having a crucial impact on the material realm. This is the development of new 'parallel practices' that have been set up by offices such as Asymptote, UN Studio and AMO, the digital branch of OMA. These practices, initiated by

Below: Hani Rashid, Guggenheim Virtual Museum

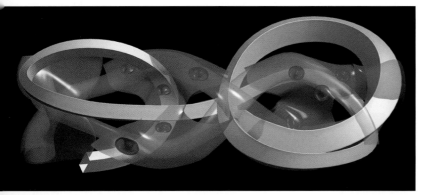

projects such as Asymptote's informational model for the New York Stock Exchange, bring a new meaning to the digital realm.[10] The Virtual Guggenheim Museum project, in particular – in essence a 3D interactive interface for the Guggenheim 'virtual' collections – where users navigate their way through fluid and morphing digital 'landscapes' rather than click their way through pages, reveals a whole new terrain of potential work within the architectural office. It is one to which architects are eminently suited because they have always been designers of imaginary spaces. One thinks here of the vital tradition within architectural culture of utopian projects – from Piranesi to Boullée to Lebbeus Woods and beyond – that has 'shadowed' the development of architecture in the physical realm.

And yet these practices are not completely divorced from the material world. They feed back into a physical realm. Asymptote's New York Stock Exchange project led directly to the actual fabrication of a material space. Meanwhile the Virtual Guggenheim Museum project serves as an indirect reference to various material Guggenheim museums, much as advertisements *refer to* material items of consumption. In a 'promotional culture', as Andrew Wernick has described it, the parallel world of the image serves to 'promote' the physical world.[11] But this process may operate in both directions. There is a reciprocity between the two domains, and, as with the case of advertising, memories of an advertisement– a catchy jingle, a striking image, a witty comment – carry forward and influence our understanding of the material domain, just as memories of the motility of the body inform our navigation of the digital domain. AMO and UN Studio exploit this interface to some considerable effect. Their digital work for Prada and Skim.com respectively is linked to designs for material shops. What this highlights is how these two domains support one another. The digital feeds off the material, no less than the material feeds off the digital.

Traditionally architects have focused almost exclusively on the material world, conceiving of architecture within the limited spectrum of 'built' construction. It is time, perhaps, to expand this outlook, and renegotiate the territory of the architect. Architects – in their traditional mould – have become an endangered species. The

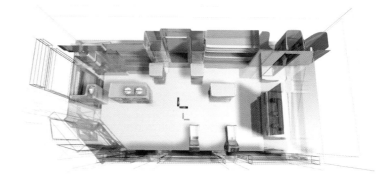

Above: UN Studio, skim.com, shop interior

profession of architecture has come under threat, as developers, builders, surveyors and others have colonised the space once reserved exclusively for it. A common response to this threat has been a form of indignation, and a sentimental appeal to the restoration of the primacy of the architect by reigniting traditional values. Such a response is inevitably doomed to failure in a culture whose values have themselves mutated.

A better strategy might be to follow the example of Asymptote, UN Studio and AMO, and be proactive in expanding the field of architectural enterprise into new territories, such as the digital realm. Indeed, one can envisage a time in the not too distant future – as soon as online informational systems have increased their capacity and speed of operations – when websites such as Amazon.com will no longer be 2D scroll down lists and click through pages, but 3D interactive 'fly through' spaces. And who better to design these spaces than architects? The emergence of these parallel practices reveals a new field of operations for architects. It may not be long before a substantial percentage of architectural graduates moves into this realm, and perhaps it is time to think through the ramifications of this for the future of not only our educational system, but also our whole architectural framework.

The answer, as Jeffrey Inaba observes, is not to speculate idly about the future, but to plan for the 'now', and to undertake thorough research in order to recognise emerging trends. But to plan for the 'now' is not to remain locked into some obsolete paradigm of the past. Rather it is to continually renegotiate and interrogate one's position, and to respond afresh each time to the challenges of the moment. Digital technologies offer one such challenge. It is time to respond to that challenge.

Notes

1 Sherry Turkle, *Life on the Screen*. New York: Simon & Schuster, 1995. See also Marc Augé, *A War of Dreams*, trans. Liz Heron. London: Pluto, 1999; Judith Butler, *Bodies that Matter*. London: Routledge, 1995.

2 See Sherry Turkle, 'Cyberspace and Identity'. In *Contemporary Sociology* 28, November 1999, pp. 643–648.

3 Douglas Rushkoff, *Children of Chaos*. London: Flamingo, 1997.

4 Simon Marvin, Andrew Gillespie and Nick Green, 'Bricks versus clicks: Planning for the digital economy'. In James Wilsdon (Ed.) *Digital Futures: Living in a Dot-Com World*. London: Earthscan, 2001 pp. 200-218.

5 See p. 58.

6 See p. 60.

7 Kenneth Frampton, *Tectonic Culture*. Camb., MA: MIT Press, 1996.

8 Neil Leach, *The Anaesthetics of Architecture*. Camb., MA: MIT Press, 1999, pp.3–4.

9 Neil Leach, *Millennium Culture*. London: Ellipsis, 1999, pp.32–33.

10 We should perhaps be cautious of using the expression 'virtual reality', especially in the Deleuzian sense of that which has yet to be realised. The term 'virtual' implies a denigration of that realm – an 'almost' reality. Even Hani Rashid's otherwise useful term, 'second order reality', implies a hierarchy of realities. Meanwhile the very term 'reality' must be treated with extreme caution. As such the 'digital realm' is a far more satisfactory term than 'virtual reality'.

11 Andrew Wernick, *Promotional Culture*. London: Sage, 1991.

DIGITAL CULTURE

THE DIGITAL RENAISSANCE
Douglas Rushkoff

So often we hear people using the word 'revolution' to describe the current overwhelming cultural shift fostered by technology and new media. However overwhelming it might be, can we really describe the current transition as a revolution? For me, the word 'revolution' evokes images of a violent upheaval and guillotined heads. There's certainly very little progress implied by revolution; it's simply someone spinning around in circles.

Digital culture may be marginally revolutionary in the sense that it is characterised by what so many companies and institutions have called 'thinking outside the box' – a willingness to challenge conventions and consider meta-narratives. But this notion of thinking outside the box and gaining perspective is not simply moving in a circle. We are coming to a new understanding of what had always been considered literal reality: we are seeing it instead as a picture of reality. Our new tools are also leading us to feel empowered enough to adjust the frame around that picture. Such an upscaling of perception, intention, and design is better described as a 'renaissance'.

Literally 'renaissance' means the rebirth of old ideas in a new context. It is a reconfiguring of the constructed ways we experience the world in order to reconnect with it, and the adaptation of our cultural lenses to conform to our changing vision. In the original Renaissance, a number of discoveries and inventions changed our most basic experience of the real. Perspective painting allowed us to create representations of reality that simulated dimensionality. The discovery that the world is round and the ability to circumnavigate it radically redefined our notion of space and our sense of agency. Furthermore, the development of calculus allowed us to relate planes to spheres and spheres to four-dimensional fictional objects, performing conceptual calculations never before possible. The printing press allowed the widespread distribution of ideas and data, connecting people in expanded social and political communities. The first signs of globalisation and the resulting cross-cultural pollination emerged. Coffee from Morocco, which began trickling over to Europe during the next century, encouraged people to stay up late at night and talk, giving rise to a 'bohemian' culture and the Enlightenment, which were dedicated to challenging conventional models of reality through new perspectives.

The late twentieth century brought discoveries and inventions, the collective impact of which could be considered a renaissance of at least equal magnitude. While perspective painting allowed Renaissance artists to create two-dimensional images, the holograph now allows us to create three-dimensional representations that approximate our vision even more closely. By manipulating the laws of perspective, some Renaissance painters created deliberately skewed or 'trick' representations of reality, challenging the reliability of our vision and suggesting the possibility that illusion exists in reality as well. The mechanics of the holograph offer a similar challenge, because when a holographic plate is shattered into many pieces, the image is not fragmented. Each shard of the plate contains a smaller image of the entire original, suggesting that fractal relationships may underlie many of our illusions as well as much of our reality. The underlying technology of holographs further extends our understanding of dimensionality, and has been used to understand everything from society to brain anatomy.

While Renaissance explorers discovered that the world was round, modern scientists discovered atomic energy and took us to the Moon. Having already mastered the Earth through exploration, we were now able to explore beyond it, to see it as an object from another position in space, and even to destroy it. Meanwhile, chaos maths and systems theory opened up complex conceptual possibilities in much the same way that calculus had for Renaissance mathematicians.

The computer and the internet changed communication, publication and the idea of community to a degree comparable with the printing press. LSD and psychedelics, like the coffee beans of the Renaissance, had people staying up late together and experimenting with the status quo.

A renaissance is a shift in perspective, the shift from living within a model to moving outside of it; or, as video gamers might express it, from game to 'meta-game'. Young people who spend a lot of time immersed in video game environments understand this phenomenon well. There are two ways one can learn to play a game. The first is to read the rules, practise, and use old-fashioned trial-and-error. The second is to find the magazines and websites that share the secret codes to help one avoid traps, win levels and gain special advantages in the game. Are the people using these 'cheat sheets' really playing the game? Certainly, but the game they're playing is the meta-game.

Likewise, there are moments when we, as society, as a culture, or even as individuals, shift from simply playing the game by the rules to playing the meta-game and changing the rules. These are renaissance moments. Renaissance moments happen when we experience a shift in perspective so that the stories, models and languages that we have been using to understand our reality are suddenly up for grabs. But these renaissance moments are transitory, because almost as soon as our perspectives are shifted, we settle into new conventions. Alas, the possibilities opened by our new perspective close up, and we once again mistake the map for the territory. We forget that the new stories and metaphors we have developed are just that, and we mistake them for literal history.

But before things have been locked down, ideas compete for consensus. The challenge, and the opportunity, during these moments is to make a positive impact in that struggle. For me, this means preserving the notion that the ideas that win consensus approval may be useful, but they are still arbitrary.

I would argue that we are currently in a time of renaissance, still in the process of assimilating the results of a shift in perspective caused by remarkable technological progress. We are still aware that the shift is going on, and hoping to preserve some aspect of our new-found sensitivity into the next phase of human society. It's akin to the realisation many people have in the heightened state of awareness caused by a mystical or psychedelic experience: the person on his visionquest wonders how he will be able to remember that state of awe or insight once the experience is over. He wonders how he can plant a seed or landmark of some kind that

he will remember when he returns to waking state consciousness.

Likewise, those of us aware of the power of the current renaissance are attempting to preserve and extend the notion that much of reality itself is open source, and that the 'codes' by which we organise our experiences are more accessible than we generally assume. For artists, cultural producers and, of course, architects, there is an imperative to influence what will become the new consensus, and to mark it with a sense of possibility that will help us maintain a sense of agency over our own collective and individual perspectives.

A lucky beneficiary of the digital renaissance, I have been encouraged to believe that our reality is, indeed, open source — or at least that much of what we have been regarding as permanent 'hardware' is, indeed, only 'software' and subject to change. For me, the most important insight of cyberculture is that we all have access to its codes; we are all potential reality-programmers.

Media is the realm in which our access is negotiated. I used to stay up nights wondering: what is media? It was a perplexing question. A zipper is media; open, it means one thing and closed, another. A face is media; we read people's appearance and expressions for information about them. Even our DNA is media, arguably the best media nature has developed, capable of sending codes through the millennia. Ultimately, the only thing that isn't media is a person's most essential consciousness — one's agency, will and intention. As consciousnesses swimming in media, we create and control narratives to negotiate reality and our places within it. Through competing stories we can negotiate over 'what' is going on. But by making up rules and creating tools through which those stories will be told, we negotiate about the 'how', the meta-story.

Renaissances are, in part, the moments when we pull out of a particular story for long enough to consider the way in which it is being told.

The game and the meta-game, the stories and the way stories are told, have largely been regulated and controlled for the last few centuries.

As Aristotle well understood, stories work by creating a character whom the audience likes and having that character make a series of decisions which put him in terrible danger. This brings the audience into a heightened state of tension about this poor character who has made all these wrong decisions. Then, once the audience can't take it any more, the storyteller invents a solution. In a Greek play that solution might have been Athena coming down to save the day.

This same storytelling technique has been honed for centuries, and perhaps has been perfected by the advertising industry which has exploited the mainstream mediaspace for its ability to tell very influential little stories called commercials. In 28 seconds, we identify with an aggravated executive, following him into his hellish day, up the incline plane of tension. Because we are a captive audience, with no access to the tools of storytelling, we must take that pain-relieving pill with him at the end of the commercial to relieve our anxiety. The storyteller chooses which pill the listener has to swallow at the end of the story – whether it is a new president or an old religion.

Cyber culture, based on an ethic of interactivity, releases the captive audience from the spell of the story and offers them the opportunity for active participation instead.

The television remote control represented the first in a series of liberating interactive technologies. Imagine a man sitting in his La-Z-Boy chair in 1958, with popcorn on his lap, watching a painful commercial. The TV programmer is dead-set on throwing this poor man into a terrible state of anxiety. If the viewer wants to get out of that imposed state of tension, he's got to move the popcorn off his lap, lift himself out of his chair, walk up to the TV and turn the channel – using perhaps 50 calories of human labour. If he sits through to the end of the commercial, however, only ten calories of anxiety may be used up. The brain is lazy; it makes the lazy decision. It will take the ten calorie option and submit to the programming.

After all, the material on TV is called programming for a reason; it's designed to program us as we sit passively in our seats. But the remote control changes the equation. Imagine a 14-year-old today, watching a commercial and feeling the first signs that he's being put into an imposed state of tension. With the .0001 calories that it takes to press a button, he's out of tension and out of the arc of that story. Kids with a remote control watch TV in a new way, following ten stations at once, surfing back and forth through different stories. When they experience TV like this they're not watching television at all, but watching *the* television, deconstructing it as *television*.

The second liberating interactive device was the videogame joystick. For most of us, the inaugurating videogame experience was Pong. And, perhaps amazingly, we probably still remember that first moment we played. Pong was a simple game based on ping-pong, with two white squares on either side of the screen that moved up and down in conjunction with movements on a control knob. People remember their first time playing Pong the way they remember where they were when Kennedy was assassinated. This isn't because Americans loved table tennis so much and were so happy to have the convenience of practising it on TV. It wasn't about the literal meaning of the metaphor; it was about experiencing something on the television as metaphor. It was a thrill just to move the little white square up and down on the screen, to control the pixel. We had never had control of the pixel before. The TV screen was the holy and inaccessible realm of newscasters and movie stars, a magical place where things just appeared. But, just as the remote control deconstructed television's stories, the joystick demystified its technology, making it an accessible medium and rendering it safe.

Finally, the computer mouse and the keyboard turned the receive-only monitor into a portal through which we could express ourselves. The mouse and keyboard spawned a do-it-yourself or 'DIY' internet culture in which people created, uploaded and shared their own content. In a sense, people were the content; we used technology to connect with other people.

The resulting cyberpunk culture was a renaissance culture. It was a chaotic space, where new ideas could spring up from almost anywhere. It was a gift economy in which new programs were created and shared for free. It was a community, where new members were introduced and escorted around as if they had just bought a home in a fantasy suburb. Best of all, internet users came to understand that the mainstream mediaspace no longer represented their reality. From now on, internet users would represent their own.

But almost no one was making money on the internet. Not that this bothered any of the internet's actual users, but families with internet connections were watching three or four hours less TV a week, seeing fewer commercials, and buying less TV-advertised products. Further, people who are having fun and feeling connected to other people are less easily coerced into purchases. So the effects of the remote control, the mouse and the joystick had to be undone. In the interests of the investment community, the internet was restyled as an online mall.

First, the mediaspace deconstructed by the remote control had to be put back together. Companies developed concepts such as sticki-ness, attention economy and eyeball hours in an effort to keep people glued to websites as they were once glued to TV stations. In response to panic-inducing articles from the mainstream media about a channel-surfing culture and decreasing attention spans, attention deficit disorder diagnoses and Ritalin prescriptions went up over 100 percent. Children's ability to enact renaissance was curtailed through drugs.

In order to regain control of the pixel, first liberated by the joystick, professional designers re-mystified the computer's interface so that it was no longer two-way. Users were forced to rely on the 'wizards' built into their software programs to work magic they didn't understand. Consider the increasing opacity from DOS to the Macintosh, and Macintosh to Windows2000. Look at the colourful and confusing interfaces used on the World Wide Web compared with the text-only bulletin boards of the early internet. The only way to participate on the Web is through the mouse; the only opportunity to use the keyboard is to enter one's credit card infor-mation. The increasing and deliberate opacity of new interfaces is designed to keep us out.

Finally, in order to undo the DIY culture that had grown out of the keyboard and the mouse, commerce replaced community and content replaced people as the soul of the net. It was announced that, rather than a *communication* age, we were in an 'information age' because information is data that can be bought and sold.

No longer able to deconstruct, demystify or do our own media, we ended up succumbing to an entirely new story about the promised new media: money.

The new story competing for consensus approval was based on the idea of a pyramid. Some young person comes up with an idea – a business plan. Then a pyramid with different levels of investor fills in beneath him. Angel investors take the top position; lower down are a few rounds of 'qualified' investors and invest-ment banks and, finally, at the very bottom, an Initial Price Offering (IPO) on NASDAQ. This final ground level is called 'going public'. Of course, by the time the general public was buying shares online, the people at the top of the pyramid had executed an 'exit strategy' and disappeared, taking away their money as the pyramid collapsed beneath them.

In the flux generated by our technological renaissance, e-commerce and the dot.com speculative market were reduced to a business fantasy: NASDAQ's claim to the meta-narrative. The pyramid schemes eventually failed, because all pyramid schemes eventually run out of money. Their collapse was aided, in part, by the internet's own structure and function. It is so organic and interactive in its make-up that it shrugs off interventionist government controls and, with a bit more effort, the corporate attacks that follow.

So, now that the dot.com pyramid scheme has failed to establish itself as the overarching metaphor of the digital age, digital reality – and perhaps our social reality – is once again up for grabs.

As long as we can maintain our renaissance sensibility and our awareness of the implications of the open source reality in which we live, we have access to enormous opportunities for cultural progress. These opportunities suggest profound implications for artists, designers and architects.

People who have been exposed to the internet and to interactive and virtual systems are more conscious of how any system is designed and constructed. We understand that our world is made up of intentionally designed interfaces. Spending so much time in virtual space, we are more aware of real space and the way it shapes interaction. We are more sensitive to the power, deliberateness and sacredness of interacting with real objects in real space.

We want a building to express a sense of our relationship to it. We want a room to be made for how we use it. With so much taking place via phone, fax and email, we want to be able to appreciate the live proximity of other people; we want to sit together on comfortable furniture and hear each other clearly. We are more aware of how spaces coerce us and more resistant to that coercion. We don't want to be induced to eat faster by brightly coloured walls or to walk faster through intentionally claustrophobic hallways. We recognise the way mirrored lobbies make us self-conscious or the way that pillars and façades declare power or opulence. We are more fluent in the codes and less easily convinced by them. We have a new appreciation of the authentic. An old railway station or carriage house becomes valuable for its authentic connection to the past, as a stable landmark in a time of flux and disconnection.

Right now, as a result of our renaissance sensibility, the definitions and conventions of our reality are becoming the component parts of a new language. Nothing is just itself, because its identifying characteristics become a self-conscious manifestation of its underlying essence. Listen to the way young people talk: 'That house is so *house*!' 'That library is so *library*!' Exactly what's going on there? It is a conscious reframing of our reality as iconography.

It's a form of self-protection, really. A defence. We are trying to focus on the mediated feeling of things. We want to stay awake in renaissance awareness as long as possible before the next reality template concretises and the self-conscious similes become tight metaphors. We now see that 'this is *like* that', '*sort of like*' that – it is '*as if*'. But we know that eventually 'it is *like*' and 'it is *as if*' will collapse into 'it *is*'. The world *is* that. It is transparency and accessibility lost yet again.

At the same time, however, there is a great longing to let go, to trust that the world is not trying to do something to us. People long to walk into a space and feel that, for once, they are not being manipulated. Can architecture do this? It can try. Artists in other media have been working on this problem for centuries. Shakespeare often writes prologues for his plays in which a character lets the audience in on the metaphor: 'Oh pardon gentles all, that we would

presume that the stage would represent…'. It's a modesty and honesty that give your audience permission to relax. They are not going to be messed with. If we can communicate this sort of goodwill in ritualised contexts, we should be able to do it in the real world of buildings and plazas as well.

It is the responsibility of architects in particular to realise that genuine social engagement and genuine discourse are what will keep people out of the traps and trances they are now at pains to avoid. If you can create spaces that foster this kind of interaction and discourse, spaces that facilitate people as people rather than subjugating them to other intentions, it will prolong our sense of freedom and possibility.

We must create buildings and spaces that serve people, rather than the other way around. The pyramids in Exodus provide an example of what happens when people are made slaves to buildings. They are dehumanised. Similarly, first and foremost the design of a bank building or corporate headquarters is meant to serve the corporation, the non-human icon of the 'brand', and the credo of the corporate mission statement. That's why the architect is hired and the articles are written. It's why the money is spent. But, in reality, that building will provide the spaces where hundreds of people spend the majority of their time, all day, five days a week, sometimes for years. Should they serve the building and the brand it represents, or can the equation be reversed?

Can these spaces support the human beings working within them on levels beyond their roles as employees? Can they facilitate more than just a sense of obligation?

How can the current shifts in perspective, developments in technology and experiences of interactivity be applied to this field in order to empower people and make them a priority? Can an architect make a career out of challenging metaphors rather than enforcing them? Given the cost of real buildings, who would pay for buildings that functioned in this way?

I'd like to see architecture that looks less like theme parks, temples or monuments and more like living communities of people. So far, at least, this architectural renaissance has been limited to the internet space. And, even there, it's been a struggle.

FORGET HEIDEGGER
Neil Leach

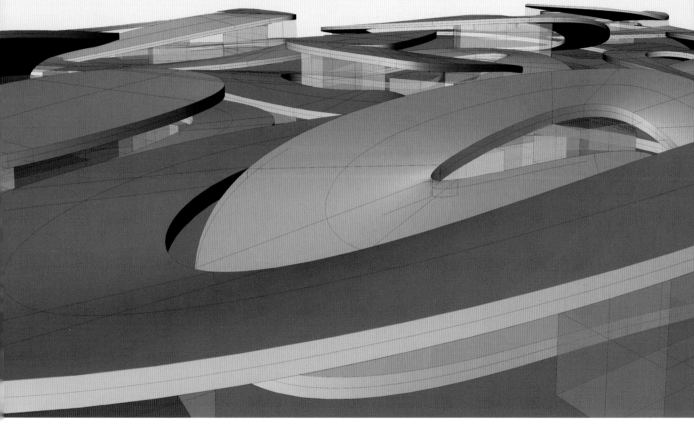

Introduction

Imagine yourself in what is perhaps an all-too-familiar scenario. You walk into a hotel room, a slightly grotty hotel room perhaps. The walls may be somewhat dirty, paint is peeling from the furniture, and there may be a musty smell. Initially you feel a sense of alienation. The room is unfamiliar. You don't feel at home in it. Nevertheless you unpack your bags, putting your washbag in the bathroom and hanging your clothes in the wardrobe. Gradually, as you lay out these familiar objects, the room seems less alienating. But what is most curious is that after a night or two spent sleeping in the room, what once seemed alienating and unfamiliar gradually becomes familiar, to the point that you begin to feel at home there. Maybe you even become slightly fond of it, with its shabby furniture and musty smells. You start to feel cosy there, and almost do not want to leave. Somehow — almost imperceptibly —

a shift has happened. What once appeared grim and alienating now appears familiar and homely.

This is a phenomenon with which we are all too familiar and yet, to my mind, no one has yet attempted to analyse it fully. It applies equally to questions of design: what once seemed ugly may appear less objectionable after a period of time. And it applies also to questions of technology. Take the example of satellite dishes. At first sight they may appear unfamiliar and out of place, but before long they have been accepted as part of the familiar language of the street. The same principle, no doubt, applied to traffic lights before them. And the same principle applies — so obviously — to digital technology today. Even the most seemingly alienating of technological forms can soon become absorbed within our symbolic horizons, such that they no longer appear so alienating.

This page: Spela Videcnik and Rok Oman, housing project, Graz, Austria

Of course the situation is often not that simple. Other factors may come into play. There may be some further consideration – an unpleasant association, for example – that prevents you from ever feeling at home in a particular environment. Yet such factors appear merely to militate against what seems to be an underlying drive to 'grow into', to become familiar and eventually identify with our environment. It is as though there is a constant chameleon-like urge to assimilate that governs human nature.

What, then, is going on here? What exactly *is* this process of 'growing into', becoming fond of, familiarising oneself with our environment? How does this mechanism operate? And more especially, within the context of this particular enquiry, how might this phenomenon prompt us to rethink the question of digital technology? How might, for example, the overtly negative stand taken by certain theorists on the supposedly alienating effect of technology be revisited in the light of these observations? Can technology be viewed more positively? All these questions are addressed to an architectural culture still dominated in certain areas by a broadly Heideggerian outlook, a culture which remains largely critical of technology in general, and reluctant to embrace digital technology in particular.

Heidegger and the Question Concerning Technology

What, then, was Heidegger's attitude towards technology? Technology is a crucial concern throughout his work, but the issue is addressed most explicitly in his essay 'The Question

Concerning Technology'.[1] Heidegger was not opposed to technology as such, but rather he saw in technology a mode of 'revealing', and it was here that the danger lay. 'The essence of modern technology,' as he puts it, 'lies in enframing. Enframing belongs within the destining of revealing.'[2] For Heidegger, the problem lies in precisely this 'destining' of this revealing, in that it 'banishes man into the kind of revealing that is an ordering'.[3] And this form of 'revealing' is an impoverished one as it denies the possibility of a deeper ontological engagement: 'Above all, enframing conceals that revealing which, in the sense of *poiesis*, lets what presences come forth into appearance.'[4] Rather than opening up to the human it therefore constitutes a form of resistance or challenge, in that it 'blocks' our access to truth: 'Enframing blocks the shining-forth and holding sway of truth.'[5]

What we find in our contemporary age, according to Heidegger, is a condition in which humankind treats nature as a form of resource, something to be exploited, stockpiled and so on. 'Everywhere everything is ordered to stand by, to be immediately on hand, indeed to stand there just so that it may be on call for a further ordering. Whatever is ordered about in this way has its own standing. We call this the standing-reserve [*Bestand*].'[6] And it is this sense of 'standing-reserve', rather than *poiesis*, that lies at the heart of modern technology: 'The essence of modern technology shows itself in what we call Enframing... It is the way in which the real reveals itself as standing-reserve.'[7] The problem is not so much of nature being devalued as standing-reserve, but of humankind finding itself in the same condition: 'As soon as what is concealed no longer concerns man even as object, but exclusively as standing-reserve, and man in the midst of objectlessness is nothing but the orderer of the standing-reserve, then he comes to the very brink of a precipitous fall; that is, he comes to the point where he himself will have to be taken as standing-reserve.'[8]

Technology therefore comes to be associated with a form of alienation. It prevents humankind from being in touch with a richer form of revealing which operates within a more poetic dimension. But it is important to stress that the danger lies not in technology, but in its essence: 'What is dangerous is not technology.

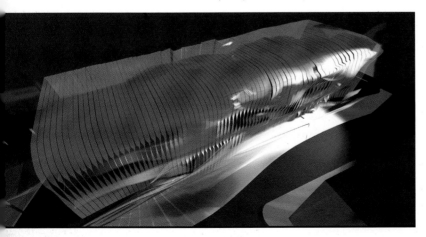

Technology is not demonic; but its essence is mysterious. The essence of technology, as a destining of revealing, is the danger.'[9]

Needless to say, Heidegger's comments on 'truth' are as deeply unfashionable in contemporary theoretical circles as is his belief in 'essences'. And even attempts by more recent thinkers in this intellectual tradition, such as Gianni Vattimo, to update Heidegger's thought for a postmodern world of 'difference' and 'differals' of meaning, can do little to redeem such a position. The question will always remain: 'Whose truth?' And this refers to all forms of human engagement. As Félix Guattari comments on the subject of technology: 'Far from apprehending a univocal truth of Being through *techné*, as Heideggerian ontology would have it, it is a plurality of beings as machines that give themselves to us once we acquire the pathic or cartographic means of access to them.'[10]

Heidegger's approach always threatens to reduce human beings to a single, universal individual, and to collapse the subject into the object, so that the agency of the interpreter is somehow overlooked, and 'meaning' is deemed to be unproblematically 'given'. Yet we might more properly approach such questions from an individual perspective, and treat meaning not as some universal 'given', but in symbolic terms as that which may vary from individual to individual. Symbolic meaning – like beauty – lies in the eye of the beholder, but is no less real for that. And symbolic meaning, as Fredric Jameson reminds us, is 'as volatile as the arbitrariness of the sign'.[11] An object might mean one thing to one person, and quite the opposite to another. This is not to sanction relativism, so much as to

highlight the need to acknowledge the agency of the interpreter and the perspective from which an interpretation is made. As such we might do better to retreat from such abstract universals and address the specificity of the concrete situation.

What such thinking fails to interrogate is how our understanding of the world is always mediated. It fails to address questions of consciousness. What is important, surely, when we address objects in the world is to consider not only the objects themselves but also the consciousness by which we know those objects. The phenomenological tradition does not perceive this as an area of concern. It therefore fails to grasp the very fluid and dynamic way our engagement with the world takes place. And this includes technology. Just as humans invest and subsequently transfer notions of 'home' by cathecting it from one dwelling to another, so they take a more dynamic and flexible attitude to technology. They may come to invest it with meaning, and to forge an attachment to it, which serves ultimately to overcome any initial resistance to it. As such, they may reappropriate it from the realm of standing-reserve.

In sum, what needs to be brought into the frame is the notion of 'appropriation'. Heidegger, to be sure, has been criticised elsewhere for overlooking the question of 'appropriation'. As Derrida argues convincingly, the whole principle of hermeneutics is based on a form of undisclosed appropriation – 'claiming' – where the agency of the interpreter in making that interpretation is not fully acknowledged.[12] But by 'appropriation' I refer here to the process of

This page and opposite:
Spela Videcnik and Rok Oman, offices of Ove Arup Partnership

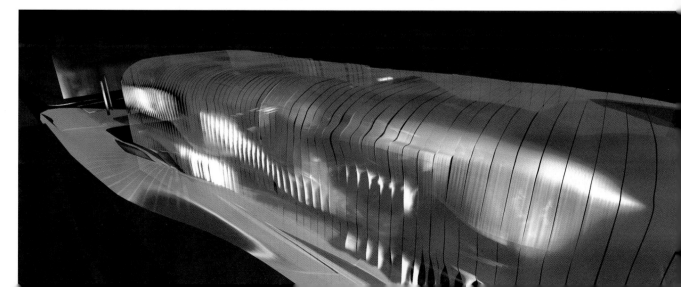

'familiarisation' over time. Just as one can question whether the 'authenticity' or indeed 'inauthenticity' (in Heideggerian terms) of an artefact will endure once memory of its creation is lost, so technology can never be seen to be the enduring site of alienation. Technology is always open to poetic appropriation.

Heidegger's somewhat monolithic attitude towards technology needs to be challenged. Those who argue that technology is the perpetual source of alienation clearly overlook the potential for human beings to absorb the novel and the unusual within their symbolic framework. We need to adopt a more flexible, dynamic framework that is alert to the very chameleon-like capacity for psychical adaptation that is a fundamental aspect of what it is to be human. It may be, of course, that we can locate an opening in Heidegger's thought, and argue, as does Ingrid Scheibler, that Heidegger also allows for what he terms 'meditative thinking', and that this can be deployed in the realm of technology so as to forge a less deterministic relationship between human beings and technology.[13] But such strategies will tend to bear the character of an apology, a qualification to an earlier argument. The sheer force of Heidegger's critique of technology puts to the fore calculative thinking as the dominant mode of engagement, and it is not at all clear when, if ever, calculative thinking gives way to meditative thinking.

Moreover, we need to adopt a more open attitude towards technology, not least because we live in a technological age. Technology has permeated all aspects of contemporary existence, and has suffused itself within our background horizon of consciousness. We live our lives so much *through* technology that we begin to see them in terms of technology. With time not only do we accept technology, but we even begin to identify with it. We call our cars names and speak to our computers. Ultimately we even begin to constitute our identity through technology – through our cars, computers and electronic gadgetry. We *are* the car we drive, or so the advertisers would have us believe: sleek, elegant, sophisticated, rugged, adventurous, whatever. Technology can lend us our lifestyles, can lend us our identities.

Mimetic Identification

How, then, might we adopt a more sympathetic attitude towards technology? What theoretical framework might allow us to address these concerns more openly? I want to propose that the work of Walter Benjamin and Theodor Adorno on the concept of *mimesis* offers a more subtle approach to questions of assimilation and identification in general, and to the problem of the alienation of technology in particular. To quote Adorno:

This page and opposite:
Yael Brosilovski, landscape for Feminine Retreat, Bursa, Turkey

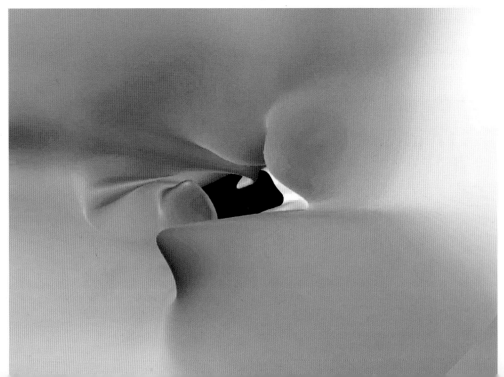

According to Freud, symbolic intention quickly allies itself to technical forms, like the aeroplane, and according to contemporary American research in mass psychology, even to the car. Thus, purposeful forms are the language of their own purposes. By means of the *mimetic* impulse, the living being equates himself with objects in his surroundings.[14]

This last sentence, 'By means of the *mimetic* impulse, the living being equates himself with objects in his surroundings', is, surely, one that holds the key to exploring the whole question of how human beings situate themselves within their environment, and points to an area in which the domain of psychoanalysis might offer crucial insights into the mechanism whereby humans relate to their habitat. It begins to suggest, for example, that the way in which humans progressively feel 'at home' within a particular building is precisely through a process of symbolic identification with that building. And equally they may come to identify with techno-logical objects. This symbolic attachment is

something that does not come into operation automatically. Rather it is something that is engendered gradually, in Adorno's terms, through the '*mimetic* impulse'.

Mimesis here should not be understood in the terms used by, say, Plato, as simple 'imitation'. Nor indeed does it have the same meaning that Heidegger gives it. Rather mimesis in Adorno (as indeed in Walter Benjamin) is a psychoanalytic term – taken from Freud – that refers to a creative engagement with an object. As Adorno defines it, it is 'the non-conceptual affinity of a subjective creation with its objective and unposited other'.[15] *Mimesis* is a term, as Freud himself predicted, of great potential significance for aesthetics.[16]

To understand the meaning of *mimesis* in Adorno we must recognise its origin in the process of modelling, of 'making a copy of'. In essence it refers to an interpretative process that relates not just to the creation of a model, but also to the engagement with that model. *Mimesis* may operate both transitively and reflexively. It comes into operation both in the making of an object and in making oneself like an object. *Mimesis* is therefore a form of imitation that may be evoked both by the artist who makes a work of art, and also by the person who views it. Yet *mimesis* is richer than straight imitation. In *mimesis* imagination is at work, and serves to reconcile the subject with the object. This imagination operates at the level of fantasy, which mediates between the unconscious and the conscious, dream and reality. Here fantasy is used as a positive term. Fantasy creates its own fictions not as a way of escaping but as a way of accessing reality, a reality that is ontologically charged, and not constrained by an instrumentalised view of the world. In effect, *mimesis* is an unconscious identification with the object. It necessarily involves a creative moment on the part of the subject. The subject creatively identifies with the object, so that the object, even if it is a technical object – a piece of machinery, a car, a plane, a bridge – becomes invested with some symbolic significance, and is appropriated as part of the symbolic background through which individuals constitute their identity.

It is important to recognise here the question of temporality. Symbolic significance may shift, often dramatically, over a period of time. What was once shockingly alien may eventually appear reassuringly familiar. The way in which we engage with architecture must therefore be seen not as a static condition, but as a dynamic process. The logic of *mimesis* dictates that we are constantly assimilating to the built environment, and that, consequently, our attitudes towards it are forever changing. Our engagement with the built environment is never a given, static condition, but an ongoing process of constant adaptation. While books have been devoted to 'weathering', to the performance of

This page: Yael Brosilovski, Landscape for Feminine Retreat, Bursa, Turkey

the building *in time*, few seem to have addressed the question of our own reception of the building itself within a temporal framework.

Mimesis therefore constitutes a form of mimicry, but it is an adaptive mimicry just as when a child learns to speak and adapt to the world, or when owners take on the characteristics of their pets. In fact, it is precisely the example of the child 'growing into' language that best illustrates the operation of *mimesis*. The child 'absorbs' an external language by a process of imitation and then uses it creatively for their own purposes. Similarly, within the realm of any aspect of design we might see *mimesis* at work as designers develop their design abilities: it is this process which also allows external forms to be absorbed and sedimented as part of a language of design.

Although *mimesis* involves a degree of organised control, and therefore operates in conjunction with rationality, this does not mean that it is part of rationality. Indeed, in terms of the dialectic of the Enlightenment, we might perceive *mimesis* as constitutive not of rationality, but of myth, its magical 'other'. *Mimesis* and rationality, as Adorno observes, are 'irreconcilable'.[17] If *mimesis* is to be perceived as a form of correspondence with the outside world which is articulated within the aura of the work of art, then Enlightenment rationality, with its effective split between subject and object, and increasing emphasis on knowledge-as-quantification over knowledge-as-sensuous-correspondence, represents the opposite pole. In the instrumentalised view of the Enlightenment, knowledge is ordered and categorised, valorised according to scientific principles, and the rich potential of *mimesis* is overlooked. All this entails a loss, a reduction of the world to a reified structure of subject/object divides, as *mimesis* retreats even further into the mythic realm of literature and the arts.

At the same time *mimesis* might be seen to offer a form of dialectical foil to the subject/object split of Enlightenment rationality. This is most obvious in the case of language. Language becomes the 'highest level of mimetic behaviour, the most complete archive of non-sensuous similarity'.[18] *Mimesis* for Benjamin offers a way of finding meaning in the world, through the discovery of similarities. These similarities become absorbed and then rearticulated in language, no less than in dance or other art forms. As such language becomes a repository of meaning, and writing becomes an activity which extends beyond itself, so in the process of writing writers engage in unconscious processes of which they may not be aware. Indeed writing often reveals more than the writer is conscious of revealing. Likewise the reader must decode the words, resorting to the realm of the imagination which exceeds the purely rational. Thus the activity of reading also embodies the principles of *mimesis*, serving as the vehicle for some revelatory moment. For Benjamin the meaning becomes apparent in a constellatory flash, a dialectics of seeing, in which subject and object become one for a brief moment, a process which relates to the experience of architecture no less than to the reading of texts.

Along with the other visual arts architecture

can therefore be viewed as a potential reservoir for the operation of *mimesis*. In the very design of buildings the architect may articulate the relational correspondence with the world which is embodied in the concept of *mimesis*. These forms may be interpreted in a similar fashion by those who experience the building, in that the mechanism by which human beings begin to feel at home in the built environment can also be seen as a *mimetic* one.

Mimesis, then, may help to explain how we identify progressively with our surroundings. In effect, we read ourselves into our surroundings, without being fully conscious of it. 'By means of the *mimetic* impulse,' Adorno comments, 'the living being equates himself with objects in his surroundings.' Elsewhere I have argued that this may be understood in terms of the myth of Narcissus.[19] The *mimetic* impulse might be seen as a mechanism for reading ourselves into the

other. We relate ourselves to our environment by a process of *narcissistic* identification, and mimetically absorb the language of that environment. Just as Narcissus saw his own image in the water, without recognising it as himself, so we identify ourselves with the 'other' – symbolically – without realising that recognition of the 'other' must be understood in terms of a *mimetic* identification with the other, as a reflection of the self. And this refers not to a *literal* reflection of our image, so much as to the metaphorical reflection of our symbolic outlook and values.

The aim throughout is to forge a creative relationship with our environment. When we see our values 'reflected' in our surroundings, this feeds our narcissistic urge, and breaks down the subject/object divide. It is as though – to employ Walter Benjamin's use of the term *mimesis* – in the flash of the *mimetic* moment, the fragmentary is recognised as part of the whole, and the individual is inserted within an harmonic totality.

Rethinking Technology

What, then, can we read into this process of assimilation that is implied in the concept of *mimesis*, and how might it prompt us to rethink the issue of technology? There are clear comparisons to be made between Heidegger's championing of *poiesis* over 'standing reserve',

Left: Yael Brosilovski, Institute for Fascist Studies, Portbon, Spain

Below: Spela Videcnik and Rok Oman, offices of Ove Arup Partnership

and the corresponding championing by Benjamin and Adorno of knowledge-as-sensuous-correspondence over knowledge-as-quantification. Both traditions would criticise the world of enlightenment rationality as an impoverished one, and indeed *mimesis* here can be seen to offer a foil to this condition. But only with Heidegger is technology assigned unreservedly to this condition.

Let us take Heidegger's example of the airliner. For Heidegger, the airliner that stands on the runway is 'surely an object… Revealed, it stands on the taxi strip only as standing-reserve, inasmuch as it is ordered to ensure the possibility of transportation.'[20] The point here is that our understanding of that airliner is defined solely in terms of its 'standing-reserve': 'The object disappears into the objectlessness of the standing-reserve.'[21] The possibility that the airliner might be viewed in any other way is not entertained. And yet airliners, as Barthes once commented of buildings, are a combination of 'dream and function'.[22] But Heidegger fails to address the crucial role that an airliner might play as a symbolic form in its own right, a vehicle for dreams, emotions and desires. As such he offers a somewhat restrictive approach to the question. In his account there is no

This page and opposite:
Yael Brosilovski, Landscape for Feminine Retreat, Bursa, Turkey

potential for the object to be withdrawn from the realm of standing-reserve. There is no potential for it to be reappropriated.

Intriguingly, Adorno also cites the example of an aeroplane, but his thinking remains more flexible. The argument of *mimesis* suggests – and indeed Adorno explicitly states – that symbolic identification may take place even with technological objects such as a car or a plane, so that they too may be appropriated as part of our symbolic background: 'According to Freud, symbolic intention quickly allies itself to technical forms, like the aeroplane, and according to contemporary American research in mass psychology, even to the car.'[23] The aeroplane is not consigned irredeemably to the realm of knowledge-as-quantification. It can be reappropriated within the realm of the symbolic. In other words our consciousness of the aeroplane is itself altered.

Adorno's further example of the car reveals how the technological has come to colonise our everyday lives not as standing-reserve, but as something to which symbolic intention is always already being 'attached'. The point here is that we have to understand that our engagement with technology involves a moment of 'proprioception'. Technology may come to operate as a form of 'prosthesis' to the human body, that is appropriated in such a way that it becomes part of the motility of the body. In driving a car we come to navigate the road *through* that car. As such, the car as an item of technology is not divorced – alienated – from the body; indeed, it becomes a form of extension to that body. What I am arguing here is not some simplistic manifesto for cyborgs, claiming that human beings can become part human and part machine. Rather I am trying to tease out the logic of *mimesis* itself. For according to this logic, human beings have absorbed technology at an unconscious level, such that they have come to operate *through* technology, as though by way of some telekinesis.

Not only this, but technology may actually influence the way that human beings think. It may itself affect our consciousness. Let us take the example of the computer. For if, as Walter Benjamin once argued, the factory worker in the modernist age comes to absorb the jolting, jarring repetitive action of the machine such that those movements are appropriated into the worker's own behaviour, so too people today have absorbed the thinking and fluid circuitry behind the computer screen. New conditions breed new ways of thinking. As Douglas Rushkoff observes, a new computer generation is emerging.[24] The computer kids of today come to behave like their computers. They identify with them, play with them, and mimic their operations. Analogical reasoning is out. Non-linear, multiple-layered thinking is in – Deleuzian surfing. Fractals, rhizomes and clones, fluidity and flux: these are the buzz words of this new generation. In such a context, those who argue against the use of the computer in the contemporary design studio are failing to address the concrete ontological reality of life today, and are doing no service to the students for whom knowledge of computer has become a 'given' within the contemporary office. It may be that the still-prevalent antipathy towards digital technology is merely a form of 'denial'. As in the case of homophobics, who often deny their latent homosexuality,[25] critics of technology may be repressing a secret fascination with technology. An individual 'in denial' may be fascinated by some personal psychic obsession but, not wishing to acknowledge it, will project that obsession onto some external object and then criticise it. But whether this antipathy towards digital technology is a form of repressed fascination or not, it is clearly out of place in what has become a highly digitalised world.

This is not to say that the computer should be accepted unhesitatingly within the studio. Indeed the lessons of those design schools that have accepted the computer wholesale would seem to indicate that the concerns expressed in *The Anaesthetics of Architecture* about the potential aestheticisation and hence anaesthetisation of social issues are borne out only too clearly in such contexts.[26] Rather it is a call for a

self-critical, theoretically informed engagement with such realms. Theory may be unable in itself to combat the potential problems of aestheticisation. Yet it may provide the first crucial step. Once a problem has been exposed, one is no longer trapped by that problem.

The consequences are all too obvious. Not only have we accepted technology as an essential part of our everyday life, such that the distinction once posed between *techné* and technology seems no longer valid, but our whole existence has become conditioned by technology. In this new digital age, as Sarah Chaplin argues, we have adopted a form of cybervisuality. An important factor, then, is our interface with that technology for technology may take many forms. Here the question of design becomes crucial. The message of *mimesis* is not that human beings will adapt to anything, so that design is unimportant, but precisely the opposite.[27] Design becomes an important mechanism for making people feel at one with their world. This relates not simply to whether a piece of technology is itself aesthetically pleasing – as is the case with the iMac computer, for example – but in the context of digital technology it relates also to the user interface – to software programming and its compatibility with human modes of operation. Far from engendering alienation, well-designed technology has the capacity to *overcome* alienation.

There was a time when Heideggerian

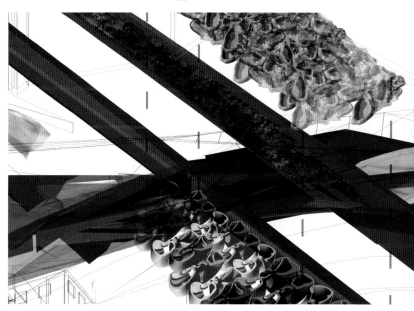

thought made a substantial and noteworthy contribution to architectural culture in challenging the spirit of positivism that was once so pervasive. But now Heideggerian thinking must not itself go unchallenged, in that it threatens to install itself as a set of fixed values out of tune with the fluidity and flux of contemporary society. And while some would criticise postmodern thought for being relativistic in accommodating plurality and difference, and questioning the ground on which any particular statement is made, surely the true relativism lies in a tradition that forecloses the possibility of even asking these questions, by doggedly adhering to an out-of-date set of values, and by failing to engage substantively with any critical discourse.

In an increasingly digital world, it is time, it would seem, to adopt a more flexible and tolerant attitude towards digital technology. It is time to break free from the shackles of the past. It is time, perhaps, to forget Heidegger.[28]

Notes

1 Martin Heidegger, *Basic Writings*. David Farrell Krell, (Ed.) New York: Harper Collins, 1993, pp. 311–341.

2 Ibid. p. 330.

3 Ibid. p. 332.

4 Ibid.

5 Ibid. p. 333.

6 Ibid. p. 322.

7 Ibid. pp. 328–329.

8 Ibid. p. 332, as quoted in Ingrid Scheibler, 'Heidegger and the rhetoric of submission'. In Verena Andermatt Conley (Ed.), *Rethinking Technologies*. Minneapolis: University of Minnesota Press, 1993, p. 116.

9 Ibid. p. 333.

10 Félix Guattari, 'Machinic heterogenesis'. In Conley (Ed.), *Rethinking Technologies*, p. 26.

11 Fredric Jameson, 'Is space political'? In Neil Leach, *Rethinking Architecture*. London: Routledge, 1997, p. 258.

12 Jacques Derrida, *Truth in Painting*. Chicago: University of Chicago Press, 1987, pp. 255–382.

13 Ingrid Scheibler, 'Heidegger and the rhetoric of submission'. In Conley (Ed.), *Rethinking Technologies*, pp. 115–139.

14 Theodor Adorno, 'Functionalism today'. In Leach (Ed.), *Rethinking Architecture*, London; Routledge, 1997, p. 10.

15 TW Adorno, *Aesthetic Theory,* G Adorno, R Tiederman (Eds), trans. C Lenhardt. London: Routledge, 1984, p. 80.

16 '…I believe that if ideational mimetics are followed up, they may be as useful in other branches of aesthetics…' Sigmund Freud, *Jokes and Their Relation to the Unconscious* (1905), trans. James Strachey. London: Routledge, 1960, p. 193. For further reading on *mimesis*, see Erich Auerbach, *Mimesis*, trans. Willard Trask, Princeton: Princeton University Press, 1953; Michael Taussig, *Mimesis and Alterity*, London: Routledge, 1993; Gunter Gebauer and Christoph Wulf, *Mimesis*, trans. Don Reneau, Berkeley: University of California Press, 1995.

17 TW Adorno, *Aesthetic Theory,* G Adorno, R Tiederman (Eds), trans. C Lenhardt. London: Routledge, 1984, p. 81.

18 W Benjamin, 'Mimetic faculty'. In Edmund Jephcott (trans.) *Reflections*. New York: Schocken, 1978, p. 336.

19 N Leach, *'Vitruvius crucifixus:* Architecture, *mimesis* and the death instinct'. *AA Files*, 38, July 1999.

20 Heidegger, *Basic Writings*, p. 322.

21 Ibid. p. 324.

22 Roland Barthes, 'The Eiffel Tower'. In Leach (Ed.), *Rethinking Architecture*. p. 174.

23 G Adorno, 'Functionalism today'. Ibid. p. 10.

24 Douglas Rushkoff, *Children of Chaos*. London: Flamingo, 1997.

25 An obvious example of this is the incident in the film, *American Beauty*, where the homophobic character proves to have homosexual leanings.

26 N Leach, *The Anaesthetics of Architecture*. Cambridge, MA: MIT Press, 1999.

27 *Mimesis* operates both in the design of the item, and in the relationship between the viewer and the item itself. It therefore follows that when a technological item has been designed with a view to a mimetic understanding of the world it will *lend itself* to being absorbed mimetically. In other words, if we are to understand *mimesis* as offering a mechanism of relating to the world, of forging a link between the individual and the environment, of offering a means – in Fredric Jameson's terms – of 'cognitively mapping' oneself within the environment, good design has an important *social* role.

28 An early version of this paper appeared in *Scroope* 12, 2000.

E-FUTURES AND E-PERSONAE
Sherry Turkle

Computers offer themselves as models of the mind and as 'objects to think with' for thinking about the self. They do this in several ways. First of all, there is the world of artificial intelligence research – Marvin Minsky once called it the enterprise of 'trying to get computers to do things that would be considered intelligent if done by people'. In the course of doing so, some artificial intelligence researchers explicitly endeavour to build machines that model the human mind. And there is the world of computational objects in the culture – the toys, the games, the simulation packages, the Internet connections. These objects are evocative; interacting with them provokes reflection on the nature of the self.

Here I'm going to focus on this second way in which computers influence thinking about self, life and mind; that is, the role of experiences with computers as evocative objects – objects to think with.[1]

Most recently, these objects have quite explicitly invited us to construct virtual selves that are built from our imaginations and the machine's possibilties. Ten years ago, our projections of self onto computers were via computer programs whose structure encouraged a model of thinking about the self that was linear and logical. Today, we project ourselves into a far wider variety of computational landscapes – we see ourselves in the virtual spaces of simulation games and create representations of ourselves in text-based virtual communities on the Internet. In both of these settings, the images of self that are reflected back to us support what to many must seem like a very 'un-computer' model of the self: a view of self as fluid and multiple.

Virtual Personae
Through networked software known as MUDs (short for Multi-user Dungeons or Multi-user Domains), people log in from all over the world, each at their individual machine, and join online virtual communities that exist only through and in the computer. MUDs are social virtual realities in which hundreds of thousands of people participate. The key element of 'MUDding' – the creation and projection of a 'personae' into a virtual space – also characterizes the far more

'banal' online communities such as bulletin boards, newsgroups and 'chat' rooms on commercial services. MUDs may seem exotic, but in fact they are representative of the social and psychological dynamics of life on the screen.

When you join a MUD, you create a character or several characters, you specify their genders and other physical and psychological attributes. Other players in the MUD can see this description. It becomes your character's self presentation. In traditional role-playing games in which the physical body is present, the player steps in and out of a character; MUDs, in contrast, offer a parallel life. Often, players on MUDs and the most avid participants in online life are people who work with computers all day at their 'regular' jobs. As they play on MUDs, for example, they will periodically put their characters to 'sleep', remaining logged on to the game, but pursuing other activities. From time to time, they return to the game space. In this way, they break up their work days and experience their lives as a 'cycling through' between the real world and a series of simulated ones. This same sort of 'cycling through' characterizes how people play with newsgroups, Internet Relay Chat, bulletin boards and chat rooms.

This kind of interaction with MUDs and other virtual environments is made possible by the existence of what have come to be called 'windows' in modern computing environments. Windows are a way of working with a computer that makes it possible for the machine to place you in several contexts at the same time. As a user, you are attentive to only one of the windows on your screen at any given moment but, in a certain sense, you are a presence in all of them at all times. You might be writing a paper on bacteriology and using your computer in several ways to help you; you are 'present' to a word processing program on which you are taking notes and collecting thoughts; you are 'present' to communications software which is in touch with a distant computer for collecting reference materials; and you are 'present' to a simulation program which is charting the growth of bacterial colonies when a new organism enters their ecology. Each of these activities takes place in a 'window' and your identity on the computer is the sum of your distributed presence.

The development of the windows metaphor for computer interfaces was a technical innovation motivated by the desire to help people to work more efficiently by 'cycling through' different applications, much as time-sharing computers cycle through the computing needs of different people. But, in practice, windows have become a potent metaphor for thinking about the self as a multiple, distributed 'time-sharing' system. The self is no longer simply playing different roles in different settings, something that is experienced when, for example, one wakes up as a lover, makes breakfast as a mother, and drives to work as a lawyer. The life practice of windows is of a distributed self that exists in many worlds and plays many roles at the same time.

This notion of the self as distributed and constituted by a process of 'cycling through' undermines many of our traditional notions of identity. 'Identity', after all, from the Latin *idem*, literally refers to the sameness between two qualities. On the Internet, however, one can be many and usually is. If, traditionally, identity implied oneness, life on today's computer screen implies multiplicity, heterogeneity and fragmentation.

In the late 1960s and early 1970s, I was first exposed to notions of identity and multiplicity. These ideas, most notably that there is no such thing as 'the ego' – that each of us is a multiplicity of parts, fragments and desiring connections – took place in the intellectual hothouse of Paris; they presented the world according to such authors as Jacques Lacan, Gilles Deleuze and Félix Guattari.[2] But despite such ideal conditions for absorbing theory, my 'French lessons' remained abstract exercises. When twenty years later, I used my personal computer and modem to join online communities, I had an experience of this theoretical perspective which brought it shockingly down to earth. I used language to create several characters. My textual actions are my actions – my words make things happen. I created selves that were made and transformed by language.

And different personae were exploring different aspects of the self. The notion of a decentred identity was concretized by experiences on a computer screen.

People decide that they want to interact with others in a multi-user computer environment. They think that they will have new access to people and information – and there is little question that they do. But they find themselves playing in MUDs. They find themselves assuming multiple personae on computer networks. They are swept up in experiences that challenge their ideas about a unitary self. They meet their double and it is a cyborg. To sum up: in thinking about identity in a culture of simulation, the citizens of MUDs are our pioneers.

Objects-To-Think-With

Appropriable theories, ideas that capture the imagination of the culture at large, tend to be those with which people can become actively involved. They tend to be theories that can be 'played' with. So one way to think about the social appropriability of a given theory is to ask whether it is accompanied by its own objects-to-think-with that can help it move out beyond intellectual circles.

For instance, the popular appropriation of Freudian ideas had little to do with scientific demonstrations of their validity. Freudian ideas passed into the popular culture because they offered robust and down-to-earth objects-to-think-with. The objects were not physical, but almost-tangible ideas such as dreams and slips of the tongue. People were able to play with such Freudian 'objects'. They became used to looking for them and manipulating them, both seriously and not so seriously. And as they did so, the idea that slips and dreams betray an unconscious started to feel natural.

In Freud's work, dreams and slips of the tongue carried the theory. Today, life on the computer screen carries theory. People decide that they want to interact with others on a computer network. They get an account on a commercial service. They think that this will provide them with new access to people and information and, of course, it does. But it does more. When people log on, they may find themselves playing multiple roles, they may find themselves playing characters of the opposite sex. In this way they are swept up by experiences that enable them to explore previously unexamined aspects of their sexuality or that challenge their ideas about a unitary self.

When people adopt an online persona they cross a boundary into highly-charged territory. Some feel an uncomfortable sense of fragmentation, some a sense of relief. Some sense the possibilities for self-discovery, even self-transformation. A 26-year-old graduate student in history says, 'When I log on to a new MUD and I create a character and know I have to start typing my description, I always feel a sense of panic. Like I could find out something I don't want to know.' A woman in her late thirties who just got an account with America Online used the fact that she could create five account 'names' as a chance to 'lay out all the moods I'm in – all the ways I want to be in different places on the system'. Another named one of the accounts after her yet-to-be-born child. 'I got the account right after the amnio, right after I knew it would be a girl. And all of a sudden, I wanted that little girl to have a presence on the net, I wrote her a letter and I realized I was writing a letter to a part of me.' A 20-year-old undergraduate says, 'I am always very self-conscious when I create a new character. Usually, I end up creating someone I wouldn't want my parents to know about. It takes me, like, three hours.' In these ways and others, many more of us are experimenting with multiplicity than ever before.

With this last comment, I am not implying that MUDs or computer bulletin boards or chat rooms are causally implicated in the dramatic increase of people who exhibit symptoms of multiple personality disorder (MPD), or that people on MUDs have MPD, or that MUDding (or online chatting) is like having MPD. What I am saying is that the many manifestations of multiplicity in our culture, including the adoption of online personae, are contributing to a general reconsideration of traditional, unitary notions of identity. Online experiences with 'parallel lives' are part of the significant cultural context that supports new theorizations about multiple selves.

In thinking about the self, 'multiplicity' is a term that carries with it several centuries of negative associations; contemporary theorists are having an easier time with descriptions of multiplicity that stress the virtue of flexibility. We see this in the work of such authors as Kenneth Gergen,[3] Emily Martin,[4] and Robert Jay Lifton.[5] The essence of the 'acceptable', flexible self is not unitary, nor are its parts stable entities. A person cycles through its aspects and these are themselves ever-changing and in constant communication with each other. The philosopher Daniel Dennett[6] speaks of the flexible self in his 'multiple draughts' theory of consciousness. Dennett's notion of multiple draughts is analogous to the experience of several versions of a document open on a computer screen where the user is able to move between them at will. Knowledge of these draughts encourages a respect for the many different versions while it imposes a certain distance from them. The social theorist Donna Haraway,[7] picking up on this theme of how a distance between self states may be salutory, equates a 'split and contradictory self' with a 'knowing self'. She is optimistic about its possibilities: 'The knowing self is partial in all its guises, never finished, whole, simply there and original; it is always constructed and stitched together imperfectly; and *therefore* able to join with another, to see together without claiming to be another.' What most characterizes these two models of a knowing self is that the lines of communication between its various aspects are open. The open communication encourages an attitude of respect for the many within us and the many within others.

Inceasingly, psychoanalytic theorists are joining social theorists and philosophers in efforts to use flexibility as a way of introducing non-pathological multiplicity. They are trying to think about healthy selves whose resilience and capacity for joy come from having access to their many aspects. For example, the American psychoanalytic theorist Philip Bromberg[8] insists that our ways of describing 'good parenting' must now shift away from an emphasis on confirming a child in a 'core self' and on to helping a child develop the capacity to negotiate fluid transitions between self states. Bromberg believes that dissociation is not fundamentally trauma driven. It is a part of normal psychological development, necessary to the 'necessary illusion of being one self'. The healthy individual knows how to be many but smooth out the moments of transition between states of self. Bromberg says: 'Health is when you are multiple but feel a unity. Health is when different aspects of self can get to know each other and reflect upon each other. Health is being one while being many.' Here, within the psychoanalytic tradition, is a model of multiplicity without dissociation; that is, multiplicity with fluid traffic across, a conscious, highly-articulated 'cycling through'.

Cycling Through and Children's Constructions

In Piaget's classical studies of the 1920s on how children thought about what was alive, the central variable was motion. Simply put, children took up the question of an object's 'life status' by asking themselves if the object could move of its own accord. When in the late 1970s and early 1980s I studied children's reactions to a first generation of computer objects that were physically 'stationary' but which nonetheless accomplished impressive feats of cognition (talking, spelling, doing math and playing tic-tac-toe), I found that the focus had shifted to an object's psychological properties when children considered the question of its 'aliveness'. So although the presence of computational objects disrupted the classical Piagetian story for talking about aliveness, the story children were telling about computational objects in the early 1980s had its own coherency. Faced with intelligent toys, children took a new world of objects and imposed a new world order, based not on physics but on psychology.

In the 1990s, that order has been strained to the breaking point. Children will now talk about computers as 'just machines' but describe them as sentient and intentional. Faced with ever more complex computational objects, children are now in the position of theoretical bricoleurs or tinkerers, 'making do' with whatever materials are at hand, 'making do' with whatever theory can fit a prevailing circumstance. They cycle through evolution and psychology and resurface ideas about motion in terms of the communication of bits.

My current collection of comments about life by children who have played with small mobile robots, the games in the 'Sim' series, and Tierra includes the following notions: the robots are in control but not alive; would be alive if they had bodies; are alive because they have bodies; would be alive if they had feelings; are alive the way insects are alive but not the way people are alive. The Tierrans are: not alive because they are just in the computer; could be alive if they got out of the computer and got onto America Online; are alive until you turn off the computer and then they're dead; are not alive because nothing in the computer is real. The Sim creatures are: not alive but almost-alive; they would be alive if they spoke; they would be alive if they travelled; they're alive but not 'real'; they're not

alive because they don't have bodies; they are alive because they can have babies; and finally, for an 11-year-old who is relatively new to SimLife, they're not alive because these babies don't have parents. She says: 'They show the creatures and the game tells you that they have mothers and fathers but I don't believe it. It's just numbers, it's not really a mother and a father.' There is a striking heterogeneity of theory here. Different children hold different theories and individual children are able to hold different theories at the same time.

In the short history of how the computer has changed the way we think, it has often been children who have led the way. In the early 1980s, for example, prompted by computer toys that spoke, did math, and played tic-tac-toe, children disassociated ideas about consciousness from ideas about life, something that historically had not been the case. These children were able to contemplate sentient computers that were not alive, a position that adults are only now beginning to find comfortable. Today's cyborg children are taking things even further; they are pointing the way towards a radical heterogeneity of theory in the presence of computational artifacts that evoke 'life'. In his history of artificial life, Steven Levy[9] suggested that one way to look at where artificial life can 'fit in' to our way of thinking about life is to envisage a continuum in which Tierra, for example, would be more alive than a car, but less alive than a bacterium. My observations suggest that children are not constructing hierarchies but are heading toward parallel, alternating definitions.

Today's adults grew up in a psychological culture that equated the idea of a unitary self with psychological health and in a scientific culture that taught that when a discipline achieves maturity, it has a unifying theory. When adults find themselves cycling through varying perspectives on themselves ('I am my chemicals' to 'I am my history' to 'I am my genes') they usually become uncomfortable. But such alternations may strike the generation of cyborg children who are growing up today as 'just the way things are'.

Children speak easily about factors that encourage them to see the 'stuff' of computers as the same 'stuff' of which life is made. Among these are the ideas of 'shape shifting' and 'morphing'. Shape shifting is the technique used by the evil android in 'Terminator II' to turn into the form of anything he touched, including people. A 9-year-old showed an alchemist's sensibility when he explained how this occurs: 'It is very simple. In the universe, anything can turn to anything else when you have the right formula. So you can be a person one minute and a machine the next minute.' Morphing is a general term that covers form changes which may include changes across the animate/inanimate barrier. A 10-year-old boy had a lot to say about morphing, all of it associated with the life style of 'The Mighty Morphin' Power Rangers', a group of action heroes who turn from teenagers to androidal/mechanical 'dinozords' and 'mega-zords' and back. 'Well,' he patiently explains. 'The dinozords are alive; the Power Rangers are alive, but not all the parts of the dinozords are alive, but all the parts of the Power Rangers are alive. The Power Rangers become the dinozords.' Then, of course, there are seemingly omnipresent 'transformer toys' that shift from being machines to being robots to being animals (and sometimes people). Children play with these plastic and metal objects and, in the process, they learn about the fluid boundaries between mechanism and flesh.

I observe a group of 7-year-olds playing with a set of plastic transformer toys that can take the shape of armoured tanks, robots or people. The transformers can also be put into intermediate states so that a 'robot' arm can protrude from a human form or a human leg from a mechanical tank. Two of the children are playing with the toys in these intermediate states (that is, in their intermediate states somewhere between being people, machines and robots). A third child insists that this is not right. The toys, he says, should not be placed in hybrid states. 'You should play them as all tank or all people.' He is getting upset because the other two children are making a point of ignoring him. An 8-year-old girl comforts the upset child. 'It's okay to play them when they are in between. It's all the same stuff,' she says, 'just yucky computer "cy-dough-plasm".' This comment is the expression of a cyborg consciousness as it expresses itself among today's children: a tendency to see computer systems as 'sort of' alive, to fluidly 'cycle through' various explanatory concepts, and to willingly transgress boundaries.

To sum up: When today's adults 'cycle through' different theories, they are uncomfortable.

Such movement does not correspond to the unitary visions they were brought up to expect. But children have learned a different lesson from their cyborg objects. Donna Haraway characterises irony as being 'about contradictions that do not resolve into larger wholes… about the tension of holding incompatible things together because both or all are necessary and true'.[10] In this sense, today's cyborg children, growing up into irony, are becoming adept at holding incompatible things together. They are cycling through the cy-dough-plasm into fluid and emergent conceptions of self and life.

Readership in a Culture of Simulation

Simulations, whether in a game like SimLife or in a physics laboratory or computer-aided-design application, do teach users how to think in an active way about complex phenomena as dynamic, evolving systems. And they also get people accustomed to manipulating a system whose core assumptions they may not under-stand and which may or may not be 'true'. Simulations enable us to abdicate authority to the simulation; they give us permission to accept the opacity of the model that plays itself out on our screens. Paul Starr[11] has pointed out that this very abdication of authority (and acceptance of opacity) corresponds to the way simulations are sometimes used in the real worlds of politics, economics and social planning. Perhaps screen simulations on our personal computers can be a form of consciousness raising. Writing about the 'seductions of Sim', Starr makes it clear that while it is easy to criticise SimCity and SimHealth for their hidden assump-tions, we tolerate opaque simulations in other spheres. Social policymakers regularly deal with complex systems that they seek to understand through computer models used as the basis for actions. Policymaking, says Starr, 'inevitably re[lies] on imperfect models and simplifying assumptions that the media, the public, and even policymakers themselves generally don't understand'. He adds, writing about Washington and the power of the Congressional Budget Office, America's 'official simulator', '…We shall be working and thinking in SimCity for a long time'. So, simulation games are not just objects for thinking about the real world but also cause us to reflect on how the real world has itself become a simulation game.

The seduction of simulation invites several possible responses. One can accept simulations on their own terms, the stance that Starr was encouraged to take by Washington colleagues who insisted that, even if the official models are wrong, they have to be used to get anything done. This might be called simulation resignation. Or one can reject simulations to whatever degree possible, the position taken by the MIT physicists who saw them as a thoroughly destructive force in science education. This might be called simulation denial. But one can imagine a third response. This would take the cultural pervasiveness of simulation as a challenge to develop a new social criticism. This new criticism would discriminate among simulations. It would take as its goal the development of simulations that help their users understand and challenge their model's built-in assumptions.

I think of this new criticism as the basis for a new class of skills: *readership skills for the culture of simulation*. On one level, high-school sophomores playing SimCity for two hours may learn more about city planning than they would pick up from a textbook but, on another level, they may not know how to think about what they are doing. When I interview a tenth-grader named Marcia about SimCity, she boasts of her prowess and reels off her 'Top ten most useful rules of Sim'. Among these, number six grabs my attention: *Raising taxes always leads to riots*.

Marcia seems to have no language for discriminating between this rule of the game and the rules that operate in a 'real' city. She has never programmed a computer. She has never constructed a simulation. She has no language for asking how one might write the game so that increased taxes lead to increased productivity and social harmony. And she certainly does not see herself as someone who could change the rules. She does not know how to 'read' a simulation. Marcia is like someone who can pronounce the words in a book but doesn't understand what they mean. She does not know how to measure, criticize, or judge what she is learning. We are back to the idea over which the Mass-CUE teacher stumbled when trying to describe the notion of an 'appropriate' level at which to understand computers and the programs that animate them. When Oliver Strimpel[12] talked about wanting to use the computer museum as a place to teach the power of a transparent

understanding of the layers of the machine, he was talking about understanding the 'naked' computer. As we face computers and operating systems of an increasingly dizzying size and complexity, this possibility feels so remote that it is easy to dismiss such yearnings as old fashioned. But Marcia's situation — she is a fluent 'user' but not a fluent thinker — re-poses the question in urgent terms. Marcia may not need to see the registers on her computer or the changing charges on a computer chip, but she needs to see *something*. She needs to be working with simulations that teach her about the nature of simulation itself, that teach her enough about how to build her own that she becomes a literate 'reader' of the new medium.

Increasingly, understanding the assumptions that underlie simulation is a key element of political power. People who understand the distortions imposed by simulations are in a position to call for more direct economic and political feedback, new kinds of representation, more channels of information. They may demand greater transparency in their simulations; they may demand that the games we play (particularly the ones we use to make real life decisions) make their underlying models more accessible.

We come to written text with centuries long habits of readership. At the very least, we have learned to begin with the journalist's traditional questions: who, what, when, where, why, and how. Who wrote these words, what is their message, why were they written, how are they situated in time and place, politically and socially? A central goal for computer education must now be to teach students to interrogate simulations in much the same spirit. The specific questions may be different but the intent is the same: to develop habits of readership appropriate to a culture of simulation.

Walt Whitman once wrote: 'There was a child went forth every day. And the first object he look'd upon, that object he became.' We make our technologies, our objects, but then the objects of our lives shape us in turn. Our new objects have scintillating, pulsating surfaces, they invite playful exploration; they are dynamic, seductive, and elusive. They encourage us to move away from reductive analysis as a model of understanding. It is not clear what we are becoming when we look upon them.

Notes

1 Sherry Turkle, *Life on the Screen: Identity in the Age of the Internet.* New York: Simon and Schuster, 1995; Sherry Turkle, *The Second Self: Computers and the Human Spirit.* New York: Simon and Schuster, 1984.

2 Sherry Turkle [1978], *Psychoanalytic Politics: Jacques Lacan and Freud's French Revolution,* 2nd Revised Edition. New York: Guilford, 1990.

3 Kenneth Gergan, *The Saturated Self: Dilemmas of Identity in Contemporary Life.* New York: Basic Book, 1991

4 Emily Martin, *Flexible Bodies: Tracking Immunity in American Culture from the Days of Polio to the Age of AIDS.* Boston: Beacon Press, 1994.

5 Robert Lifton, *The Protean Self: Human Resilience in an Age of Fragmentation.* New York: Basic Books, 1993.

6 Daniel Dennett, *Consciousness Explained.* Boston: Little, Brown and Company, 1991.

7 Donna Haraway, *Simians, Cyborgs and Women: The Reinvention of Nature.* New York: Routledge, 1991.

8 Philip Bromberg, 'Speak that I May See You: Some Reflections on Dissociation, Reality and Psychoanalytic Listening.' *Psychoanalytic Dialogues* 1994, 4 (4): 517–547.

9 Stephen Levy Artificial Life, New York: Pantheon Books (1992: 6-7) DETAILS?

10 Donna Haraway, 'The Actors are Cyborg, Nature is Coyote, and the Geography is Elsewhere: Postscript to "Cyborgs at Large"'. In Constance Penley and Andrew Ross (eds.), *Technoculture.* Minneapolis: University of Minnesota Press, 1991.

11 Paul Starr writing in *The American Prospect* (Spring 1994)

12 Oliver Strimpel, Executive Director Ementus, Computing Museum, Boston, MA

CYBERVISUALITY: RECODING PERCEPTION

Sarah Chaplin

'We are born as new hard drives, and culture formats us.'
Douglas Coupland, *Microserfs*[1]
'The sky above the port was the colour of a television, tuned to a dead channel.'
William Gibson, *Neuromancer*[2]

Visuality has been an important concept in new art history, offering a revised understanding of the relationship between looking and meaning. It is a way of saying that everything we see is preconditioned by what we already know and think. At the very same moment that we take in visual stimuli, we are also interpreting them on the basis of what we have already experienced. We are assigning meaning to what we see, consciously and subconsciously at all times, and thus Hal Foster, editor of *Vision and Visuality*, asserts 'Visuality makes sight a social fact'.[3] In the same volume, Norman Bryson expresses the comprehensive scope of visuality and differentiates it from its physiological counter-part, thereby foregrounding the importance of mediation in understanding visuality: 'Between the subject and the world is inserted the entire sum of discourses which make up visuality, that cultural construct, and make visuality different from vision, the notion of unmediated visual experience.'[4]

To speak of *cyber*visuality is to extend this cultural construct a stage further, in order to suggest that the nature of this insertion is now becoming suffused with our understanding of the virtual. It indicates the emergence of a new discursive emphasis upon which visuality is predicated, brought about by means of different technologies of mediation. Cybervisuality implies that we have to some extent absorbed or acquired the capacity to perceive and process visual information in a slightly different way, and that the visual logic of computer-mediated communication is in some senses becoming naturalised. Cybervisuality may therefore be regarded as a specific cultural consequence of our progressive individual and collective exposure to the look and feel of virtual worlds and experiences. In this chapter I will show how this gives us a fresh conceptual purchase on visual experience and I will also analyse various

conceptual modifications and recodings of perception that are intended to address the wide-reaching impact of computer-mediated communication as we begin a new millennium. I will give examples of the physical effects of this recoding, and lastly make a few observations about design practice in relation to cybervisuality.

Jonathan Crary hinted at the emergence of cybervisuality in his introduction to *Techniques of the Observer*[5] in which he remarked that: 'Increasingly, visuality will be situated on a cybernetic and electromagnetic terrain where abstract visual and linguistic elements coincide and are consumed, circulated and exchanged globally'.[6] Crary described this transformation in terms of 'a sweeping reconfiguration of relations between an observing subject and modes of representation that effectively nullifies most of the culturally established meanings in terms of observer and representation', and drew attention to the implications of technologies such as 'CAD, synthetic holography, flight simulators, computer animation, robotic image recognition, magnetic resonance imaging, ray tracing, texture mapping, motion control, virtual environment helmets, and multispectral sensors,' which in his view are effectively 'relocating vision to a plane severed from a human observer'.[7]

Crary's observations embrace both the technological and cultural consequences of cybervisuality, calling attention to the need to understand changing relations between participation and meaning, and the ontological/phenomenological impact which such techniques might have upon the (post)human observer, affecting their relationship to the spaces they occupy and the nature of their interaction within those spaces, virtual or otherwise. In attempting an initial delineation of cybervisuality it will be important to take account of both aspects from a variety of theoretical and historical perspectives, and to problematise the roles of perception, representation and subjectivity within the discourses of visuality.

From the outset, it is necessary to acknowledge and critique the inherent ocularcentrism present within Western discourse since the Enlightenment, a task which Martin Jay undertook in writing *Downcast Eyes*. Jay discusses the 'ocular permeation of language' and 'visually imbued cultural and social practices', charting a shift from an oral culture to one based on writing in which 'visual bias is firmly entrenched',[8] to one which is now seemingly image-based. Jay also charts the parallel technological developments of such visual 'prostheses' as telescopes, microscopes, camera, cinema, etc., suggesting that in terms of visual perception 'the threshold between what is "natural" and what is "cultural" is by no means easy to fix'.[9] Rather than attempting to locate this threshold, Jay cites several psychologists and philosophers whose work justifies a culturalist, intentionalist reading of visual experience. In particular, he quotes Marx Wartovsky who wrote in *Picturing and Representing* that 'human vision is itself an artefact, produced by other artefacts, namely pictures'.[10] In other words, Jay infers that 'all perception is the result of historical changes in representation'.[11] This might seem like an argument for the tail wagging the dog, a reverse scenario not unlike the two quotations which appear at the beginning of this chapter. It is nevertheless a powerful scenario that helps establish the basis for a perpetual recoding of perception, of which cybervisuality emerges as the most recent reconfiguration.

Sight is not only a social fact, but a culturally situated social fact, occurring at a specific juncture in time and space, a point which Jay also underscores. He argues a case for the cultural variability of visual experience: given that people speak different languages, 'the universality of visual experience cannot be automatically assumed.'[12] By this formulation, we must speak of a plurality of cybervisualities, both within a culture and across cultures, according to differences in ethnicity and outlook brought about by socio-economic, educational, political, cultural, geographical and generational factors.

Mounting a similarly diachronic and historiographical thesis, Donald Lowe, in his book *The History of Bourgeois Perception*,[13] charts five distinct phases of perception from the Middle Ages to the present day, positing that we have now moved beyond the fourth, or 'bourgeois', phase which was heralded by the various extensions of sight such as photography and cinema, and have now reached the fifth, 'corporate capitalism', which Lowe argues is characterised by the use of electronic media. This yokes together the ideology of multinational market economics with the technological means to effect this on a global stage, a situation which epitomises not only the basis for globalisation but also the prevailing context for cybervisuality. It is a context based on a 'specular economy'[14] where images are seen as both endlessly proliferating on the one hand and tightly controlled in terms of access and reproduction rights on the other, which in turn both sustains the media and conditions public perception.

Lowe's paradigm shifts now seem too broadly periodising to be an accurate, dynamic means of conceptualising perceptual changes that are currently taking place, particularly in response to virtual technologies. In considering the term 'virtuality', N Katherine Hayles

© SARAH CHAPLIN

approaches an information-driven economy from a slightly different angle and offers a 'strategic definition': 'virtuality is the cultural perception that material objects are interpenetrated by informational patterns', which in her view 'implies a widespread perception that presence/absence is being displaced and pre-empted by pattern/randomness'.[15] Citing the example of the Human Genome Project, Hayles asserts that this new-found perception reverses the privileging of materiality over pattern (a modernist mindset) such that 'it constructs information as the site of mastery and control over the material world'.[16] She is also at pains to point out that this is actually a cultural fantasy, since all pattern/information needs matter and embodied experience to make it apparent to human perception in the first place.

Above: Travelators connecting The Mirage casino to Treasure Island, Las Vegas

Hayles' argument presents a clear case for the emergence of at least one aspect of cybervisuality: this specific cultural perception could not have come about were it not for our progressive and intensifying exposure to digital information and our encounters with virtual environments. She expresses the relationship between perception and technology as a reciprocity in performative terms: 'the perception facilitates the development of the technologies, and the technologies reinforce the perception.'[17] If it is true that we are caught in a seemingly endless perceptual loop, then what could the future hold?

Kevin Robins' text *Into the Image* ruminates in the last chapter over the question 'Will images move us still?' and in doing so offers certain recommendations, partly phenomenological, partly revisionist, about how we might come out of this apparent cultural impasse with regard to perception in the context of an image-driven, high-tech culture. Quoting Arnasson, Robins argues for a more 'open sensibility' to the visual, in which 'visual perception would be linked to "a rediscovery and articulation of the opening to the world that is constitutive of the human condition." How we look at the world relates to our disposition towards the world'.[18] In achieving this goal he defers to David Phillips, who suggests that we 'take into account the persistence and durability of older modes of visuality'.[19] Phillips' notion of perception

differs from Crary's transformational predictions discussed earlier, in that he believes 'vision operates instead as a palimpsest which conflates many different modes of perception – a model which applies both to the history of vision and to the perception of a singular observer.'[20] This model serves Robins' purpose, which is precisely to denigrate the uncritical embrace of digital technology and the prevailing tendency to regard it as revolutionary. He is anxious rather to embed within his recoding of visual perception a politicised, democratic and empowering role for image mediation, a Marxist project which seems somewhat naive and unrealisable.

In contrast to Robins' palimpsest, John Johnston presents a radically post-human development in relation to the recoding of perception in positing the notion of 'machinic vision'.[21] Johnston's definition of the term presupposes 'not only an environment of interacting machines and human-machine systems, but a field of decoded perceptions that, whether or not produced by or issuing from these machines, assume their full intelligibility only in relation to them.'[22] In other words, at the most basic level, there are some kinds of perception that are now only available to computers, what Paul Virilio refers to as 'sightless vision'.[23]

This is a Deleuzian proposition in which Johnston glosses the term 'machinic' to imply an assemblage rather than a mechanical or organic form. The decoding of perception is thus a Deleuzian strategy that effects deterritorialisation, producing its own lines of flight that counter stratification within the system. In other words, what Johnston is pushing for is a way of thinking that uses the notion of machinic to indicate 'a becoming of perception in relation to machines that necessarily also involves a recoding.'[24] Deleuze's analysis of the cinema is pertinent in terms of the transformation of perception: in his text 'Cinema 1' he posits the notion of 'gaseous perception' which applies to the way in which images that are in a state of universal variation are apprehended, nullifying the distinction between objectivity and subjectivity. This kind of extra-human perception is perhaps also unrealisable, and is not something we can claim to have experienced, but it provides a partial conceptual grasp of what the future might hold in terms of cybervisuality and the recoding of perception.

Right: Shopping mall interior, Los Angeles

© SARAH CHAPLIN

While much of Johnston's own thesis is quite abstract, he also puts forward an intriguing and somewhat paradoxical analysis of the impact of virtual reality, which concurs with Crary's prediction regarding the relocation of vision to a plane severed from the observer. Johnston argues that although virtual reality seems at first to be the antithesis of machinic vision, in that it 'replaces the act of looking with an electronically simulated experience of an entirely artificial visual world'[25] it nevertheless has the effect of simultaneously displacing and replacing the body, collapsing the world into the machine, whereby the eye becomes 'a vision machine operating in a closed loop'.[26] Thus, he concludes, 'VR brings about both an absolute deterritorialisation of the body and a total recoding of perception'.[27]

Another way of considering 'machinic vision' in relation to virtual reality is put forward by Slavoj Žižek (p.122) in which he suggests that we must conceive of the computer as a 'machine à penser', a thinking machine, for the simple reason that it has gone beyond its instrumental function and has inscribed itself into our symbolic universe, displaying a whole panoply of second order meanings. Extending this notion in order to explore the idea of the virtualisation of reality, it can be argued that many of the spaces we inhabit have also gone beyond their instrumental function as a result of our experiences of virtual reality in one form or another, and therefore also exert a whole range of second order meanings, embodying a different logic of participation and subjecting people to a new set of rules. This is part of the sweeping reconfiguration and nullification of culturally established meanings which Crary identified.

In order to clarify and substantiate some of the factors I have been discussing which affect the recoding of perception and the development of the condition of cybervisuality, I want now to examine a few examples where experience of the virtual has had a retroactive correspondence, thereby effecting a perceptual recoding of ordinary, everyday experience; that is to say, where a technique or feature encountered in a virtual environment manifests itself either as a reconfigured perception of existing conditions or as an actual physical reconfiguration.

The ability to perceive simultaneously multiple images from different and sometimes notional viewpoints is a facility that has been regularly visualised in cinematic, televisual and other media imagery, affording it an almost normalised status, such that we can easily conjure up mental images of the world appropriating the visual language and viewpoints of new visual apparati: we can 'see' the Earth from outer space, we can reproduce in our mind's eye a surveillance-type image of the Earth's surface as if from a passing satellite; we respond to images presented to us from the point of view of CCTV, and understand them not only as the quintessential panoptic viewpoint that has meaning in terms of policing and security, but also as part of a televisual language, with the rise of reality TV. *Big Brother*[28] and other programmes like it that follow the voyeuristic formatting of CCTV imagery, turn the wide-angle surveillance camera into a form of entertainment that quasi-guarantees the audience a sense of realism – conferring upon this visual medium the paradoxical impression of an unmediated yet necessarily mediated visual experience.

Further to these static examples of ontologically ambiguous, virtualised visual perceptions, our perception of certain strategies or behaviours found in physical environments may be undergoing a recoding as a result of our experience of online and gaming environments: the use of travelators, lifts and escalators in leisure spaces acts effectively like hyperlinks in a web-based environment, connecting two or more spaces together with a simple accelerated device, which overcomes the inconvenience of distance. The use of live spaces which facilitate semi-virtualised forms of movement thus starts to approximate the way in which people navigate through virtual space, and evidences the extent to which cybervisuality can have implications for the design specifications of built space. This is countered by a tendency in game environments to utilise lifts and other spatial linking devices as metaphors for moving avatars between levels which connect non-contiguous spaces that are nevertheless sequential in narrative terms.

In his analysis of the spaces of consumption, Norman Klein has drawn attention to the similarities between shopping malls and computer games,[29] showing how they share the same operational logic, aiming to keep people

Above: Segaworld entertainment centre, Trocadero, London

© SARAH CHAPLIN

Above: Themed map of
San Diego

'there' as long as possible, enclosing them inside an interiorised world, and so on. Their historical development can also be paralleled: early games/malls offered simple generic experience of winning/shopping, a strategy which has now been augmented with greater thematic complexity and a more elaborate interplay/overlapping of consumption and entertainment. Shoppers' attention is as sought after as the attention span of a gamer, with concept designers and space syntax experts being employed to work on mall layouts and airport retail concourses to ensure that spatial linkages and continuities maximise opportunities to browse and partake of the total retail offer.[30] Lines of sight are analysed on plan, which take account of the eye-level point of view of the shopper in the same way as computer games take advantage of this situated form of participation.

This is perhaps all the more apparent in an environment which explicitly revolves around gaming: Segaworld, located in the centre of London, as a space dedicated to playing computer games in a semi-public setting has been designed and lit to feel more 'virtual', that is to say, to give it a more artificial quality, bringing it closer to the elusive nature of machinic perception. Escalators seem to exist in free space, encapsulated in bands of neon, and the main spaces are experienced sequentially, moving from the top level downwards, much like progressing through levels in a game.

In terms of the cartographic representation of real spaces, it is interesting to note that many contemporary tourist maps of downtown urban areas now use a game-like interface to communicate the main points of interest. Such tactics are synonymous with the way in which landmarks are encountered in a computer game, picked out in pseudo-3D, like a cartoonified SimCity. Orientation within many urban entertainment centres is now given in terms of a suggested itinerary which tourists are invited to undertake in order to derive the most enjoyment from the place, a strategy which again borrows from the sequencing of a computer game experience.

In some cities, the game-like map itself is not enough to sustain the experience of a number of prominent 'destination' landmarks: at one time it was sufficiently exciting to ride up to the top of the Empire State Building in a state-of-

the-art elevator and enjoy the thrilling view from the top. Now, in order to safeguard visitor numbers to this classic New York tourist attraction, it has been bundled as a virtualised encounter with the real: a simulator ride takes you from the top of the Empire State Building on a hair-raising flight over the streets of Manhattan, employing a pseudo-game narrative (the voice-over is in the second person), which goes out of control. This renders a visit to the Empire State Building a programmable event, no longer dependent on time of visit (visibility, night, day, season, etc.), instead encapsulating a virtualised Manhattan and turning it into a real ride which supplies the same rush as a computer game, and heightens the experience of the real city.

These are all in effect second order meanings evident in pre-existing physical environments, where the primary function of the environment has become somehow eclipsed by its secondary function, intended to create a space in which symbolic meanings and interpretations can be played out. This layering of meaning takes us away from our primary purpose or point of contact with that environment, and engages us with more exciting and dynamic secondary interpretations/use values. It subjects spaces to a new perceptual conditioning, such that marketing and lifestyle experts can make their messages speak louder than the less vocal preferred meanings supplied by the architect or designer at the outset.

Second order meanings can communicate in a form of shorthand, omitting a level of detail which is not deemed necessary, since they do not have to fulfil the same functions. In extreme cases of second order meanings, the supplier of first order meaning is no longer present, although its actual referent may exist elsewhere: it is no longer something to which we need to have direct access for the purposes of enjoyment. In the case of the Venetian, Paris, and even to an extent the New York New York resort casinos in Las Vegas, it is a fact that most American visitors to Vegas have not actually visited these places firsthand; rather their previous contact with them was virtual or mediated – something encountered only on TV, at the movies or in magazines. The designs for these themed architectonic creations are therefore constructed soundbite-style from a series of well-known cultural landmarks which are bricolaged together to provide the right amount of visual iconography needed to symbolise these cities. Conversely, it is increasingly the case that when we do have the opportunity to experience 'the real thing', it is so thoroughly proscribed by our mediated encounters with that place, that it can only be experienced as something that has been overly mediated and therefore reified: an exotic beach holiday is experienced as stepping into a film or an advertisement.

These are just a handful of indications as to how we are resolving some of the ontological and representational dilemmas that cybervisuality poses for us. There is much work to be done. Design practice needs to develop its own awareness of cybervisuality and it needs to respond to and also bring about the recoding of perception if it is to remain effective in terms of creating the kinds of environment that people can relate to in the twenty-first century. Design professionals need to be able to develop a revised understanding of perception that might lead to the creation of more exciting ontologically hybrid spatial conditions.

Similarly, in order to understand more clearly the process by which virtual experience is affecting contemporary consciousness, cultural theorists need to develop more detailed studies of some of the ambivalent representational aspects of computer games, science fiction films and online environments to ascertain which metaphors are dominant, which operational systems are presupposed, and which aesthetic codifications are being established. From this analysis it will become clear which aspects of our lived experience are being mediated in virtual settings, and what the perceptual effect is of then mapping that mediation back onto lived experience, thereby creating ever more complex forms of cybervisuality.

Many of the leisure spaces we now occupy are as algorithmically determined as spaces encountered in a computer game, in that their parameters are fixed, the mode of engagement with them is totally scripted, and the sequencing and outcomes are a known quantity. Disney/MGM operates this system *par excellence*, bringing about a gradual convergence of their actual and virtual environments, all of which are designed to entertain whilst maximising consumer loyalty, docility and economic profitability. It is therefore increasingly important to understand the effects that the spatial strategies of corporate capitalism are having on public perception, and the recoding that this is necessarily precipitating.

My initial interest in cyberspatial technologies[31] was triggered by a concern about the effect of mapping of habits, nomenclature and assumptions of our actual existence onto the virtual, and the fact that this might hinder its ongoing development into a completely different medium not based analogously on other known forms. Elsewhere I have argued in the context of feminist discourse that cybervisuality might come to represent a shift towards a non-objectifying scopic regime, and offer a way for visual culture to engage with both technologies of gender and the gendering of technology.[32] It therefore now seems productive to consider the issues of mapping or representing in reverse our tentative and provisional understanding of the virtual onto our actual existence, since this presents a different kind of problematic, offering a way of probing and recoding collective perception, machinic, gaseous or otherwise, and of rehearsing our responses, our tactics and our modes of cultural appropriation. Cybervisuality might then have the possibility of becoming not simply a salient fact of contemporary existence, but an active theoretical tool in directing the future of our engagement with the virtual.

© SARAH CHAPLIN

Left: Exterior of the Venetian, Las Vegas

Notes

1 Douglas Coupland, *Microserfs*. London: Flamingo, 1995.

2 William Gibson, *Neuromancer*. London: Grafton, 1984, 1986, p. 9.

3 Hal Foster (Ed.), *Vision and Visuality*. Seattle: Bay Press, 1988, p. ix.

4 Norman Bryson, 'The gaze in the expanded field', Ibid., p.91.

5 Jonathan Crary, *Techniques of the Observer*. Cambridge: MIT Press, 1990

6 Ibid. p. 1.

7 Ibid.

8 Martin Jay, *Downcast Eyes*. Berkeley: University of California Press, 1992, p. 2.

9 Ibid. p. 3.

10 Marx Wartovsky, Ibid. p. 5.

11 Jay, *Downcast Eyes*, p. 5.

12 Ibid p. 9.

13 Donald Lowe, *The History of Bourgeois Perception*. Brighton: Harvester, 1982.

14 Sadie Plant, 'On the matrix: cyberfeminist simulations'. In David Bell and Barbara M Kennedy (Eds), *The Cybercultures Reader*. London: Routledge, 2000, p. 332.

15 N Katherine Hayles, 'The condition of virtuality'. In Peter Lunenfeld (Ed.), *The Digital Dialectic*. Cambridge: MIT Press, 1999, p. 69.

16 Ibid. p. 72.

17 Ibid. p. 69.

18 Kevin Robins, *Into the Image*. London: Routledge, 1996, p. 164.

19 David Phillips, quoted Ibid. p. 165.

20 Robins, *Into the Image*, p. 165.

21 John Johnston, 'Machinic vision'. *Critical Enquiry*, Vol.26, Autumn 1999.

22 Ibid. p. 27.

23 Paul Virilio, *The Vision Machine*. Bloomington: Indiana University Press, 1994, p. 59.

24 Johnston, 'Machinic vision', p. 29.

25 Ibid. p. 40.

26 Ibid.

27 Ibid.

28 *Big Brother*, Channel 4, 2000.

29 Norman Klein, 'Scripted spaces: Navigating the consumer built city'. In Sarah Chaplin and Eric Holding (Eds) *Consuming Architecture*. London: Wiley, 1998, p. 80.

30 See Bill Hillier, *Space is the Machine*. London: Cambridge University Press, 1996.

31 Sarah Chaplin, 'Cyberspace: Lingering on the threshold'. In Neil Spiller (Ed.), *Architects in Cyberspace*. London: Wiley, 1995, pp. 32–35.

32 Sarah Chaplin, 'Cyberfeminism'. In Fiona Carson and Claire Pajaczkowska (Ed.), *Feminist Visual Culture*. Edinburgh: Edinburgh University Press, 2000, pp. 265–280.

THE CULT OF THE NOT YET

Richard Coyne

Digital technology bears a great burden. Not only is it required to meet our growing expectation of ever more sophisticated and enabling inventiveness, but it is also required to bear responsibility for major social and cultural transformations. For media commentators such as Marshall McLuhan and his followers, instant and incessant communications are returning society to a tribal state of idealised, happy and democratic union.[1] We are becoming citizens of a global village. It seems that such claims to transformation have accompanied other major and identifiable technologies. Media theorist James Cary notes that the same transformative role was attributed to steam power, railways, electricity, and atomic power,[2] and we see similar promise accompanying space travel, robotics, genetic engineering and reproduction technologies. At their more modest, such claims focus on the promise of efficiencies in production, an enhanced ability to solve difficult problems, increased profits, and new business opportunities. More extravagantly, the increased connectivity and greater access at affordable cost empower individuals and auger a more egalitarian and democratic society. (Here we could be talking of the railways, the motor car, the telephone or the internet.) For extreme enthusiasts, digital technology is the culmination of an inexorable progression. Not only does it usher in a new phase in social improvement, but of biological evolution that somehow implicates machines. We are on the way to having our thoughts and bodies transferred to machines and participating in a networked digital transfiguration, a *Star Trek*-inspired global mind meld.[3]

How does a technology acquire responsibility for such extravagant possibilities? I would like to conjecture three conditions that prime a technology for inflated expectation and overstated capabilities. First, the technology needs to be named. The technological world is complex and diffused, implicating institutions, social systems, history and myriad interacting technological systems. There needs to be a way of condensing this reality of the complex of relations to an identifiable entity. In the manner of metonymy, there has to be some part of the fabric of our complex world that can be named to stand in for the larger picture. Why or how this is the case is as much a question of the nature of language as it is of the nature of specific technologies. 'Digital technology' is one rubric that has been identified. 'The computer', 'information technology', 'digital media', 'new media', 'digital communications' have also served this role; and in the domain of architecture is found 'computer-aided design (CAD)' and 'virtual architecture'. Lately the internet, the Web and mobile technologies have taken over a metonymic role in accounting for the large and ill-defined complex of systems waiting to be named.

Second, what is named has to fit within a technical agenda, which is simply to say that its development can be identified in terms of measurable trajectories: such as bigger, smaller, faster, closer, further. The railways readily submitted to the quanta of journey time, speed, numbers of connections and miles of track. The digital realm measures itself in terms of processing speed, storage capacity, bandwidth and number of network connections, each of which can appear as curves on a graph showing increase. Such vectors sustain the narrative of progress and are capable of translation by analogy to society as a whole. Through metaphor, quantity is readily equated with quality.[4] More is readily equated with better. Society is capable of improvement analogously to the way that more nodes increase network connectivity, and finer printed circuits increase processor speeds. Society can be reconfigured analogously to the reconfiguration of components on a circuit board or elements in a CAD database.

Third, the technology is a candidate for being presented as totalising. Measurable trajectories fit readily into narratives of restoration. Each technological improvement takes us closer to a complete whole, where every city is connected by lightning-fast railways, safe travel is open to everyone, you can go anywhere at any time. Digital technology presents the spectre of instant communications, totally ubiquitous digital devices in communication with each other, including computers woven into the fabric of our clothing or even implanted in our bodies. The technology is potentially restorative of our fractured world, uniting us with one another and unifying humans and machines. Similarly, the eighteenth-century technology pundit may have claimed that steam is purest white, suffuses through our world, is clean and gives life to the dried-out fabric of our weary existence. Subsequently, electricity dealt in the positive and negative and united them in a productive life-giving charge. Now, digital technology is a play of zeros and ones.[5] They ultimately unite in restoring a long-lost primordial communion. If the technology lends itself to such narratives of restoration and unity, then it seems it is a ready candidate for assuming inflated responsibility for social transformation.

Considering these three conditions linguistically, the technology functions in terms of metonymy, metaphor and analogy to claim the capability of bringing about social restoration, transformation and reconfiguration. Alternatively, in terms of Heidegger's philosophy of technology, we have become technological beings, infatuated with control and instrumental causality, and are slaves to the necessity of explaining everything in the same reductive terms. Technology becomes a cause. We have adopted a totalising world picture, a technological conceit that is at once limiting and inevitable.[6]

Irrespective of how it gains its power of explanation, a technology inevitably fails to meet its promise, if for no other reason than that it simply reaches its technical limits. As the asymptotes of the graphs come into view the law of diminishing returns dictates that it is too expensive to take the technology further. Or perhaps the technology becomes integrated inconspicuously into social practices, as have the motor car, the telephone and automatic teller machines. The name (computer, digital media, digital communications, CAD, virtual architecture) can become lost, as the complex interdependencies of the social and technological systems become apparent. Society can become inured to extravagant claims made for the technology. There may also be concerted resistance to the technology. In the obvious case we are persuaded that the technology might be socially deleterious, as with nuclear power, defence technologies and genetic modification. Or a nostalgia for simpler technologies may come into play.

Contrary to their promise, evidence of the inadequacies of digital technology abounds. The social transformations do not seem to take place. The putative positive change of increased communications imposes new burdens on labour. New forms of drudgery and exploitation emerge. Charges have been levelled at the exploitation of labour in digitised telephone call centres and the isolation of networked home working.[7] Digital technology is capable of displacing people from interesting, fulfilling work and turning them into information workers, continuing the dehumanising aspects of industrialisation.[8] At the level of our micro-practices with computers we are familiar with failing software, bugs, crashes, computer viruses, and the costs and demands imposed by inexorable updates to software, hardware and operating systems. The technology is anything but invisible as one wrestles with new instructions, supposedly intelligent online manuals, esoteric commands and obscure icons. Like it or not, you have to be a computer hobbyist to keep up. For a while there was a joke circulating around the internet that working with the software of one particular well-known company was analogous to having to be an amateur car mechanic in order to drive a car.

Digital technology is characterised by the 'not yet', a term developed at length (with no reference to the digital world) by Ernst Bloch in his treatise on Utopia and the future, *The Principle of Hope*.[9] Is software reliable? Is the world a better place as a result of digital communications? Does CAD make architectural practice more efficient? Are virtual walkthroughs of buildings realistic? Is digital architecture inhabitable, immersive and compelling? Well, not yet, but it will be. The concept of the future assumes an important role in the face of the increasing inadequacies of digital technology to the promises made of it. The future serves as a repository for the unfulfilled ambitions of digital technology. For Bloch and the phenomenological tradition, the 'not yet' is a suitable name, a place holder, for the condition of being unsettled in the face of hopes and desires. Our primordial condition is of care and expectation, the concept of the future follows, as a particular form of explanation of our involvement in the world of technology.

The future is the way the 'not yet' is revealed when we wish to exert our interest in control, in the face of the unrealised promises of technology. 'Future' names the part of the time vector extending from the present, and which is contiguous with the past. It lends geometrical legitimacy to the play of extrapolation, prediction, goal setting and method. Time constitutes the axis on the graph showing progression to bigger, smaller, faster, further, closer. Unrealised expectations gain expression as 'misfit variables',[10] and constitute goals to be achieved. The RIBA series on Future Studies is perhaps motivated by a desire to control the destiny of architecture, a rightful duty of a professional organisation. If we can predict how digital technology is shaping up then we can control how we position ourselves in relationship to it, instrumentally and rationally.[11]

But there is another tradition in play that frustrates this ambition. This is the romantic legacy of utopian speculation, to which the architectural tradition is also a party. This is the inspirational and sometimes anti-rationalist dreaming of the first person vision: 'I see the future, and it is digital.' As remarked by architectural historians,[12] architecture provided a rich medium for the expression and exploration of Utopia (as made overt in Futurism and Expressionism), a role now largely taken over by the media of science fiction, film, computer games, and speculations about digital technology. The future is here the non-place of the ideal, the restored whole, problematised in the best fiction as a struggle with a dystopian obverse, or at worst sentimentalised as a New-Age melding of mind, body, soul, nature and artifice. One problem for a professionally oriented Future Studies dialogue is disentangling the utopian from the instrumentally predictive. Speculative and utopian narratives may inspire, but do they show us how to prepare for new forms of architectural practice?

But the dialogues that cluster around the poles of instrumental and romantic speculation have already run their course in the social sciences and humanistic disciplines, such as sociology, politics and literary study, though the imperatives of digital technology seem to have cleared a space for their revival. Architects speculating about electronic futures seem to be given licence to fall back on outdated forms of

argument: appealing either to case studies of how they set and solved technical problems (a kind of instrumental pursuit), or time-worn excesses of utopian speculation (a neo-romanticism).

Even the Marxist and neo-Marxist legacies of critical architectural theory seem to be side-lined in much of the discourse on digital architecture. Marx provides a dour line of critique which does not capture the imagination in the same way as giddy speculation about reconfigured digital futures. The kill-joy Marxist legacy came out against the concepts of Utopia, as an ideological pursuit. Marx long ago identified the problem of the replacement of labour by machines. With more colour, Baudrillard and others present the concealing and masking effects of technology. Capitalism distracts and masks the current unsatisfactory condition by directing labour to pin the fulfilment of unrealistic and unrealised expectations on a utopian future. Labour can be inured to its toil by promise of something better.

But narratives of the 'not yet' can do more than describe what 'may be'. In the manner of good science fiction, a computer game or a work of surreal art, they can provoke through our capacity to let the absurd do its work. The supposed, and nonsensical, human/machine hybrid known as the cyborg, which apparently we are all becoming, can serve as a shock to those who believe in the goal of integrated and whole personalities in tune with some natural order. The cyborg serves as a surreal object thrown into the context of our discourses on digital technology. The claim is that whether or not we have prosthetic implants we are perhaps provoked to re-think who and what we are.[13] The prospect of virtual architecture, an ambiguous, distributed form of space-making that is as much process as product, perhaps provokes us into thinking anew what architecture is, and what it is to practise as an architect. Whether or not we now try to design virtual buildings, the concept of architecture without bricks and concrete may already be informing what we do. In this and other respects, the computer (and its metonymic variants the internet, the WAP phone, the virtual construction) serves as a surreal object thrown into the fabric of our expectations. It distorts and unsettles the fragile warp and weft of professional certitudes.

Whether such speculative provocations are productive is a pragmatic question. The value of a narrative, like the meaning of a word, is in its use, and use is subject to ever-changing context. It is perhaps the task of Future Studies to find suitable names for entities that might challenge and provoke in ways that illuminate the changing contexts of architectural practice. This task is already far removed from the blind assumption that digital technology is the prime mover of radical transformation, and rhetorical ploys aimed at causing us to gasp in breathless wonder at what may yet be achieved, while ignoring the failed promises of the moment.

Notes

1 Marshall McLuhan, *The Gutenberg Galaxy: The Making of Typographic Man*. Toronto: University of Toronto Press, 1962.

2 James Cary, *Communication as Culture: Essays in Media and Society*. London: Routledge & Kegan Paul, 1989.

3 Richard Coyne, *Technoromanticism: Digital Narrative, Holism and the Romance of the Real*. Cambridge, MA: MIT Press, 1999.

4 George Lakoff and Mark Johnson, *Metaphors We Live By*. Chicago, IL: University of Chicago Press, 1980.

5 Sadie Plant, *Zeros and Ones: Digital Women and the New Technoculture*. London: Fourth Estate, 1998.

6 Martin Heidegger, *The Question Concerning Technology and Other Essays,* trans. W. Lovitt. New York: Harper and Row, 1977.

7 Graham Scott and Robert Scott, 'Ethics and the human aspects of technological change: Call centres, a case study'. *International Journal of Design Sciences and Technology* 2000, 8(1): 25–35.

8 Jeremy Rifkin, *The End of Work: The Decline of the Global Work-Force and the Dawn of the Post-Market Era*. London: Penguin, 2000.

9 Ernst Bloch, *The Principle of Hope,* trans. Neville Plaice, Stephen Plaice and Paul Knight. Oxford: Basil Blackwell.

10 Christopher Alexander, *Notes on the Synthesis of Form*. Cambridge, MA: Harvard University Press, 1964.

11 Richard D Coyne, *Designing Information Technology in the Postmodern Age: From Method to Metaphor*. Cambridge, MA: MIT Press, 1995.

12 Iain Boyd Whyte, 'The expressionist sublime'. In Timothy O. Benson (Ed.) *Expressionist Utopias: Paradise, Metropolis, Architectural Fantasy*. Los Angeles, CA: Los Angeles County Museum of Art, 1993, pp. 118–137.

13 Katherine N Hayles, *How We Became Posthuman: Virtual Bodies in Cybernetics, Literature and Informatics*. Chicago, IL: University of Chicago Press, 1999.

DIGITAL CITIES

E-BODIES, E-BUILDING, E-CITIES
William J Mitchell

It is now a commonplace observation (to the point of weary cliché) that the explosive combination of tiny, inexpensive electronic devices, increasingly ubiquitous digital networking, and the world's rapidly growing stock of digital information is dramatically changing our daily lives.[1] But what does this condition suggest, concretely, for architectural and urban design strategy in the twenty-first century?

The Cost of Being There
In order to develop some useful answers to this question, I shall begin by adopting a rather brutally reductionist perspective. Specifically, I shall assume that there are three types of costs associated with assigning particular activities to specific urban locations: *fixed* costs, *interactive* costs and *churn* costs.[2] And, in each case, there are corresponding benefits, which for mathematical simplicity can just be treated as negative costs. The new technological context affects all of these (but in different ways and to different extents), and changes the balance among them. The ultimate result is a new mix of space types in the city, together with new spatial patterns at all scales.

Fixed costs, such as rent, are intrinsic to a location.[3] The corresponding benefits, such as the pleasures of climatic and scenic attractions, are valuable advantages that cannot be changed by transportation or telecommunication connections. (You cannot pump the sybaritic attractions of a beach through a wire.) Very often, location decisions are made by trading off these fixed costs and benefits against other types of costs and benefits. For example, you might choose to live in the reasonably priced, leafy outer suburbs to gain quiet and greenery, but you might pay heavily for this in terms of the time and cost of commuting to a job in the central city. In general, consideration of fixed costs and benefits produces spatial patterns in which activities cluster at locations characterised by unusual local attractions or by invitingly low rents.

Interactive costs of assigning an activity to a location are those that result from interactions with other activities. For example, there may be substantial flows of goods between a factory and some warehouses. If the warehouses are nearby, then the resulting yearly transportation costs are low. However, if the warehouses are distant, the costs will be higher. Since everything cannot be adjacent to everything else, consideration of interactive costs and benefits usually produces location patterns in which highly interactive activities are located centrally, minimally interactive activities go to the periphery, and closely inter-linked activities are as near to each other as possible.

Churn costs are those that result, over time, from moving activities around.[4] For example, if you move an office to another floor there will be associated transportation, renovation and trans-action costs. If you rely on a lot of heavy, fixed equipment, then churn costs will be high and you will have an incentive not to move – even if your location is not ideal from other viewpoints. Conversely, if you work with only a portable laptop and cell phone, your costs of picking up and moving will be low. In general, high churn costs produce stable spatial patterns, while low churn costs encourage a more nomadic condition.

Actual architectural, urban and regional spatial patterns result largely from overlays, interactions and balances of patterns produced by fixed, interactive and churn costs and benefits.[5] On an isotropic plane, interactive costs would dominate to produce patterns that responded very directly to traffic flow and accessibility considerations. But in complex and differentiated topography, the intrinsic advantages and disadvantages of particular places play a bigger role. And the high churn costs associated with permanent construction and sunk investments tend to lock in established urban spatial patterns; nomads think little of relocating and reconfiguring their tent encampments when they need greener pastures.

The Revenge of Place
Now, what are the effects of electronic interconnection on these costs, benefits and associated patterns?

First, the effects on fixed costs and benefits are minimal; network connections do not change the climate or the scenery. It follows that, when other types of costs are reduced by electronic interconnection, fixed costs and benefits begin to dominate. In other words, if you can locate anywhere you will locate where it's particularly attractive in some way. I shall refer to this phenomenon as the *revenge of place*.

One extreme manifestation of the revenge of place is the much-hyped (and even occasionally instantiated) 'electronic cottage' located deep in the woods, high in the mountains, or on some idyllic island. Electronic connectivity provides necessary economic, social and cultural linkages to the wider world, while self-contained power generation, water collection and waste recycling systems keep everything working. It is the sort of thing that Robert Louis Stevenson had in mind, albeit relying upon the earlier interconnection technologies of the steamship and the international mail, when he moved his dwelling and the site of his work to Apia in the South Pacific.

A more common and practical manifestation is the affluent telecommuter village, such as is now being seen in the vicinity of Paris or in resort settings such as Aspen or Camden, Maine. Here the attraction is the picturesque, charming and generally exclusive small community. The inhabitants are very high-end knowledge workers (stock traders, software wizards, script writers) who can now work electronically to a large extent, and who can afford very high-quality personal transportation (limousines, light aircraft) when they need it.

Fragmentation and Recombination

The most obvious effects of electronic interconnection are on interactive costs and benefits. The whole point of digital telecommunications systems is that they reduce spatial and temporal interdependencies among activities; they make it possible to do things at a distance, and to conduct transactions asynchronously. This does not mean (as some have suggested) that the 'friction of distance' simply disappears so that you can locate anything anywhere. Rather, it means that spatial and temporal linkages among activities are *selectively* loosened. Internet distribution drastically reduces the cost of getting recorded music from producer to consumer, for example, and it eliminates trips to the record store, but you still have to drag your body from your residence to the dental surgery when you need a filling.

This selective loosening allows latent demands for proximity to manifest themselves; proximity requirements that could not previously be satisfied, since they were dominated by other requirements, now come to the fore. Furthermore, latent demands for quality of place also begin to take over; if you can telecommute, for example, you might relocate to a scenic but hitherto hopelessly inaccessible location. The resulting phenomenon, as activities regroup, is *fragmentation and recombination* of building types and urban patterns.[6]

Fragmentation and recombination processes sometimes result in decentralisation to reach larger markets, to get closer to customers, and so on. But they can also produce centralisation, motivated by efforts to achieve economies of scale, or to take advantage of knowledge spillover effects. And they can yield mobilisation of certain activities, as these activities float free of traditional locational ties and thereby become easier to relocate in response to dynamic conditions such as changes in labour markets. (It all depends, of course, on what latent proximity demands are lurking.) All these things, and more, can take place simultaneously, producing complicated and sometimes apparently contradictory spatial outcomes.

The death of the branch bank vividly illustrates the complexities of fragmentation and recombination. Not so long ago, branch banks were a prominent building type on any high street. Then came automated teller machines (ATMs), followed by electronic home banking. Face-to-face interactions with a teller during banking hours were replaced by electronically mediated remote interactions at any time of the day or night. The space for retail banking systems fragmented and decentralised; ATMs are now found on street corners, in airport terminals, in gambling casinos – in short, wherever people may need cash – while electronic home banking transactions can be conducted from anywhere there is internet connectivity. Simultaneously, electronic commerce technology allowed back office functions to cluster for efficiency and to relocate to places where the labour market was attractive – often offshore. The old branch banks were shut down in their thousands, and a radically new spatial pattern, involving different building types (large-scale back-office facilities, call centres) emerged. Banking organisations were no longer represented by their dignified high street façades, but by screen logos on ATM and personal computer screens.

Electronically mediated retailing of books and similar articles has generated parallel effects, with the additional twist of restructuring transportation as well as spatial patterns. A traditional urban bookstore is a place to store books, to advertise them, to allow customers to browse among them and make selections, to conduct purchase transactions across a counter, and to pursue necessary back-office activities such as ordering and inventory tracking. All these activities need to be clustered tightly together within a well-defined spatial envelope, because of requirements for face-to-face interaction, efficient circulation of stock and customers, visual supervision and physical security. And there are some inherent contradictions; it is desirable, for instance, to offer customers the largest stock of titles possible, but capacity to do this is limited by expensive, highly constrained urban real estate. But an operation like Amazon.com changes the rules of the game. It virtualises and radically decentralises the browsing and purchasing functions, it shifts book storage from local storage points to huge, highly automated warehouse and distribution centres at national airline hubs (where huge numbers of titles can be kept in stock economically), and it mobilises back-office work by exploiting electronic commerce technology for maintaining relationships with customers and suppliers. Amazon back-office employees could be located just about anywhere, but it turns out that they are largely located in downtown Seattle – because that's where they want to be. Overall, under this pattern, the local bookstore disappears, residences and offices become decentralised sites for retail transactions, the national distribution centre emerges and is located to minimise interaction costs, and the back-office work gravitates to attractive urban locations (for higher-level employees) or to rural locations where the land is cheap and the labour market is depressed (for lower-level employees).

It is immediately obvious that new transportation patterns will result from all this. Where books were once delivered in medium-sized shipments to intermediate storage points provided by local retailers, then carried home by customers, they are now delivered in large shipments from publishers to national distribution centres, from where they travel in small packages, by air and van, directly to homes and offices. Some places get more traffic, others get less. Certainly, as a result of electronic retailing, I make fewer trips to go shopping but there are now more delivery vans on my street.

Of course, that is not the *only* way to change the rules of the book retailing game. An increasingly attractive alternative is to store books on online servers, and to download them on demand to sophisticated machines that do high-quality printing and binding. Instead of physically distributing after manufacture, you electronically deliver before manufacture. This fragments traditional, centralised factory space and recombines it with retail space.

Erasing Incompatibilities

The converse to spatial attraction produced by high interaction between activities is spatial repulsion resulting from incompatibility. One of the major moves of nineteenth- and twentieth-century urban planning was to separate residential suburbs from the noise, traffic and pollution of urban industrial areas. In general, the central idea of land use zoning has been to cluster compatible activities together and to separate them from incompatible ones. (Of course, there is lots of room for contention about the definitions of 'compatible' and 'incompatible'.)

But the information work that is such a crucial part of today's economy, supported by networked electronic devices, is not like factory work. It does not generate noise and pollution, it does not necessarily require large concentrations of workers in one place, and it does not generate large amounts of delivery traffic. Therefore, the incompatibilities with residential land uses are greatly reduced or eliminated, and reintegration of the home and the workplace becomes an increasingly attractive possibility. Fine-grained, mixed-use neighbourhoods created from live/work dwellings can begin to re-emerge.

Similarly, the activities associated with online retailing are not like those associated with suburban shopping malls. When you order goods online, you do not need access to a big-box facility stocked with goods and serviced by big trucks, nor do you need a large parking lot. You do need space in your home to conduct the transactions, and you do need some convenient way to receive deliveries – either by being at home, by providing some sort of secure delivery locker (maybe a refrigerated one in the case of food), or by making arrangements with a neighbourhood delivery point such as a mom-and-pop corner store. This potentially reintegrates fine-grained retail activities with the neighbourhood, separates them from large-scale storage and distribution functions, and displaces those big-box functions to regional transportation nodes, unvisited by customers, on the urban periphery.

This electronic erasure of long-standing incompatibilities creates conditions for re-establishing traditional neighbourhood patterns, as advocated by the American New Urbanists, and as suggested by the Urban Villages proposals of Prince Charles.[7] We have seen these patterns emerging in certain high-tech hotspots, such as the SoHo area of Manhattan, and the South of Market (SoMa) district of San Francisco. This is not a matter of ignoring the genuine problems addressed by traditional zoning strategies, nor one of sentimental hankering after the virtues of pre-industrial small-town life, but a realistic response to emerging post-industrial conditions.

Tunnel Effects

In addition to producing fragmentation and recombination, and allowing new spatial patterns to emerge (or traditional patterns to re-emerge) by erasing incompatibilities, radical reductions in interactive costs can generate profoundly antispatial interdependencies among towns, cities and regions.

Traditionally, there have been strong interdependencies among geographically clustered activities, but much weaker interdependencies among widely separated activities. A city might have strong economic, social and cultural linkages to its agricultural hinterland and to nearby provincial towns, for example, but much more tenuous relationships to distant corners of the world. The development of transportation networks enabled stronger linkages and interdependencies at a distance – among trading cities, in particular – but the 'tyranny of distance' remained potent.[8] There was substantial congruence between place and community.

Now, in contexts where interactions among activities can effectively be supported by electronic interconnection, very strong interdependencies can develop at a distance. Thus the information technology clusters of Silicon Valley and Bangalore are very closely linked to one another and highly interdependent. Hollywood (a world centre for film production) and London's Soho (a remarkable concentration of post-production facilities and talent) have become increasingly symbiotic as high-speed electronic interconnections have linked them ever more effectively. And, as everyone knows, the world's major financial centres are now strongly interconnected through sophisticated electronic linkages to form a global system. Such 'tunnel effects', which unevenly warp accessibility surfaces, are becoming increasingly common.[9]

As many have noted, this condition generates dramatic slippages and discontinuities within the urban fabric. A high-rise office building in Jakarta may function as a node in the global financial networks, while the surrounding urban kampongs belong to a completely different economic, social and cultural order. A campus workplace in Bangalore may be almost indistinguishable from one in Palo Alto, but the cows amble down the dusty road outside. A telephone call centre in Sydney may exist to serve customers in Hong Kong. Being in the right time zone can now be far more important than being in the right neighbourhood.

At worst, it is easy to imagine these distortions, slippages and discontinuities becoming chasms, destroying any sense of cohesive local community, and producing an urban fabric of juxtaposed but socially and culturally disconnected fragments held in a matrix of common physical infrastructure.[10] At best, one might imagine combining the virtues of small-town cohesiveness (provided spatially) with the opportunities and excitement of cosmopolitan connections (provided electronically) to a wider world. Finding ways to get the balance right will be one of the great design and planning challenges of the coming years.

We will not achieve this goal by conceiving of electronic interaction as a direct (though perhaps inferior) substitute for face-to-face. Nor will we get there by treating social interaction as a zero-sum game in which time devoted to one mode is time subtracted from another. We will do better to consider some of the subtler ways in which digital and physical space may intersect. Consider, for example, the common problem of providing network access on a university campus. One approach is to network desktop computers in dormitory rooms; in this case, spatial organisation and network configuration clearly conspire to produce fragmentation and isolation. Some students will almost never come out of their rooms. An alternative approach is to combine wireless laptop computers with a system of inviting, informal public study spaces: sidewalk cafés, common rooms, nooks and crannies off public spaces, shady spots under trees, and so on; this combination of digital and physical arrangements activates social spaces, promotes accidental encounters, and allows students to create informal study groups as they wish, while retaining all the advantages of electronic connectivity.

Electronic Mobilisation

Whereas these various effects of the digital revolution on interactive costs derive from loosening of spatial and temporal linkages among activities, the effects on churn costs follow from miniaturisation and dematerialisation. For example, office work used to require filing cabinets filled with paper, a desktop and a typewriter; now the desktop has virtualised and shrunk to a laptop screen, files are accessible online, the typewriter has transmuted into word-processing software, and the telephone fits into a pocket. It was slow and expensive to move all your stuff from one office to another, but now it is effortless to pick up your laptop and your cell phone to relocate. And you can work just about anywhere: not only in an 'official' workspace, but also at home, in an aeroplane seat, at a customer location, on a park bench, or in a café. It isn't that we all turn into full-time telecommuters; face-to-face interaction still has its important uses. But work hours and locations become far more fluid and adaptable to changing circumstances.[11]

Simply put, wireless networking increases mobility, reduces churn costs, and provides flexibility to reorganise and regroup rapidly and efficiently in response to changing conditions. The effects are felt in a wide range of contexts, from design offices rearranging themselves to take on new projects to kids in the street with cell phones organising raves and protests on the fly.

Attentive Architecture

A second significant consequence of electronically enabled miniaturisation and dematerialisation is the increasing prevalence of electronic tags, sensors and sophisticated control systems in buildings. HVAC and lighting systems have long had electronic sensors and controls, of course, and electronic security systems are commonplace, but the tags and sensors are now getting smaller, cheaper, more versatile and more ubiquitous. Some of them are wireless. And they are being integrated into standard IP networks (that is, they become part of the internet) rather than operating as specialised proprietary systems.

Potentially, we can think of all the devices and appliances in a building as smart objects that can sense and respond to their changing environments, and can operate as servers in peer-to-peer networks (a sort of architectural Napster) within buildings.[12] Even a single light bulb might incorporate sensors, intelligence, network connectivity and TCP/IP capability; you could send email to it and get a reply. The ultimate consequences of this will be profound, and they are probably not yet fully imaginable, but the first-order outcome will surely be to enhance the versatility of spaces. A given space, through electronic intelligence and functionality, will not only be more responsive and efficient, it will also be programmable for wider ranges of activities.

We should be careful to distinguish flexibility and multifunctionality achieved through electronic reprogramming of services from the 1960s and 1970s strategy of providing modular, reconfigurable spaces and partition and furniture systems. This older strategy tended to produce characterless architecture, and it often foundered on the inconvenience and high labour costs of actually moving things around to accommodate new requirements. But electronic reconfiguration can be swift and effortless. In a classroom or conference space, for example, speakers might define pre-sets for lighting and audio-visual equipment, and simply invoke their personal configurations as they take their turns at the podium. In a hotel room or office cubicle, you might download your complete personal work environment as you entered.

Rethinking Programming, Design and Construction

These reductions in interactive and churn costs, together with reductions in specialisation and enhancements of the versatility of spaces, challenge the characteristic modernist practice of beginning an architectural project by developing a detailed space program.[13] Such programs typically enumerate the specialised spaces that will be required in a building, tabulate their floor areas and technical requirements, and specify their proximity requirements. But increasingly, under the conditions I have described, the need is less for specialised spaces providing fixed-in-place resources, and more for electronically serviced, diverse, interesting and humane habitats that can support a nomadic style of habitation. The boundaries among different building types are blurring, spaces are becoming more multifunctional, and satisfaction with complex adjacency and proximity requirements is becoming less critical.

All these conditions also come close to home for architects. They apply to the activities of design and construction, just as they do to other professional and production fields. They regroup and restructure design and construction tasks, redistribute them spatially, and ultimately change the material processes and formal languages of architecture. CAD/CAM digital models replace paper documentation, electronic telecommunication supports geographically distributed design and construction teams, and electronically mediated mass-customisation techniques supplant strategies of component standardisation and industrial mass production – as manifested, in the extreme, in industrialised component building.

Frank Gehry's Bilbao Guggenheim was the first great architectural triumph to emerge from these new conditions.[14] Digital modelling was at the heart of the design, fabrication and onsite assembly processes, the design and construction team was spread across the globe from Santa Monica to the Veneto, and the complex, non-repeating forms were made feasible through clever exploitation of advanced CAD/CAM production capabilities.

Unfortunately, some of the post-Gehry blob projects that we have seen can be dismissed as fairly mindless NURBS-mongering. But this should not obscure the fact that an important new direction is vigorously emerging, particularly among students and the more adventurous younger practitioners.

Summary: New Conditions and Strategies

I do not mean to suggest, of course, that these new material conditions determine architectural and urban form in any simple way. But they are powerful current realities, independently of whatever techno-enthusiasts or techno-sceptics may wish. They create new ground for generation of socio-spatial systems in particular contexts. And they open up new opportunities for responding to particular cultural and political goals.

Here then, as a brief guide for the perplexed, is my checklist of the concrete architectural and urban consequences most worthy of critical consideration, design investigation and debate. First, as spatial and temporal linkages among activities selectively loosen, we will see fragmentation and recombination of familiar building types and urban patterns. Second, with the electronic erasure of some traditional incompatibilities, it will make increasing sense to recombine the home and the workplace, and to favour fine-grained, mixed-use neighbourhood patterns rather than coarse-grained, single-use zoning. Third, as unique local advantages (such as a beachfront location or historic significance) gain in relative importance compared to the diminishing benefits of mere accessibility, we will encounter the revenge of place. Fourth, as tunnel effects radically warp time and space, and as local and remote interactions continually compete for attention, we will have to find effective, electronic/spatial strategies for getting the balances and complementarities right. Fifth, as places become more versatile through electronic augmentation, as adjacency and proximity requirements become less critical, and as personal mobility increases with the growing use of portable wireless devices, we will see a decline in the power of the program to organise architectural form. And finally, as CAD/CAM design and construction replace paper-based processes, and as design and construction processes globalise, we will see ways of making places that privilege variety, complexity and local responsiveness rather than the standardisation, repetition and tight spatial disciplines characteristic of the industrial era.

Notes

1 A wide ranging, insightful introduction to these changes is provided by Manuel Castells in *The Rise of the Network Society*. Oxford: Basil Blackwell, 1996.

2 This approach is directly based upon a classic formulation of location-allocation problems. See Tjalling C. Koopmans and Martin Beckmann, 'Assignment problems and the location of economic activities'. *Econometrica* 1957, 25(1): 53–76.

3 This standard terminology may be slightly confusing. Fixed costs, such as rents, clearly may vary over time. They are fixed in the sense that they are independent of interaction effects with activities at other locations.

4 Facility managers in large organisations are acutely aware that churn costs can be very significant over time. And real estate agents and removal companies largely make their livings from dealing with churn.

5 Given a set of activities to be assigned, a set of available locations and relevant cost data, the task of assigning activities to locations in the least costly way can be formulated as a quadratic assignment problem. Such problems are difficult to solve for large numbers of activities and locations, but computer software exists for generating good solutions in reasonable time. By running this software, it is possible to explore the spatial effects of varying the relative magnitudes of fixed, interactive and churn costs. See Robin S. Liggett, 'Optimal spatial arrangement as a quadratic assignment problem'. In John S Gero (Ed.) *Design Optimization*. New York: Academic Press, 1985, pp. 1–40.

6 The phenomenon of fragmentation and recombination is explored in more detail in William J Mitchell, *City of Bits: Space, Place, and the Infobahn*, Cambridge, MA: MIT Press, 1995, and William J Mitchell, *E-topia: Urban Life, Jim – But Not As We Know It*, Cambridge, MA: MIT Press, 1999. See also Thomas Horan, *Digital Places: Building Our City of Bits*, Washington DC: Urban Land Institute, 2000, and Joel Kotkin, *The New Geography: How the Digital Revolution is Reshaping the American Landscape*, New York: Random House, 2000.

7 See Andreas Duany, Elizabeth Plater-Zyberg and Jeff Speck, *Suburban Nation: The Rise of Sprawl and the Decline of the American Dream*, New York: North Point Press, 2000; Peter Calthorpe and William Fulton, *The Regional City: Planning for the End of Sprawl*, Washington: The Island Press, 2001; and Urban Villages Forum, *Urban Villages: A Concept for Creating Mixed-Use Urban Developments on a Sustainable Scale* (2nd edn), London: The Urban Villages Group, 1992.

8 Geoffrey N Blainey, *The Tyranny of Distance*. Melbourne: Sun Books, 1966.

9 Stephen Graham and Simon Marvin, *Splintering Urbanism: Networked Infrastructures, Technological Mobilities and the Urban Condition*. London: Routledge, 2001.

10 A version of this dystopian scenario is developed in Martin Pawley, *Terminal Architecture*. London: Reaktion Books, 1997.

11 Jack M Nilles, *Managing Telework: Strategies for Managing the Virtual Workforce*. New York: John Wiley, 1998.

12 For an introduction to the relevant technology see Neil Gershenfeld, *When Things Start to Think*. New York: Henry Holt, 1999.

13 John Summerson, 'The case for a theory of modern architecture'. *RIBA Journal* 1957, 64: 307–310.

14 William J Mitchell, 'Roll over Euclid: How Frank Gehry designs and builds'. In *Frank Gehry, Architect*. New York: Guggenheim Museum, 2001, pp. 353–-363.

URBAN AGENCY –
MAKING INTERFACES INFLAMMABLE:
PUBLIC ACCESS, EXCESSIVE MANIFESTATIONS,
CONNECTIVE CONFRONTATIONS AND
TACTICAL WITHDRAWALS

Yvonne Wilhelm, Christian Huebler and Andreas Broeckmann
(Knowbotic Research)
Interviewed by Wilfried Prantner for the Film + Arc Biennale, Graz, 1999

Your work and thought have always centred around a problematic and complex notion of territory within data space and electronic networks, which you have described variously as spaces of action or events – concepts which have also been used to describe the fluctuating political, social, cultural realities of the city in contrast to its spatial organisation. To what extent is your recent interest in urbanity related to fundamental qualitative similarities between the spaces opened by electronic networks and those traditionally supported by and created within the architectures of the city?

Our interdisciplinary practice places itself outside an architectural framework. When we talk about problems of urban spaces, we mean the urban as an assemblage which is constituted not so much by built forms and infrastructures, but as a heterogeneous field that is constituted by lines of forces, by lines of action and interaction.

These lines form the co-ordinates of an urban topology that is not based mainly on the human body and its movements in space, but on relational acts and events within the urban. These can be economic, political, technological or tectonic processes, as well as acts of commu- nication and articulation, or symbolic and expressive acts. The urban field that we are talking about is therefore quite different from the physi- cally defined spaces of events and movements. Rather, we are interested in what the relation between the spaces of movement, the spaces of events and the relational, machinic 'spaces' might be. It does not really make sense to oppose the city and the networks in the suggested way. We don't read the city as a representation of urban forces, but as the interface to these urban forces and processes. Therefore, the city in our under- standing features not as a representation, but as

Above: *IO_dencies* Tokyo, Artlab exhibition at Hillside Terrace, Tokyo, 1997, Photo: Canon Artlab

an interface which has to be made and remade all the time.

Following the interface thinking of Otto Rössler,[1] we don't take the world as 'the world in which we live', but as the interface through which we perceive and act. Electronic media are not 'the world of data and information' in which we now live because the 'real world' doesn't function any longer, but they have the potential to inter- face certain symbolic and expressive activities and thus are able to interface the existing urban processes. The goal is not so much to insist on the differences between different 'worlds', but to articulate the differences and overlaps between the various interfaces' tactics and modes of acting. Our projects investigate how far electronic interfaces can be the means for such heteroge- neous articulations: dealing with interfaces means to deal with intermediary variables (Saskia Sassen) and 'distortions' (Rössler).

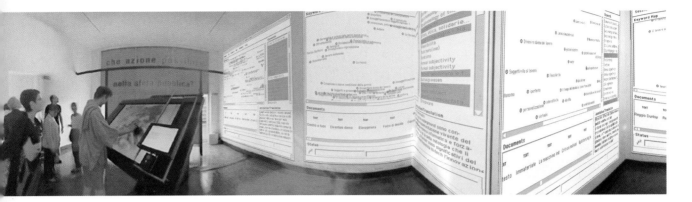

Above: *IO_dencies* lavoro immateriale, exhibition at Venice Biennale, Austrian Pavillon 1999 Photo: Gerhard Koller

Those occur through the temporary coupling of several processes unfolding on different time scales in the interface. To deal with intermediary variables, to allow for such distortions, to make them conceivable is what could make the interface 'inflammable'.

While you follow the approach of opening architecture towards mediated space, the fields of events or non-locations you seek to generate within computer networks are supposed to transgress architecture by constituting an area that coincides with the event itself. Such technologically supported environments aim to be perpetually 'under construction', to provide an interface whose form is not constructed by the artist but results from the collaborative usage of it and hence has the potential for serving as a public field of agency. Is not the *IO_dencies* project, in drawing on data and parameters employed by traditional urban planning, in danger of relapsing, as it were, into construction: of constructively contributing to a kind of advanced urban design, for which your experimental data spaces may serve as a model or at least a complementary element by which it may come to terms with the unpredictable processes of the heterogeneous and fragmented urban field?

You refer to experimental settings which Knowbotic Research developed in the past.[2] Our current work tries to push non-locations towards fields of agency and we are rather doubtful if the term 'under construction' may turn the attention in the right direction.

Our recent projects are not meant as urbanistic solutions, but they seek to formulate questions about such urban interfaces, about visibility, presence and agency within urban assemblages. We aim at experimental topologies of networked intervention, which are able to offer a connective form of acting inside urban environments, between heterogeneous forces and in multiple, differentiating ways. The relation to the concrete city environment is maintained through working with young local architects and urban planners who are searching for other ways of dealing with the problems and challenges of the city they live in. The aim, however, is not to develop advanced tools for architectural and urban design, but to create events through which it becomes possible to rethink urban planning and construction. The question we raise is: what can be done if we accept that urban environments, systems of complex dynamics, cannot be planned and constructed any more in a traditional modern sense?

Urbanism in exploding megacities with high social inequalities means that city space is delimited and planned only for about one-third of the inhabitants; the rest of the people stay outside the walls of the capitalised space. It would be politically precarious to speak of this other two-thirds, the so called illegal city as a non-location. In our studies we found clear needs for relevant forms of agency which are able to deal with the complex processes of urban exclusions. These forms of agency don't have to deal so much with the re-articulation of territory, but they have to invent and produce existential interfaces in order to avoid political, economic and cultural isolation.

IO_dencies explores the phenomenon of urban agency and distributed networked subjectivities on different levels. Initially, it seeks to develop innovative ways of reading and notating city environments, drawing out their energetic and dynamic elements. This provides the basic data for the following, collaborative manipulations of specific urban strata. We outline interfaces that are able to transcode the analysed data and facilitate different forms of access to the urban.

Analysis, interface development and practical collaborative involvement are all part of a connective process that represents an inquiry into the structures and the points of potential transformation in urban environments.

Could you elaborate more precisely on what Knowbotic Research calls 'connective interfaces' and describe their difference to the failed urban participatory models of the 1970s?

It is characteristic of the forms of agency that evolve in networked environments that they are neither individualistic nor collective, but rather connective. While individualistic and collective diagrams assume a single vector, a single will that guides the trajectory of the action, the connective diagram is mapped onto a machinic assemblage. Whereas the collective is ideally determined by an intentional and empathetic relation between actors, the connective is an assemblage which rests on any kind of machinic relation and is therefore more versatile, more open, and based on the heterogeneity of its members.

To act connectively in this context can mean simultaneously different things: to use functional ways of acting, to open up moments of conflict and rupture, to disperse and repulse actors where no interaction is possible. Thinking about open interfaces means that you let it evolve from a starting or catalytic point, so that the dynamic processes can get going. We will give you an example: the complex working conditions like those in the *IO_dencies* experiment in São Paulo create multiple irritations between the participating local urbanists and the producing institutions, the programmers, the hard- and software, misunderstandings and wrong expectations. These distortions are present in the project without causing it to fail. On the contrary, they generate new developments. It is vital to become sensitive to the weakness of interfaces and to the potential forces that they bear. One aim is to recognise them and to turn them into tendential forces (IO_dencies) which may become effective sooner or later.

The connective interfaces we are working on attempt to give the users' actions and interventions into the urban conditions a presence over time. The complexity of the project environments is constructed on the temporal axis. The aspect

of space is of lesser importance. Thus the project prioritises the topology of agency over the topology of space. The visualisation seeks to support not the orientation and mobility in space, but to enhance the mobility of action in time.

What we are surprised about ourselves is this new, differentiated vocabulary that is emerging in relation to working with electronic networks: such interfaces tie together, fold, collapse, repulse, extinguish, weave, knot. All these activities, which are obviously not germane to our projects, make it necessary to rethink 'networking' as a multi-functional, highly differentiated set of possible actions.

In a passionate defence of the physical city, the British geographer and urbanist, Kevin Robins, has recently criticised current celebrations of cybercities and virtual communities (e.g. William Mitchell *City of Bits*) as conforming strikingly with Modernist notions of urbanism, in being driven 'by a desire to achieve detachment and distance from the confusing reality of the urban scene'.[3] Invoking literary descriptions of the city from Robert Musil's *The Man Without Qualities* to Juan Goytisolo's *Landscapes After the Battle*, Robins defines urbanity as something that is essentially disorderly and chaotic, something that is 'about embodied and

Below: *2=IO_dencies* São Paulo, exhibition at V2 Rotterdam 98, Photo: Jan Sprij

situated presence, proximity, contact'.[4] **In your own works and texts you seem to draw on a similar opposition between the urban (as that which is fragmented, non-homogeneous, incomplete) and the technological (which is seen as continuous, closed, discrete). Although your interest lies in creating intermediary fields or interfaces between those two realms rather than in playing off one against the other, you clearly claim urban qualities for the spaces you create, by describing them as comparable with the 'urban structures of megapoles'. Could you elaborate on your sense of the urban and how it relates to that found in the countless digital cities?**

Our projects respond to one dominant mode of the urban, that is, its overwhelming, unbounded, uncontrollable experiential qualities. In this sense, we agree with Robins' observation about the 'confusing reality of the urban scene', and in this sense, we also agree with his criticism of digital cities and virtual communities. However, we are doubtful that this chaotic and disorderly nature of the urban is necessarily dependent on 'embodied and local situated presence'.

French urbanist Henri Lefebvre wrote in 1970 that the urban as such is never a completed reality, but it is a potentiality, an 'enlightening virtuality'.[5] The path of urbanisation, however, never comes uni-directional and does not necessarily lead to a transglobal urban zone.

The heterogeneous and permutating assemblage of materials, machines and practices which we call the urban implies a globalstratum that is locally embedded. If the urban is something that one can work with, into which one can intervene, or become a part of, then it is important to understand its forces and layers, and also to understand how it interlaces the global with the local.

Before engaging with the complex of the local–global relationship, can you specify your concept of an urban machinic and explain what kind of machinic agencies Knowbotic Research is aiming at?

The urban is a complex machine, consisting of multi-directional processes of connection and separation, of layering, enmeshing and cutting, which leads to ever different formations.

It gives the impression that it can be channelled and controlled, that it can be ordered and structured. The city is always an attempt at realising this order which, however, is nothing but a temporary manifestation of the urban.

The machinic urban is always productive and accidental, in contrast to the 'anti-production' of a fixed city structure. But its productivity lies in the creation of discontinuities and disruptions; it dislodges a given order and runs against routines and expectations. We can clearly observe this tension between the urban and the city wherever the city appears dysfunctional and unproductive, e.g. where real estate speculations are prepared that will disrupt an area within the city, or where a natural catastrophe or political instabilities will cause a rapid influx of large numbers of people. In these cases, the 'finance machine' and the 'political machine' have an inscribing impact on a local urban situation.

The human inhabitants of cities are not the victims of such machinic processes, but they form part of them and follow, enhance or divert given urban flows and forces. Contemporary analytical methods of the urban environment no longer distinguish between buildings, traffic and social functions, but describe the urban as a continuously intersecting, n-dimensional field of forces: buildings are flowing, traffic has a transmutating shape, social functions form a multilayered network. The individual and social

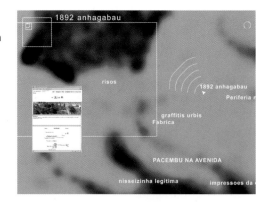

groups are codetermining factors within these formations of distributed power.

Drawing on Guattari's notion of the machinic, we describe the interface as a machine in a complex aggregate of other machines. The machinic character of the urban means that there are multiple modes of intervention, action and inscription in the urban formation. The relation between space and action is of crucial importance. There seems to be a reluctance on the part of many architects and urban planners to consider 'action' as a relevant category. Instead, built spaces are much more closely identified with and, it seems, made for certain types of behaviour. The distinction between behaviour and action is a significant one, behaviour being guided by a set of given habits, rules, directives and channels, while action denotes in our practice a more unchannelled and singular form of moving in and engaging in a given environment.

The suggestion here would be to move on from thinking about a topology of forms, behaviour and space to a topology of networks, a topology of agency, of events and of subjectivity.

One major issue addressed in your present project *IO_dencies* is the question of the 'cultural identity' of the cities investigated – Tokyo, São Paulo – and the interrelation of local and global forces. Now on the one hand, the peculiar character of these cities emerges in the urban profiles provided by local architects and urban planners; on the other hand, and more importantly, you argue that 'cultural identity' can no longer be located in the architectural structures of the mega-cities, but might be relocated in the activities of local and translocal agents who, by means of data networks, form a new kind of 'connective'. From your experience with the project so far, what are your preliminary conclusions regarding the shape of cultural identity as it emerges through the co-operation of local and global forces?

What is referred to as the global is, in most cases, based on a technical infrastructure rather than on lived experiences. The electronic networks form a communication structure which allows for an immediate and easy exchange of data over large distances. But the way in which people use these networks is strongly determined by the local context in which they live, so

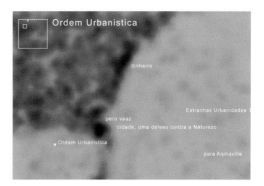

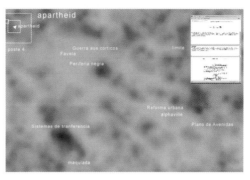

This page and opposite:
IO_dencies São Paulo, Internet interface (native applet), 1998 Credit: Knowbotic Research

that, as a social and cultural space, electronic networks are not so much a global as a translocal structure which connects many local situations and creates a heterogeneous translocal stratum, rather than a homogeneous global stratum. The activities on the networks are the product of multiple economic, social and cultural factors emerging from this connective local–translocal environment. We don't deny the existence of the global but don't see it as the most important field for developing new forms of agency.

We were intrigued by the polemical hypothesis of the Generic City that Rem Koolhaas formulated in 1994. Suburban nightmares and recent Asian boomtowns viewed under the sobering, cynical, pragmatic – dare we say Dutch – daylight. Is the Generic City the city without a history, without the burden of an identity? Implicit in Koolhaas' suggestion is the relentless growth and the unstoppable expansion of the Generic City. In the twenty-first century, he seems to say, the Generic City will become the norm rather than the exception.

For the project *IO_dencies*, the Generic City would be the counter-argument to the necessity for developing tools and interfaces that are locally specific and respond to cultural and social circumstances which distinguish one place from another. In taking the *IO_dencies* project from Tokyo to its next destination, São Paulo, the level and the quality of difference, that is, specificity, were at the heart of the preparations.

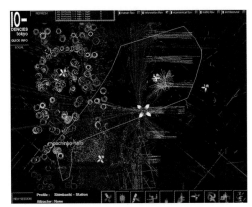

What became clear to us very quickly was that cities are and become 'generic' only in certain segments. Like many other cities with a colonial past, São Paulo is an intensely segmented city, with social, racial, economic and cultural borders dividing it like the Berlin Wall – a metaphor that was quoted to us quite regularly. This segmentation protects the Generic City, while other quarters, or segments located outside the city boundaries, are decidedly 'un-generic', 'dirty' and 'specific'.

The Generic City is identity-less. Yet, identity is not something that is the same for a whole city. People have or develop a clear sense of 'home' even in the most decrepit of neighbourhoods. Local people have an intuitive knowledge that allows them to distinguish between a street in Kreuzberg and Mitte, between Manhattan and Brooklyn, between Bras and Pinheiros. The identity that is constructed in such urban environments is a heterogeneous composite of different symbolic matrices – social, cultural, familial – that are local as much as they are translocal. A possible counter-hypothesis to Koolhaas would therefore be that only a few places are generic cities, and only a fraction of these will remain generic for longer periods of time. The generic is not the end, but a beginning, starting characteristic of many human settlements.

The project *IO_dencies* asks how urban characteristics, suspended between local and global activities, are enhanced, transformed or eradicated, and it investigates whether the extension of the urban environment into electronic spaces might allow for changed qualities of urbanity. Is communication technology the catalyst of the Generic City, or is it the motor for another, transformed notion of urbanity and public space?

In Tokyo, the technological permeation of social space is accepted without the social resistance that we know in Europe. Technology is used in particular to make the ritualised social communication even more perfect, smooth and characterless or 'generic'. Digitalisation is supposed to prevent any kind of social noise or economic disturbance. In Tokyo, the *IO_dencies* project therefore developed software structures that could create a noisy, irritating decentralised network topology of experimental events between the urban actors.

In São Paulo, in contrast, we were confronted with a ruptured, fragmented and exploding (in terms of social/political/economic inequalities and exclusions) urban space. Here, there were fewer technological strategies, a different order to the public sphere and different parameters of public forms of agency. For São Paulo, we are enabling the collaborative articulation of the personal lived experiences of the participants. The São Paulo interface allows the participants and internet users to express, condense and confront their daily urban know-how and 'street knowledge' on several concrete and intuitive levels.

Yet, if the observation about a certain constructiveness of your current project is correct, then how does it relate to your claim that your work is intended to enable intervention and resistance? Where, specifically, would you place the locus of resistance and intervention both as a capability of your machinic constructs as such and as a possibility of the user within the fields of action thereby created? In terms of the Deleuzian notion of the machine as that which interrupts a flow, how does the internet-aggregate of *IO_dencies* cut into the given physical spaces and the lived urban experience of the urban quarters investigated?

IO_dencies does not offer networked experiments to an abstract or global 'audience', but addresses small groups of people/participants who share our interest in questioning critically the political potential of the new media and looking for individual ways of participating and intervening in their local urban situations. Urbanists and architects are frequently disappointed by the methods and models of agency that are dominant in planning offices. *IO_dencies* tries through several workshops in each city to initiate a concrete process inside the group of participants which allows for a specific form of locally and translocally determined collaborative actions, accompanied by software processes which try to support the individual needs inside the group communication.

In a previous project, *Anonymous Muttering* (1996), we had posed the question about the possibilities of agency and intervention in urban environments from a very intuitive, yet also rather critical point of view. The project does this by confronting visitors with an experience of high intensity of urban processes which they can influence without being able to control. The frustration sparked by the lack of feedback on one's action highlights the degree to which processes of subjectification rely on the feedback that we receive on our actions.

Contemporary cities are covered with successful and failed attempts at leaving such traces and creating such feedback loops. The noise from roaring cars and ghetto blasters, the ubiquity of graffiti and tags, stickers and other lasting marks, even temporary and permanent pieces of architecture are clear attempts at creating a lasting visibility and presence in the urban environment. Viewed from a cultural and from a political perspective, however, this kind of visibility is rather powerless if it is not coupled with opportunities to act and to intervene in the public arena. A possible hypothesis that follows from the experience of Anonymous Muttering is that in complex machinic systems like the urban, effective intervention is only possible in the form of a connective agency within which the different individual and machinic tendencies and potentials are combined and connected. This form of agency would not develop its strength through being localised and aimed at a certain goal or a certain political enemy, but would be composite, heterogeneous, dynamic and, to a certain degree, subjectless.

IO_dencies works in a very different way and tries to develop interfaces that allow for a more conscious engagement with urban forces. We are becoming more sensitive to the specific local circumstances, and we have to formulate the interfaces in a way that makes it possible for people to insert and develop elements of their cultural identity.

The goal is to find out whether it is possible, in a situation where the city itself is being deprived of many public functions, to develop electronic interfaces which open up new forms of agency and public access, and whether network interfaces can become useful in local as well as in global contexts.

Another question is how far the 'larger context' can be incorporated at all, and whether it might be more useful to concentrate on the construction of small machines for the engagement with small terrains. The *IO_dencies* point towards an event-driven micromedia economy and a political locatedness in networks.

And finally, in which way are your technologically supported machines for urban intervention indebted to the urban explorations of the Situationists and their current revivals? If the urban consists in the fields of action and event that emerge and may be constructed against the spatial order of the city, then could not the mental and emotional landscapes of the Situationists and their followers be considered as a kind of low-tech virtuality which intersects with what you are trying to achieve?

The political analysis of the Situationists seems to remain caught in a certain obsolete analytical vocabulary, but an aspect where they were way ahead of what we are doing at the moment was the way in which they integrated passion into their activities. We are, it seems, currently too much tied up in the fight against the functionality

This page and opposite:
IO_dencies Tokyo, Internet interface- Hinode passenger terminal (java applet), 1997 Credit: Knowbotic Research

of the so-called information society, and we are thinking critically about the lack of excess, of irrationality, of relevant openness.

What we are looking at is the oscillation and transformation of potential agencies and potential subjectivities in the interface, and we are testing what the political effects might be. The way in which the tendential clusters have been configured formally, the different interventions can enhance and collapse each other. These tendential clusters of events, these multiplying and splintering forces torpedo any notion of 'construction'. By working with force fields, intensities, energy fields as formal elements of the projects, we move away from the analytical, rational conjunctive models towards open, unpredictable results. What we try to do is offer alternative models of agency to those that are currently available on the internet, where information is segmented and packaged as commercial goods, and where communica-

tion and the engagement of the subject can be easily controlled. Operating with the open qualities of a data set also means that it can be modified by each project participant, the data are connected to the local knowledge of the participant and that there is no obligation to 'think global'.

A question that we are trying to tackle through the *IO_dencies* project is whether it is possible to build interfaces that can intervene into information processes, that can bridge the tension between conscious and goal-oriented action and accidental, directionless fields of forces, and that can thus bring forth new forms of group subjectivisation and heterogenisation. The aim would be an open interface that allows a bandwith of agency between public access, excessive manifestations, connective confrontations and tactical withdrawls. Such micropolitical interfaces have to be outlined, coded and activated!

Projects Description

In the search for new forms of urbanity the influence of media technologies on the perception of and on the engagement with social constructed spaces becomes evident. Under the conditions of telecommunication, digital networks, distributed production systems and global financial markets the traditional concept of city as a spatial, temporal and political defined place cannot be any longer circumscribed within the dimension of the local. Together with young urban planners, economists and political theorists Knowbotic Research investigated in several megacities the specific cultural and political interrelationships of city, work, public sphere and electronic networks. Starting from local workshops (software concepts, theoretical constructions, urban readings) the interdisciplinary participants developed online cartographies (mental maps) which were collaboratively exchanged and reworked in networked processes enabled by groupware environments. The cartographies consisted of collaboratively organised textual, visual and auditory materials,

whose relationships between the participants were visualised as force fields and intensities through visual attractor and clustering systems. Knowbotic Research developed a special physical feedback interface to deal with these online cartographies and their force fields. The interface, in the shape of an architectural construction and drawing table, interpreted the complex relationships of the urban data sets in the cartographies as magnetic force fields and enabled a sensual experience via a handheld magnet which could be moved over the projection surface of the data visualisations.

Some examples of material in the urban cartographies: *IO_dencies* São Paulo: the mythical role of technologies for immigrants of the north of Brazil; interviews with people of favelas on self-organised job markets and porter-economies; the regulation of the real estate market by law, in the Italy project: new forms of political (immaterial) action in the new public domain.

Notes

1 Das Flammenschwert oder *Wie hermetisch* ist die Schnittstelle des Mikrokonstruktivismus? 96

2 The Anonymous Muttering project, 1996.

3 Kevin Robins, *The City* 7 [1997], p. 41.

4 Ibid., p. 42.

5 Henri Lefebvre, *La Révolution urbaine.*, 1970

TELEPHONY
Sadie Plant

A quick look back to some of the ideas around digital culture which emerged in the mid-1990s reveals both disappointments and pleasant surprises. Much of the internet has acquired the attributes of a shiny shopping mall, with channelled information akin to interactive TV, and many of the ideas which only recently seemed subversive – for example viral communication – are now commonplace marketing tools. On the other hand, there are parts of the world in which digital communications technologies have assumed some very different and more promising roles.

Last year I spent four months in Peshawar, Pakistan – a city which has become home to a vast number of Afghan refugees whose families are distributed all around the world. And there the internet has become a crucial means of communication. Few people have their own phones or computers, but there are internet clubs and cafés on every corner of some districts of this city. Afghan culture is highly segregated: women and men live quite separate lives; when they are out of the house, many women wear the chadoree, which completely envelopes them from head to toe and provides just a screen through which the eyes can see. Society is not as tightly controlled as it is in Afghanistan, but things are not so different in Peshawar.

Hardly surprisingly, the city's first internet clubs catered only for men. One or two provided screened-off areas – as is often the case in cafés and restaurants – for women, but few men were willing to let their daughters and wives enter such shared spaces. But when I was there, there was great excitement. The owners of Mars, one of the city's most successful and slick internet clubs, had opened Helen's, a women-only internet space.

It is difficult to grasp the extensive implications of this kind of development. What happens when women who just a year or two ago only had access to information filtered through the censorious hands of male relatives, now gain access to information about everyday life in other cities, other cultures, and chat with people with whom they would never have come into contact before?

Check the history of a browser in Peshawar and it is clear that the majority of sites accessed by male users are related to sex and pornography. Political sites are also popular: Taliban sites and those put up by the Afghan opposition mean that young men in Peshawar can even access video footage of their comrades in the mountains. The Web is also widely used to access information about migration and study abroad. These last themes are also popular amongst female users. But email, online chat and access to academic information are by far the most popular uses of the internet by Peshawar's women, who have now begun to make contact with a virtual social world which would have been unthinkable just a year ago.

The dispersal of the Afghan population round the world has undoubtedly encouraged the growth of the internet in Peshawar. It is still, of course, the case that fixed-line telephones are rare in many parts of the developing world. But something else has shifted on this front. I was one of many writers and theorists in the 1990s who completely failed to notice the quiet revolution unfolding before us: the appearance of the mobile phone.

It has been said that the landline telephone 'arrived at the exact period when it was needed for the organisation of great cities and the unification of nations'.[1] Perhaps the mobile phone has now arrived to suit a new era of mobility: all over the world, people are moving and migrating for work, often to cities from more rural areas. The numbers of refugees, tourists and travellers have soared in the last 20 years: business travel and tourism alone have tripled in that period. And because the circulation of commodities, money and information has also gained a new sense of momentum, even people who go nowhere face new instabilities as traditional structures of employment, family, community and cultural life are disturbed. The mobile encourages such movements; it also serves to repair or replace the connections they may break.

A hundred years after the fixed line telephone, wireless technologies are accompanying a new wave of social and cultural change. First appearing as a car phone in the late 1970s, the mobile phone remained large, costly and relatively rare for nearly 20 years. For some time, it was closely and even derisively associated with certain strata of corporate and administrative life. But it soon began to leak into the wider world. When it proved to be as useful to drug dealers as to other sales executives, the mobile became the prime example of William Gibson's cyberpunk observation that 'the street finds its own use for things'.

In some parts of world the mobile is already an established means of accessing the internet, playing games, downloading music and accessing a wide range of other wireless services. But it owes much of its popularity to SMS, the short message service which allows people to send short text messages between mobile phones and from computers to mobiles. Even though SMS was a peripheral feature to which no marketing attention was initially drawn, its use has spread like wildfire. Some fifteen billion text messages are now sent world-wide every month; many of these are from the Philippines, where less than 6 percent of people have a mobile phone and few can afford to make phone calls, but more than fifty million text messages are transmitted every day.

The fixed-line telephone changed the architecture of its day, making new constructions, new spaces and new urban relationships possible. The classic example is the skyscraper, which would have been unthinkable without the telephone − all those telegraph boys running up and down between the floors or continually using the elevators to take messages would have made the internal traffic problems insurmountable. Is it possible that the psychogeographical landscape − and even the actual geography − of the city will change once again to suit the new possibilities of mobile communication?

If the fixed-line telephone brought communications links into the workplaces and homes of the developed world, the mobile puts them straight into the hands of unprecedented numbers and varieties of individuals. It is so close and personal that it is experienced as a kind of detachable sense organ; a more-or-less permanent appendage which can, like other organs, accompany its users wherever they go. Mobiles are not quite prostheses, but they are highly personal devices, carried close to the body and

often deployed almost as easily and automatically as any other body part. Many of the psychological and social implications of such a technology have yet to be assessed, although Neil Leach has alerted us to the narcissistic, even isolating and atomising implications of this piece of technology.[2] But the personal nature of this connectivity also represents an important redistribution of the cultural resources associated with the ability to communicate, and it seems to me that its growth and popularity mark a significant devolution of many different kinds of economic and social power.

In Dubai I met a small-time trader who told me that the mobile has multiplied his opportunities to make contacts and do deals as he moves between cities and ports. The short, instantaneous messages and calls to which the mobile lends itself are perfectly suited to the small and immediate transactions in which he is engaged. He now has access to intelligence about the movements of goods, ships, competitors and markets. Information once way beyond his reach is now at his fingertips. Many other workers use the mobile to circumvent the systems that would otherwise govern their lives. Taxi drivers who once talked to their passengers en route now spend their journeys on their mobiles, talking to friends and family, but also making contact with other drivers, keeping up to date with traffic conditions, and often getting extra business from short-circuiting the radio control. Bar girls and prostitutes find that the mobile gives them more economic independence. Truck drivers use their mobiles to find the work that will allow them to ensure that they never return with an empty load.

Although many parts of the world are still miles and years away from a fixed-line telephone, the mobile has already found its way to several regions and communities that have often found themselves excluded from telephony and on the margins of technological change. The mobile can be vital to regions where fixed-line telephone services are unavailable, inefficient or prohibitively expensive, and the social, economic and political impact of the mobile is often greatest in such hands. Even when it is beyond the financial means of most individuals, its collective use can bring it into play: in the poorer areas of even the most developed cities of Asia and the

West, there is often someone selling mobile call time, text message services, and even internet access. In the more remote parts of several developing countries, including Swaziland, Somalia and the Côte d'Ivoire, the mobile is being introduced in the form of payphone shops in villages which have never had landlines. In rural Bangladesh, these shops and the women who run them have become new focal points for the community.

Recent upheavals in the Philippines suggested that the mobile has political potential too. When President Estrada went on trial in January 2001, mobilisation found a new meaning as protestors used text messaging to keep up-to-date with meetings, events and mass gatherings. The local press referred to them as the 'text brigade'. Access to a mobile is also access to a world of information and, as events in the Philippines made clear, the mobile means that people can co-ordinate their actions and change their behaviour almost as quickly as they can communicate. Mobiles have recently played crucial roles in several other political campaigns: the co-ordination of England's environmental protests, Germany's anti-nuclear campaigners, Mexico's Zapatistas, prison rioters in Turkey and Brazil, and anticapitalist activists in Seattle, Prague, Quebec and Genoa.

The mobile introduces a new sense of speed and mobility to social life. Its connections are direct and immediate; responses to its calls can be spontaneous and fast. Loose arrangements can be made in the knowledge that they can be firmed-up at a later stage; people can be forewarned about late or early arrivals; arrangements to meet can be progressively refined. Everything becomes provisional and contingent: people, spaces and times remain in flux, suspended in a matrix of possibilities until a meeting actually occurs – everything is virtual

until the parties, the places and the moments come together to make it real. In cities, these aspects of this new mobility change the experience, the possibilities, the parameters of urban life. But it is not just the psychogeography of the city – and perhaps its architecture – which is changed by the introduction of such mobile connectivity: the images, maps, perceptions and, indeed, the geopolitical architecture of the whole world are changed as well. It is this that makes me slightly uncomfortable about some of the antiglobalisation rhetoric which is kicking around at the moment. It is crucial to oppose the corporate formations which are seeking control of social, economic and technological life, but quite another to confuse them with the kind of grassroots globalisations which are amongst the more energising and positive effects and concomitants of digital culture. The mobile phone – cheap, simple and effective – is both a cause and an effect of this new mobile connectivity.

Cutting across distinctions between genders and ages, as well as regions of the world and levels of economic development, the mobile is the first hi-tech device to fall into so many hands so fast. Its rise has been rapid and extensive, and also remarkably quiet: although it emerged at a time of great intellectual interest in communications technologies, the mobile has often been regarded as rather too prosaic to merit serious attention. This failure to notice its emergence left many industrial analysts, academic researchers and cultural commentators surprised by the pace and nature of its growth which, for a while, proceeded in its own discontinuous, piecemeal way. Although it is now being heavily marketed, the mobile phone is a fascinating and instructive example of the ability of new media to find their own uses, users and ways around the world.

Notes

1 Herbert N Casson, *The History of the Telephone*. Chicago: A.C McClurg & Co., 1910.
2 Neil Leach, *Millennium Culture*. London: Ellipsis, 1999, pp. 91–92.

DIGITAL LIFESTYLES AND THE FUTURE CITY

Andrew Gillespie

As a geographer, my concern with the built environment is in terms of its overall spatial form, rather than with individual buildings or ensembles of buildings. In this chapter, I consider the implications of so-called 'digital futures' for the spatial form and functioning of British cities; the plural, *cities*, is important, as I believe that our perceptions of urban problems and the means of addressing them have been distorted through an overly London-centred lens.

The policy context for envisioning the future city can be stated clearly as a desire to bring about an 'urban renaissance'.[1] Realising this vision will require an emphasis on urban concentration, in which urban sprawl is contained and higher densities are achieved through promoting brownfield rather than greenfield development. Achieving such reconcentration, however, runs the risk of producing chronic congestion, so the necessary concomitant of an urban concentration policy is the reduction of 'unnecessary travel', particularly that made by car, and the promotion of public transport.

Tools for Sustainability?

Against this policy background, in which more sustainable urban forms and less travel-intensive lifestyles are to be promoted, some have seized upon the potential of digital technologies to act as 'tools for sustainability'. Central to this possibility is the concept of 'e-materialisation', in which physical goods and physical movements are substituted by electronic equivalents. For example, e-commerce has the potential, according to the American commentator Joseph Romm, to substitute electronics and software for material products, electronic delivery for movements of goods by road, and websites for buildings.[2]

We cannot, however, assume that this potential will be realised. As Evan Davies notes, 'our experience so far suggests that the benefits of technology are typically directed towards making us richer, rather than greener'.[3] And, we might add, the benefits of distance-shrinking technologies such as digital communications seem to be directed towards generating more, rather than less, movement. The assumption that 'digital lifestyles' – the new ways of living, working,

shopping and being entertained that are facilitated or enabled by digital technologies – are going to result in less travel, and hence contribute to more sustainable urban forms, appears to be highly dubious. Indeed, it is my contention that by expanding the 'activity spaces' within which daily life is conducted, these *digital* lifestyles are best understood as extensions of the *motorised* lifestyles that became established in the second half of the twentieth century; by making distance easier to overcome, they effectively contribute to the decentralisation of both people and activities within extended metropolitan regions. Far from being 'tools for sustainability', therefore, digital technologies seem to be in direct conflict with the realisation of the compact city, urban renaissance vision which underpins contemporary urban policy.

The Decentralisation of Employment

To explore this contention further, I propose to examine the implications of one aspect of digital lifestyles – that of new ways of working linked to new technologies – from the perspective of what they mean for the future city and its spatial form. In order to demonstrate that these new ways of working represent not a break with the past but rather a deepening and extension of well-established trends, it is necessary to understand the context within which these new ways of working are being deployed; this context is that of the long-established relative decentralisation of service jobs from major cities to their surrounding hinterlands.[4]

According to the analysis of Ivan Turok and Nicola Edge,[5] between 1981 and 1996 Britain's conurbations lost 500,000 jobs, a decline of 6.2 percent. Manufacturing jobs declined by over one million in this period, but the decline was offset by a rise in service employment. Jobs in the private services grew by 651,000 (18.1 percent) in the conurbations between 1981 and 1996, with the banking, finance and business services contributing the lion's share of this growth (an increase of 589,000 or 52.8 percent). By contrast, in the towns and rural areas of Britain overall job growth was experienced (an increase of 1.68 million jobs, or 14.8 percent), due to the fall in manufacturing of 748,000 being more than offset by vigorous growth in private services (which grew by just over two million jobs, or 49.2%). The key banking, finance and business services category increased by 939,000 jobs in towns and rural areas (95.4 percent). Thus even the sector which most people would associate as being the heart of the post-industrial urban economy is decentralising in relative terms, with much more vigorous growth in banking, finance and business services being experienced in Britain's towns and rural areas than in its conurbations.

These apparently distinct spatial categories – of conurbations on the one hand and towns and rural areas on the other – are somewhat misleading. What in effect happened through the 1980s and 1990s was that jobs growth was increasingly taking place in smaller urban centres beyond the boundaries of the existing conurbations; a process of jobs decentralisation within metropolitan regions became established, just as population decentralisation had become established earlier in the 1960s and 1970s. In both cases, transportation and communications improvements, particularly those associated with the car, were instrumental in permitting this decentralisation to take place.

New Ways of Working Linked to New Technologies

How then might new ways of working linked to new technologies reinforce the established trend towards the decentralisation of service activity employment? The answer is by no means straightforward, as there are a number of distinctly different ways of working which are associated with information and communication technologies. Let us briefly examine the urban form implications of three such ways of working: home-based teleworking, teleservice centres, and mobile working.

Teleworking from home

Teleworking has of course long been over-hyped in terms of its significance, but evidence from the Labour Force Survey does suggest that it is now growing, albeit from a very small base.[6] Although it is often associated in the popular imagination with working from remote

rural areas, in fact there are important locational constraints on this type of teleworking. Except for self-employed and freelance teleworkers, most teleworking is a partial activity, undertaken perhaps one or two days a week, and hence teleworkers continue to need to be located with reasonable access to their existing workplace; and for self-employed and freelance teleworkers, access to clients continues to impose significant constraints upon location, at least for the majority of such teleworkers.[7]

Teleworking has no necessary urban form implications, in that it can be conducted from anywhere, notwithstanding the constraints in terms of access to existing workplaces and clients. We might anticipate, beyond the small number of 'lifestyle' teleworkers able to work from remote locations, that the location of teleworkers will reflect the existing residential location preferences of middle-class professionals, who constitute the main category of worker likely to be engaged in teleworking. Given that the revealed locational preferences of such people are clearly for suburban and amenity-rich small towns within metropolitan spheres of influence,[8] it can be anticipated that the growth of teleworking is likely to contribute to the continuing decentralisation of employment within metropolitan regions.

Teleservice centres

Teleservice centres constitute a very different type of digital working. These telephone call centres or web-enabled customer contact centres represent a radical innovation in service delivery, in which there is no longer a need for 'co-presence' with the consumers of the services concerned. This enables radically different service geographies to emerge, in which many local customer-serving units can be replaced by a much smaller number of single, dedicated tele-mediated service delivery centres, able to exploit economies of scale and to be optimally located in order to take advantage of low labour or property costs.[9]

The locational outcomes in terms of call centres has favoured provincial cities, with their labour pools and relative cost advantages over London and the South East of England.[10] At the metropolitan region scale, call centres have, for various reasons, tended to prefer edge- or out-of-town business park locations rather than central business districts. The reasons include, firstly, the scale and nature of the premises required: these 'customer service factories', which may house 1000 or more customer service agents, are essentially large sheds rather than office buildings in the conventionally understood sense, and as a result they tend not to be conducive to siting within conventional office districts in the centres of cities. Secondly, such property is often available on a speculative build basis on business parks, frequently with room available for expansion, an important factor given the rate of expansion in call centre operations. Thirdly, call centre operators tend to assume that their workforces will travel by car to work; in part, this assumption is self-fulfilling, as the business park locations preferred are usually not well served by public transport, but it also reflects the nature of call centre working, with shift working the norm. Whatever the reasons, call centre operators prefer ample car parking and good road access, conditions which are most easily satisfied in edge- or out-of-town business park locations.

Call centres thus represent one of the main stimuli to the decentralisation of service employment from city centres. As a new form of employment made possible by ICTs – the first call centre in Britain opened only 12 years ago – they have been able to be sited largely unencumbered by existing office property portfolios, and have displayed a clear preference for decentralised locations within metropolitan regions.

Mobile working
A very different form of technology-facilitated working is so-called mobile working, in which laptops and digital cellphones are used to support work done on the move or at clients' premises. Although mobile working is not a new phenomenon, there is evidence that it is increasingly developing in the client-oriented professions, including consultancy, computing, accountancy and law. Because of the emphasis in these new ways of working when visiting clients, there is some evidence that companies are preferring to locate in areas such as business parks, with good road access and ample parking, rather than traditional central business

districts. This varies according to the metropolitan context: it appears to have developed less in London than in some of the provincial cities although examples such as BT point in the direction of change; previously located in central London, they have moved most of their staff into new offices around the M25 in order to aid staff retention, reduce property costs and facilitate mobile and flexible working.[11]

In their very different ways, each of these new ways of working – home-based teleworking, telephone call centres and mobile working – is thus contributing to the decentralisation of employment within expanding metropolitan regions. But as Peter Hall reminds us, 'decentralisation of people and jobs and services did not begin with the digital economy… trends roll on, in the long-term, with surprising consistency. And, so far, there is little evidence that e-commerce has affected them much'.[12]

The point is that, in their urban form implications, developments in the digital economy and in digital lifestyles seem to be very much in accord with long-established trends which are leading towards more decentralised metropolitan regions. Steve Graham and Simon Marvin go further and suggest that these trends are leading towards quite new urban forms, in that we are witnessing a 'transition from traditional, core-dominated, monocentric cities towards complex, extended, and polycentric city-regions made up of a multitude of superimposed clusters, grids, and internal and external connections'.[13]

A Challenge to Planning?
These trends seem then to pose a challenge to the prevailing urban policy and planning paradigm, which as noted above is emphasising urban concentration and the need to bring about an urban renaissance. This raises the question of the extent to which planners are aware of the challenge which current trends, including that of the emergence of a digital economy and digital lifestyles, pose to the realisation of current policy goals.

One way of examining the current state of planners' awareness is to examine the new spatial development strategies, known as regional planning guidance (RPG), which have recently been prepared for each of the regions of England, following extensive consultations between local authorities and other stakeholders.[14]

The RPGs cover the period to 2016, and it would therefore seem reasonable to expect that aspects of the digital economy and digital lifestyles likely to impinge on spatial development or on spatial planning would be considered in these planning documents. In Table 1, an attempt is made to summarise whether these issues are considered in any way at all within the new spatial strategies: the role of ICTs within spatial restructuring; the significance of telecommunications infrastructure and the forces shaping its spatial deployment; the contribution of ICTs to economic development and to rural development; the implications of e-commerce for retail provision; and the travel substitution potential of ICTs.

All of the draft five RPGs examined, with the exception of that for the South East of England, have *begun* to address the social and environmental issues surrounding the digital economy, though extremely patchily and from a limited starting point. For example, the role of digital technologies in contributing to the decentralisation of employment receives very little consideration, and none of the RPGs gives any consideration to the roll-out of broadband networks within the territories for which they are planning. Further, although each of the RPGs has an emphasis on the need to reduce the demand for travel, there is little mention of the potential of teleworking or of the travel substitution potential of ICTs more generally. Perhaps most surprising of all is that in the draft RPG for the South East, the region which is at the leading edge of the UK's digital economy,[15] there is, to all intents and purposes, not a single mention of information and communications technologies and of their significance for the future spatial development of the region.

The conundrum we are left with then is that while digital lifestyles are pushing us further towards electronically-facilitated forms of mobility and towards spatially-extended metropolitan regions, urban policy and planning is trying to achieve changes in the opposite direction, towards more compact urban forms and towards reduced movement and mobility. This is not necessarily a contradiction, in that planning has often sought to modify or even reverse existing trends in order to achieve public interest goals; what *does* appear to be a problem, however, is that planners display little evidence that they are even aware of the forces that are pushing in the opposite direction to that they are trying to plan for.

We are left to conclude that planners have yet to develop the awareness, let alone the expertise or appropriate policy intervention mechanisms, that would enable them to influence the spatial development of a digital society. Somebody might be 'planning' the future digital city – the telecommunications companies perhaps? – but it certainly doesn't seem to be planners!

Below Incorporation of ICT impacts into draft regional planning guidance (RPG)

	South East Draft RPG	South West Draft RPG	North East Draft RPG	Yorkshire & Humberside Draft RPG	East Midlands Draft RPG
Role of ICTs within spatial restructuring				•	•
Significance of telecoms infrastructure		•	•	•	•
Forces shaping telecoms infrastructure					
Contribution of ICTs to economic development			•	•	•
Contribution of ICTs to rural development			•	•	•
Implications of E-Commerce					
Travel substitution potential			•	•	•

Notes

1 Urban Task Force, *Towards an Urban Renaissance: Final Report of the Urban Task Force*. London: Stationery Office, 1999. DETR, *Our Towns and Cities: The Future (Delivering an Urban Renaissance)*. Urban White Paper, DETR, 2000.

2 Joseph Romm, *The Internet Economy and Global Warming: A Scenario of the Impact of E-commerce on Energy and Environment*. Washington DC: Centre for Energy and Climate Solutions 1999. (http://www.cool-companies.org/ecom/index.cfm)

3 Response by Evan Davis to C Leadbeater and R Willis 'Mind over matter: Greening the new economy' in J Wilsdon (Ed.) *Digital Futures: Living in a Dot-com World*. London: Earthscan Publications, 2001 pp. 16–38.

4 For a discussion of this context, see A Gillespie, 'The changing employment geography of Britain'. In M Breheny (Ed.) *The People: Where Will They Work*. London: Town & Country Planning Association 1999 pp. 9–28.

5 Ivan Turok and Nicola Edge, *The Jobs Gap in Britain's Cities: Employment Loss and Labour Market Consequences*. Bristol: Policy Press for Joseph Rowntree Foundation, 1999.

6 According to figures published by Office for National Statistics (ONS), 5.8 percent of the UK workforce were teleworking in some form in Spring 2000, up from 4.3 percent in Spring 1998. UK Office for National Statistics, *Labour Force Survey*. Spring 2000.

7 U Huws, S Honey and S Morris, *Teleworking and Rural Development*. London: Rural Development Commission, Rural Research Report No 27, 1996. See also M A Clark, *Teleworking in the Countryside: Home-based Working in the Information Society*. Aldershot: Ashgate, 2000.

8 T Champion, D Atkins, M Coombes and S Fotheringham, *Urban Exodus*. A Report for CPRE. London: CPRE, February 1998.

9 R Richardson, 'Network technologies, organisational change and the location of employment'. In A Dumort and J Dryden (Eds) *The Economics of the Information Society*. Brussels: OECD/EU, 1997 pp. 194–200.

10 R Richardson and J N Marshall 'The growth of telephone call centres in peripheral areas of Britain: Evidence from Tyne and Wear'. *Area* 1996, 28(3): pp. 308–317.

11 Arup Economics and Planning and CURDS, *Changes in Working Practices in the Service Sector*, Final Report to DETR. London: Arup Economics & Planning, 1999

12 Response by P Hall, to A Gillespie, S Marvin and N Green 'Bricks versus clicks: Planning for the digital economy'. In Wilsdon (Ed.) *Digital Futures: Living in a Dot-com World*. pp. 219–220.

13 S Graham and S Marvin 'Urban planning and the technological future of cities'. In J Wheeler, Y Aoyama and B Warf (Eds) *Cities in the Telecommunications Age: The Fracturing of Geographies*. New York and London: Routledge, 2001 pp. 71–96.

14 This section draws upon material previously published in Gillespie, Marvin and Green 'Bricks versus clicks: Planning for the digital economy'. In Wilsdon (Ed.) *Digital Futures: Living in a Dot-com World*. pp 200–218.

15 Christie and M Hepworth, 'Towards the sustainable e-region'. In J Wilsdon (Ed.) *Digital Futures: Living in a Dot-com World*. pp. 140–162

GMCity~SM~: THE GENETICALLY MODIFIED CITY (2001)

David Turnbull (ATOPIA)

(GMCity and 'the genetically modified city' are service marks for a newer, better city opening for business near you...very soon)

In June 1999 a 4-page advertisement appeared in the US edition of *WIRED* magazine promoting Fairfax County in the SILICON HOLLER of Northern Virginia. As an earlier advertisement had claimed, Fairfax County is smart, smart, smart: 'Smart ideas like smart cars and smart roads are why smart companies are moving to Fairfax County.' Fair enough, but what is especially important about the *WIRED* advertisement is that it dismantles the ideas and priorities that shape a new urban area – the copywriter is masquerading as an architect, designing the city, and as will become clear, in this context the architect is also, in a sense, a copywriter. Fairfax County is built on an electronic infrastructure, and is one of the most advanced urban areas in the world in IT terms and so could be taken as evidence of an emerging pattern. (I have removed specific references to Fairfax County from the text of the advertisement in order to explore the generalisable global implications of the description.)

'Don't just think outside the box...consider a whole new ZIP code.

It all starts with a dream, imagine a fast paced career in Silicon Valley. In this dream, you see yourself as an information-age entrepreneur, zipping back and forth from your San Francisco loft to your high-tech campus, from meetings with upstart start-ups to dinners out on the town with the family.

Sooner or later, you notice cracks in the dream: A commute that takes longer than the average Internet product cycle. Street parking less common than bald eagle sightings. That loft you wanted sporting a price tag equivalent to a minor Hollywood action movie. Fear of letting your pets and children outdoors, where they might be exposed to the constant threat of marauding SUVs.

Allow us to suggest a better dream: To flourish in ...'s atmosphere of rapid technological innovation, an open mind is essential. Fortunately you'll find limitless educational resources available: three major colleges and universities – including ... – are located in ..., and nearby metropolitan ... has more than 40. Just looking to catch up on your reading? The ... public library system is the largest in ..., with a total circulation topping 2 million items; if you can't find it here, we humbly suggest you try the Library of Congress.

When you're making more at your job and wasting less on your mortgage, you'll be endlessly tempted to spend the difference on yourself. ... works hard to see that you are indulged, with more than 200 shopping centres and thousands of restaurants offering every conceivable cuisine – from world-class ... to some of the best ... food in the country.

In a mood to get out of town? Snowboard the mountains of .... Explore ...'s underground rock scene – literally – at the ... caverns of ... and .... Hike the ... Mountains and enjoy the spectacular view of the ... Valley. Or stick close to home and roam in ...'s 30,000 acres of parkland. For maximum enjoyment we suggest you bring your camera and send snapshots to your friends in ... (though you might want to straighten out your guest bedroom first)

And specific to Fairfax County: *Birthplace of the Internet. The highest proportion of software employees in the nation. Home to more ISPs and Internet start-ups than you could surf in an entire summer.*

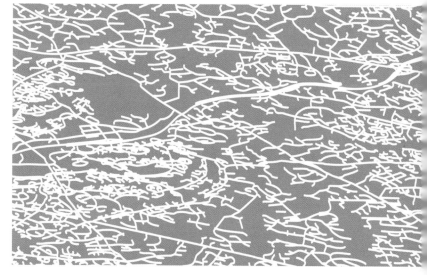

Below: Fairfax 1: GMCity~sm~: pattern 1, large-scale network.

Incredibly safe, with one of the lowest crime rates in the country. And, incidentally … is not only where you'll likely find a beautiful and affordable place to live, but also where you might find a beautiful and affordable place to park. IMAGINE THAT.'

This echoes Ebenezer Howard who, in 1898, identified the defining characteristics of the third of his three Magnets (Town ◇ Country) − a radical alternative to the polarities of the rural−urban continuum − as beauty of nature, social opportunity, fields and parks of easy access, low rents, high wages, low rates, plenty to do, low prices, no sweating, field of enterprise, flow of capital, pure air and water, good drainage, bright homes and gardens, no smoke and no slums, freedom and co-operation. The advertisement could also say, 400 square miles in area with a population of 926,573 in 1998 (close to a million now); home to the Pentagon, which is why it is the 'birthplace' of the internet; its electronic infrastructure is not superimposed on an existing structure, it is completely and irreversibly a part of it; a Foreign Trade Zone (FTZ 137) with 25,000 businesses, 79 million square feet of office space, 35 million square feet of hybrid industrial space and 15,000 acres of land planned for commercial expansion. Fairfax County has the fifth largest office inventory in the US distributed across seven businesses, a regional market of six million people and direct links to national and international markets through two major airports, Washington Dulles International Airport and the Ronald Reagan Washington National Airport, and, via Washington Union Station, the AMTRAK network.

Below: Fairfax 2: GMCitysm: pattern 2, local area network

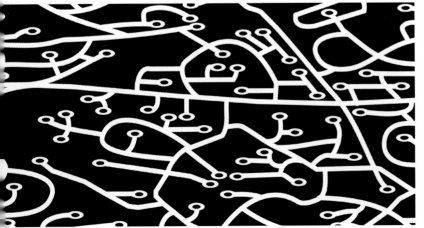

A Dream of Success

The problem: crime, danger, stress, high cost of living, congested roads, and high levels of frustration, gridlock.

The solution: relocation − great education, smart people (smart friends), good employees, high salaries, low cost of living, good lifestyle, good shops, world class food, sport, scenery, green open space, good image, happy employees, friction free living.

The urban organism which sustains this dream has been genetically modified: any problems have been designed out, happiness has been designed in. It can now be rebranded GMCitysm. As we will see this is a global phenomenon. I will borrow some organisational principles from the working lexicon of the Indian 'back office' company Daksh.com to explain the operational logics of GMCitysm. To use back office parlance is appropriate because what is at stake here is the transformation of the back office zone into a world class urban accumulation. Daksh is a Sanskrit word meaning *the utter preparedness to act immediately with supreme urgency.* Speed and preparedness are defining modes of behaviour in the GMCitysm. Daksh break down the characteristics of their organisa-tion as follows: $3xi + 3xp =$ (Investment, Influence, and Information, plus People, Platforms, and Processes). Distributed ownership, shared responsibility, a stake in the future for everyone, broadly-based decision making, 24x7x365 *bullet-proof* information architecture, constant communication, continuous self criticism, perpetual redesign − these are precisely the conditions under which the GMCitysm evolves. Fairfax County incorporates earlier city forms: the paradigmatic Edge City, Tysons Corner, discussed by Joel Garreau ten years ago, and the 'New Town' of Reston, VA. Edge Cities, at the time a new phenomenon, were not reckoned to be cities at all according to any conventional definition, being simply the accumulation of quantities: over 5 million square feet of office space, more than 600,000 square feet of retail. Edge cities were perceived as single end destinations. You just went there and came back and were predominantly non-residential. Now, only a decade later these cities are central, they are not on the edge of anywhere, they are no longer a typically American phenom-enon, they support substantial residential districts and are moving into another stage of development as they simultaneously expand and are retrofitted for new uses.

Perpetual redesign and continuous self criticism rapidly produce a city form that can be recast: GMCity$_{sm}$ is an atopical assemblage of technopolis and ecopolis, logistical zone, tourism centre, information processing hub and cluster of planned communities. It is composed according to diagrammatic strategies: codes, flow charts and models based less on what things look like than on their informational structure and pattern. To achieve the planned eradication of urban dysfunction, and to maximise attractiveness in the global economy, successful areas are cloned. Techniques of recombination are used to remove imperfections. Decontextualisation, experimental transfer from one organism to another, and systematically repeated localised adjustment – the techniques of genetic research – emerge in urbanism as the instruments of change.

Fairfax County is first generation GMCity$_{sm}$. As such it is evidence of a global trajectory of urban development that tears apart the clichés of the advocates of 'new urbanism', and the virtues of the 'traditional neighbourhood development', goes way beyond the 'generic city', and is more extreme than the 'city of exacerbated difference' theorised by Rem Koolhaas, while simultaneously upholding the demands of citizenship, empowerment and the local as a primary issue in relation to policy. Generation after generation, GMCity$_{sm}$ is systematically, genetically enriched to produce enhanced performance, by emphasising its specific strengths and heightening its local effects. When British scientists cloned a sheep, and on 27 February 1997 from Molly came Dolly, the Vatican greeted the event with the judgement that we were venturing into 'the tunnel of madness'; in the context of recent outrage about genetically modified foods and other GMOs, it is strange that there is no outrage about this kind of city. It did not enter the discourse in another guise, there was no secrecy, no Trojan Horse, it is just there. It will be argued, inevitably, that cities have always evolved through sequential, local action, but if dissolution has been the dominant tendency, then the model GMCity$_{sm}$ is predicated on the notion that a non-conservative reversal of this trend is both viable and necessary.

1 GMCity$_{sm}$ is a hub in a network of transit systems, communication and human resources. It strategically promotes the proliferation of local and regional concentrations of productive intensity. The operational and psychological effects of concentration include informational or sensory knots and hallucinatory states.

2 New proximities and continuities – informational, temporal, spatial and psychological – redefine the city. Communications networks facilitate instant access to people and places. The hard infrastructures of the twentieth century lose their pre-eminence as the soft infrastructures of intelligence and imagination – the minds of the city – link with other minds to unlock new potentials.

3 The aqueous space of the city, historically formed through the contingencies of drainage and irrigation, is now shaped by a superabundance of flows. Simultaneously, GMCity$_{sm}$ is a regulatory mechanism processing and channelling these flows – datastreams and resources rosters are subject to constant inspection and continuous redistribution to maintain a precarious steady state.

4 The topography of GMCity$_{sm}$ is almost entirely artificial. The progressive flattening of hills as the periphery is stretched marks time. The displacement of the natural topography produces vast synthetic landscapes haunted by their precondition as seabed or pulverised hill. Buildings replace topographical features which persist as names – hyper-real artefacts – spectral, nostalgia-producing moments.

5 In GMCity$_{sm}$ residual space has been abolished. Patterns of agglomeration according to use, value or economic co-dependency appear as spontaneous eruptions of form in a continuous field. This spatial organisation no longer relies on geometrical arrangement or hierarchical schema. Both landscapes and buildings conform to a logic of accumulation.

6 Ambience is manipulated to produce impact without affect. Difference is stimulated by the localised intensification of similarity. Lifestyle zones are formed by the elimination of incompatible differences and the disciplining of urban form. Idiosyncrasy is exploited for picturesque effect. Destination status is indicated by a trajectory of increasing cohesion and density.

7 GMCity$_{sm}$ is a production site for new identities and images; generic qualities are heightened to

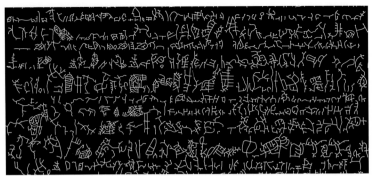

Above: Fairfax 3: GMCity_{sm}: catalogue – local road forms

become emblematic. Similarity and consistency are produced by deploying erasure and replacement strategies to reconfigure both the city and the individual psyche. A radical deterritorialisation creates the circumstances for the construction of a new condition.

8 The hypertextual structure of GMCity_{sm} produces multiple histories along regulated pathways. Constructed recall employs mnemonic devices – carefully located landmarks and icons – as testimonies to imagined pasts. These serve as the entry points to information fields where individual searches inflect, and negotiate with, the conformity of the prescribed routes.

9 The incorporation of interference in official policy realigns dynamic and destructive activism as the planned construction of creative turbulence. The interplay of strategic and errant forces accelerates the production of innovation. Localisation strategies redirect social and microeconomic forces to support the minor beginnings of large-scale effects.

10 Telescoping distinctions produces new mental states. Extremes of equivalence are established by the perpetual production of choice and the simultaneous smoothing of differences – consensus rather than conflict. New perspectives are supported by the conditions produced by the elimination of friction and an infrastructure of agreement.

It is by now abundantly clear that we are witnessing the radical transformation of cities all over the world, as a result of changes in communications technology and the accelerated growth of digital media linked to the generalised effects of globalisation. With appalling inequalities in relation to the distribution of wealth and working conditions, locally, anywhere, unprecedented volatility in the marketplace, and previously unimaginable environmental problems, the typically negative spin that this transformation is given includes the re-emergence of the Third

World in the first. The physical symptoms of the 'death of distance' are a dystopian 'geography of nowhere' with a tormented *just in time* organisational environment which every millionth of a second agonisingly confronts the perpetually imminent, potentially catastrophic effects of 'non-virtual gridlock'. In the USA, urban transformation is often characterised as the dynamic interrelationship of exurban growth, inner city decay and the increasing obsolescence of the suburban hinterland, or positively, as the populist Joel Kotkin spins it in *The New Geography*,[1] change, growth, renewal and revival more or less everywhere, based on the proliferation of choice. The 'fading charm of the European city' is also accelerating. The strategic importance of the megacities, with populations in excess of 10,000,000, which articulate the global economy, link information networks and concentrate the world's power, remains unquestionable. But embedded within, self-contained or adjacent to these massive accumulations of urban material, smaller mutant urban forms are emerging, which in their patterns of hybridisation and specialisation mime the behaviour of urbanisation in the extended field, and which conform to the model of the GMCity_{sm}. For the happily 'unenfranchised citizens of the shopping mall and the marina, the internet and cable TV' celebrated by writers like JG Ballard, emergent GMcities_{sm} can be identified by their *Silicon Something* tags[2]:

SILICON ALLEY, New York City, New York, USA,
SILICON ALPS, State of Corinthia, Austria,
SILICON BAYOU, Louisiana, USA,
SILICON BEACH, Santa Barbara, California, USA,
SILICON BOG, The midlands of Ireland,
SILICON CITY, Chicago, USA [1998],
SILICON DESERT, Phoenix, Arizona, USA,
SILICON DITCH, The M4 Corridor, west out of London, UK ,
SILICON DOMINION, State of Virginia, USA,
SILICON FEN, Cambridge, England,
SILICON FREEWAY, Southern California, USA,
SILICON FOREST, Seattle, Washington, USA and Eastern Australia,
SILICON GLACIER, Montana, USA,
SILICON GLEN, Livingstone, Scotland,
SILICON GULCH, San Jose, California, USA,
SILICON HILL, The area around Hudson, Massachusetts,
SILICON HILLS, The hills west of downtown

Austin, Texas, USA,
SILICON HOLLOW, Oak Ridge, Tennessee, USA,
SILICON HOLLER, Northern Virginia suburbs of
Washington D.C., USA,
SILICON ISLAND, St. John, Virgin Islands,
SILICON ISLE, Ireland,
SILICON MESA, North Albuquerque / Rio Rancho
area of New Mexico, USA,
SILICON MOUNTAIN, Mountaintop, Pennsylva-
nia, USA,
SILICON NECKLACE, Suburbs of Boston,
Massachusetts, USA,
SILICON ORCHARD, Wenatchee Valley,
Washington, USA,
SILICON PARKWAY, the Garden State Parkway,
New Jersey, USA,
SILICON PLAIN, Kempele, Finland,
SILICON PLAINS, Lincoln, Nebraska, USA,
SILICON PLANTATION, State of Virginia , USA,
SILICON PLATEAU, Bangalore, India,
SILICON POLDER, The Netherlands,
SILICON PRAIRIE, Lincoln, Nebraska, USA,
SILICON RAIN FOREST, Seattle, Washington, USA,
SILICON SANDBAR, Cape Cod, Massachusetts,
USA,
SILICON SAXONY, The eastern state of Saxony,
Germany,
SILICON SEABOARD, Richmond, Virginia, USA,
SILICON SNOWBANK, Area around Minneapolis
/ St. Paul, Minnesota, USA,
SILICON SPIRES, Oxford, England,
SILICON SWAMP, Indiantown, Florida, USA,
SILICON TRIANGLE, Area around Raleigh /
Durham, North Carolina, USA,
SILICON TUNDRA, Area around Ottawa, Canada,
SILICON VALAIS, Valais, Switzerland,
SILICON VALLEY NORTH, Area around Ottawa,
Canada,
SILICON VALLEY OF THE EAST, Penang State,
Malaysia [1998],
SILICON VALLEY FORGE, Philadelphia,
Pennsylvania,
SILICON VILLAGE, North Adams,
Massachusetts, USA,
SILICON VINEYARD, Okanagan Valley, British
Columbia, Canada, SILICORN VALLEY, Fairfield,
Iowa, USA,
SILICON WADI, Israel [1997], and so on and so on.

Innovation Milieux
In business in Asia the 'bamboo network' of
whispers and winks is being transformed by

more open, electronically mediated systems of
communication and 'who you know' is displaced
by 'what you know'. It is harder to be secretive
when hard facts are available on the Web. It is
easier for foreign investors to strike a bargain
when they have information to work with.
Across Europe, cities compete to attract inward
investment to support research and development,
knowledge industries, and new manufacturing
operations to replace their debilitated industrial
base. Rootless commercial interests can settle
anywhere, so qualitative issues become vital.
When the Dada poet Tristan Tzara declaimed in
1921, 'Ideal, ideal, ideal. Knowledge, knowledge,
knowledge. Boomboom, boomboom, boomboom',[3]
he was right on the money, faking it as an *idiot
savant*, anticipating the core constituents of the
propaganda issued by countless cities at the
end of the century; innovation milieux are no
longer confined to the areas around large universities in the power centres of the developed world.

To intuit the shape of the mind – the endless
diversification and bifurcation of thought –
becomes a project of urbanism when the city is
shaped by the new infrastructures of communication and exchange, the trajectories of ideas,
and transspatial networks nurturing knowledge
ecologies. The formal consequences of this
productive shift are more difficult to pin down
and need to be reassessed. Boom comes with a
price, including an apparent indifference to
architecture, and knowledge does not have a
clearly defined shape. Currently, the dominant
mode of architecture in the GMCity_{sm} is degree
zero architecture, an architecture without qualities
which can only be defined as *generic urban
substance* – houses, hybrid industrial space,
offices, parking lots, franchises, gas stations,
superstores, malls – deployed according to
logics of accumulation which, closely linked to
the behaviour of global and regional markets
and socio-economic trends, are organised
according to precisely defined global standards
and norms. Simple. Whatever is done is done
quickly. Architecture takes too long.

Since questions of identity and place defining
tactics are an important part of the 'language' of
development and are always on the agenda,
even when they are being actively denounced,
the atopical assemblage of the GMcity_{sm} poses
a problem for architecture, which demands new
responses, critically, and practically in relation to

spatial containment and address. Too often architectural responses to the problem of atopia are framed as a critique. In the past two decades many, if not most, architectural writers have been concerned in one way or another with the perceived problem of urban dissolution within an isotropic communicative space. These concerns are remarkably persistent, and while only a few designers would cite Aldo Rossi as an influence, this year many might have *The Architecture of the City*[4] buried in the back of their minds, whether they have read it or not. And they might secretly believe that the contemporary production of amorphous zones is only excusable because it represents an inconclusive time in the urban dynamic, that these zones can only exist in the City if they are thought of as moments in a process of transformation. The invective that is currently reserved for sprawl, from radicals and conservatives alike, reveals that Lewis Mumford's warning in 1961, given in his seminal collection of essays *The Highway and the City*,[5] that we were already witnessing the action of '*destructive anti-urban forces* that are artfully disguised as modern architecture and modern traffic planning' still strikes a chord. Many would agree with Vittorio Gregotti, who believes that at the centre of architecture is the concept of the project as a thoughtful way of maintaining a critical distance while engaging the context[6] and, like him, feel that not just the periphery but the consolidated historical centres of cities are under continuous attack from what he calls 'principles of oriented atopia, that is principles of settlement based on something other than the idea of place'.[7] For Gregotti, atopical typologies 'offer none of the spontaneous and temporary gathering that used to characterise spaces *"extra mura"* and have 'no need for the site…'.[8] The geographic particularity of the site linked to the idealisation of the bounded city, with architecturally articulated limits and a bucolic exterior remains as a powerful fantasy, and entropic, inconclusive urbanism is difficult to deal with. But it is too easy to claim that without the *seduction* of place, there is no place for architecture.

To operate on atopia, architecture and urbanism will have to be redefined, rebranded, repositioned like the city itself… as the engineering of atmosphere and the structuring of relation space. Increasingly, the site will be simultaneously geographic and ageographic on the borderland of the actual and the virtual, and architecture will shape the 'wormholes' that link these domains and carefully adjust the diagrams and codes of the increasingly pervasive genetically modified city.

If, like the 'Designer Children' in Lee M. Silver's *Remaking Eden, Cloning, Genetic Engineering and the Future of Humankind* (1998),[9] the inevitable, logical conclusion of systematic genetic modification is the polarisation of society into two classes − the 'Gene-enriched' and the 'Naturals' − ultimately, any fruitful relationship between the two becomes impossible. It could be that there are two city types that will, in a fundamental way, soon become completely incompatible, and that one of these will, ultimately, disappear.

Notes

1 Kotkin, Joel; *The New Geography: how the digital revolution is reshaping the American landscape*. Random House 2000

2 For an ongoing survey of Silicon, Media and Multimedia + location aka Siliconia, started in 1995 − see Keith Dawson's www.tbtf.com/siliconia.html

3 Tristan Tzara; quoted in *New York DADA* Ed. Rudolf E. Kuenzli, Willis Locker and Owens, NY 1986, p.140 'Founder explains what it means'.

4 Rossi, Aldo; *The Architecture of the City* (US Edition), Oppositions Books, MIT 1982

5 Mumford, Lewis; *The Highway and the City*, Mentor Editions, New York 1964

6 Gregotti, Vittorio; *Inside Architecture*, MIT 1996 Ch. 5, On Atopia, p .77

7 Gregotti: p. 78

8 Gregotti: p. 80

9 Silver, Lee M.; *Remaking Eden, Cloning, Genetic Engineering and the Future of Humankind,* Weidenfeld and Nicholson; 1998; Orion Books (paperback edition) 1999 − see prologue: A Glimpse of things to come; and Epilogue: Human Destiny.

DIGITAL TECTONICS

ROLLER-COASTER CONSTRUCTION

Farshid Moussavi and Alejandro Zaera Polo (Foreign Office Architects)

'This is where amateurs have an advantage over pros. A pro knows what he can deliver, and rarely goes beyond it. An amateur has no concept of his limitations and generally goes beyond them.'
Trey Gunn, *Road Diaries*, Project Two Discipline Global Mobile, 1998

Architecture is not a plastic art, but the engineering of material life. Despite the classifications, architecture is a plastic problem only if you decide that the plastic is your material. But that is just the particular case of architecture. This is what we hope distinguishes our work from other surface-complex architecture. We have grown tired of comparisons to Saarinen, Utzon or Gehry. Despite our appreciation of their work, those comparisons are based purely on the formal similarities. Formal concerns are of significance, but this association does not tell the whole story.

Gehry, for example, works in exactly the opposite direction to us: he produces a spatial effect that is subsequently implemented by means of construction. He is primarily concerned with consistency in the spatial effects. The result may be sometimes similar, but the process of reaching it is radically different. What distinguishes our work from his is fundamentally the process, as our main priority is to produce consistency throughout the process of construction and material organisation. In fact, we are interested not in having preconceived effects, but rather in exploring the materials – and here we should understand material in the broadest sense – as a part of the process. Processes are far more interesting than ideas. Ideas are linked to existing codes, operating critically or in alignment with pre-existing systems of ideas. Rather than making a project the implementation of an idea or the scaffolding of an image, what we are interested in is constructing, engineering processes on different levels.

A process is the generation of a micro-history of a project, a kind of specific narrative where the entity of the project forms in a sequence. If geological, biological or human history, for instance, have something to teach us it is that these processes of temporal formation produce organisations of a far higher complexity and sophistication than instantaneous ideas. This is perhaps the most important development brought by information technology to our practice: we can design, synthesise and proliferate specific histories, scripts for a project; write a project, as with Eisenman; introduce a sequential development rather than deploying a form, an image; proliferate; wait for the emergence of the project; write a code: let's see what happens if we are no longer trapped in the traditional compulsion to reproduce historical models, or to invent them from scratch. We do not have to produce a project as a reproduction, derivation or as the invention of a historical model. We do not need to produce complexity by making collages: we can synthesise the processes of generation as a kind of accelerated motion, adding information integrally to the construction.

This sequential, integrative addition produces ambiguous effects more capable of resonating at different levels than straightforward ideological statements, metaphors, allegories or reproductions. Through our interests in the processes of construction and engineering of material life, we get constantly involved with all sorts of technologies. And techniques are always associated with performances, producing effects, delivering services. Technique has become the domain of architectural services; but architecture as a service industry is a deadly business and it rarely delivers interesting architecture.

Opposite: Port Terminal, Yokohama, sectional compilation.

Below: Port Terminal, Yokohama, plan view

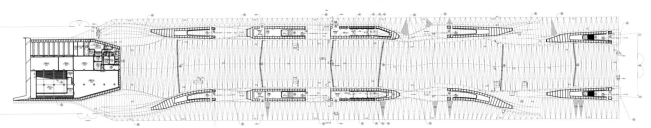

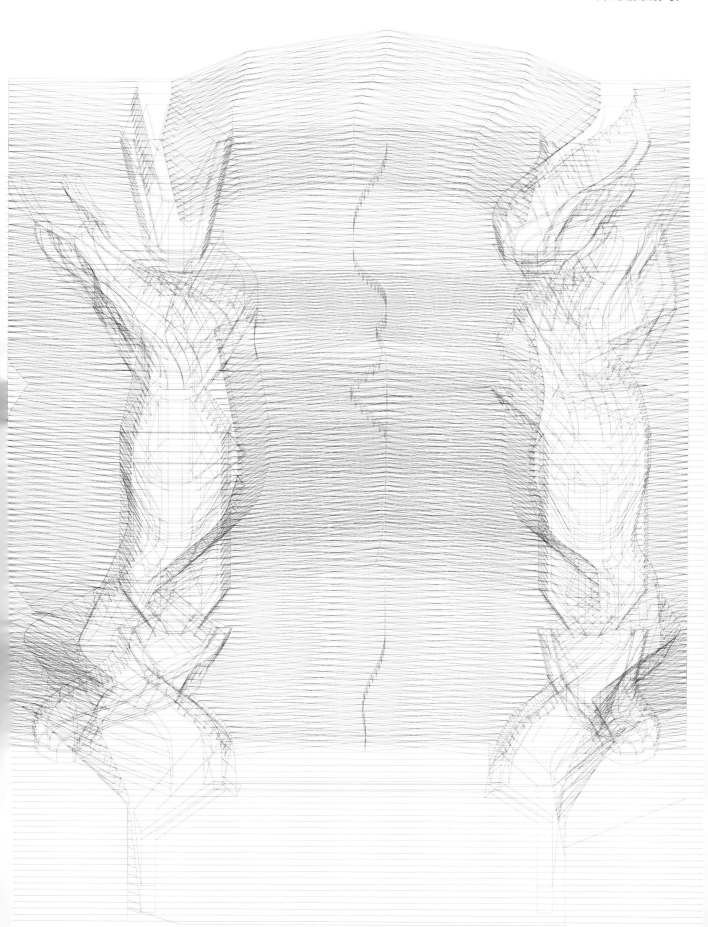

Jacques Herzog says that architects will have to become like the Spice Girls: soon, only star-architecture will be worth being involved with. The rest will be architectural services. But the concept of architectural services comes out of the coupling between architectural technology and effect: a good professional is capable of using the right techniques to produce the right effects. But what will happen if we divorce technique from service and effect? Is it possible to exploit the affective potential of architectural technique? This is where we think there may be an alternative to an architecture that masters effects – at least, *a priori* effects.

There is an enormous potential to be released, contained in the techniques of 'architectural services' that has not been exploited in itself: project management, estimation, surveys, artificial intelligence's modelling capacity. None of this has been successfully integrated in the discipline of architecture, and this is leading the profession to bankruptcy: there are stars and there are architectural services: complete schizophrenia. The real challenge is to exploit the potential of these technologies beyond their utilitarian association, and through a digitised interface to integrate them into a discipline that has not evolved for a long time, to construct a new discipline out of them.

In the production of a project of this nature, there is a very real challenge from powerful forces that threaten continuously to stratify the work, to turn it into a conventional process. If one does not take care of these forces, they may paralyse the project. If one accedes to them, they will destroy it. Greedy consultants, managers who measure work in man hours and hours per drawing, and judge people by years of experience, mediocre client representatives who mistrust anybody under fifty, uninspired

engineers who can not imagine anything beyond their calculating ruler, 'experienced' architects who feel they do not need to learn anything any more, people with a hierarchical chip in their brain – unfortunately, one has to put up with these people because sometimes the system does not recognise even the most obvious facts, such as that the people who are actually doing the jobs in every single office are under forty, and invariably under thirty. And they are the only ones able to do the job because they can use computers, because they have access to technical means that have become central to the production processes, and because they work as a research process, producing knowledge as they are producing the project, rather than accumulating 'experience'.

With Yokohama, our managers said that we would need between 30 and 40 architects working on the job. We are managing with 14. If we had followed their advice, not only would we have gone bankrupt, but we would also have sacrificed the project's sophistication, as the energy that is now concentrated in a few good people would have been lost in meetings, timesheets, minutes, and other things invented by managers to conceal their own incapacity to produce and to keep their privileged status in the hierarchy. It was perhaps our academic experience that reassured us of the value of keeping a team structure that also produces knowledge, rather than just drawings.

One of the things you learn from teaching is that there are virtually no limits to the capacity of people to produce knowledge and so on, as long as they remain motivated. It is only experience that teaches us where our limits are

This page and opposite:
Port Terminal, Yokohama, external views.

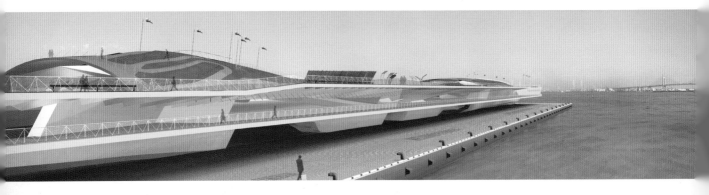

and, once we have learned that, we are finished, because our work can be calculated and measured, becomes stratified and ceases to be a weapon. It was also our academic background that allowed us to put together a dream-team of architects whose individual skills and commitment went beyond conventional measure, and whose presence could have specific impact on the work, like players in a good jazz band.

Despite the constant requirement of our client for a clear hierarchy of command, we structured the work around the production of packages, giving designers the independence to research, develop and produce the drawings for each package: partitions, glazing, ceiling, traffic, structure, mechanical services. We tried to avoid any centralisation of command, as the team was sufficiently small and close to allow us to rely on everybody to keep track of development on all fronts: individual platoons. Stir things up at work − anything to avoid stratification. Everybody goes to meetings, makes photocopies, meets contractors, makes coffee, talks to consultants, fixes computers, does accounts. Of course, it has come at a price: no 9 to 5, no holidays, no weekends.

This experiment is about pushing things to the limit, occupying everybody's life with the project for as long as it lasts and is interesting. The process is aimed at reaching maximum intensity, suspending all limitations of work and projecting it as far as possible. The structural development of the project − developed together with Structural Design Group − has become the main source of ideas for its implementation, and a trail of discovery that reaches far beyond the images that have become the better-known side of the project. The structure that we proposed in the competition was made out of a folded piece of steel, as an attempt to make the structure consistent with the general concept of the project as a folded organisation. This proposal was also advantageous in terms of its resistance to earthquake stresses and akin to the techniques of the naval industry to which the building was affiliated. The 'cardboard' structure emerged out of what was originally a reference to the local tradition of 'Origami' construction.

These references to local construction systems, both literal and culturally mediated, were an attempt to contextualise the proposal without having to resort to the mimicry of local

building. In other words, the context was introduced as a process of material organisation, rather than as an image. This sensitivity to the local will have a decisive role in the generation of the building's geometry, through the extraordinary importance that the latent asymmetry of the grounding conditions on site will play during the design development phase.

At the beginning of the Design Development stage, the structure was clearly the most critical point of the project, as the competition proposal was as interesting as it was naive, and needed substantial technical development to become realisable without betraying the original purpose. The main problem to resolve was that of the three-dimensional complexity of the structure with a geometry that was basically axial − that of folding. The outcome of the process so far has been interesting as it has opened up important geometrical and formal concerns emerging directly out of the pragmatics of the project, rather than as a kind of external formal orgeometrical ideology imposed on the project from the outside.

During the development of the Basic Design stage, we came up with a solution where the folds of the web were being woven with each other every half fold, so that we could achieve the curvature at a larger scale. This is a structural geometry that has been used, for example, by Nervi, Piano and others to make large-span shells with a kind of structural unit or cell, which is repeated along curves. But what is interesting is that the cells of the structure would become differentiated at every point of the surface, much as in an organic system.

One of the immediate implications of this system is that we removed the lower plate of the structure to simplify the construction, turning the folded metal plates into a crucial expressive trait

Above: Port Terminal, Yokohama, girders under construction

of the project: the Origami had finally become visible. At this point there was an interesting debate as to whether the structural system had to become a kind of isotropic shell with local singularities, as the computer perspectives seemed to indicate, or whether it should retain the bi-directional qualities that the plan of the building contained, becoming a system composed by two series of large-scale folds bridged by a series of transversal folds.

After testing a kind of hybrid between the original 'cardboard' type and a kind of space frame with local densification, we realised that the concentration of axial stresses along the longitudinal large-scale folds suggested that the structural type had to be altered to become a concrete-filled structure. This was the reason we decided that, despite the image of the building, the bi-directional structure was finally a more adequate structural solution. The coincidence between the ramp system and the main longitudinal girders became the primary determinant of the structural geometry, as the conflict between the symmetrical condition of the programmatic structure and the asymmetrical condition of the grounding system forced us to bend the ramps. The edges of the building were located at 15m from the pier's edges to comply with the symmetrical location of the boarding decks on both sides, while the foundations could only

reach up to 21.5m from the Shinko side and 29m on the Yamashita side.

This conflict between structural asymmetry and programmatic symmetry was already present in the competition entry, but had not been fully exploited, as it had been absorbed entirely in the lower level ramps, without affecting the geometry of the upper level. It was only when we had to start thinking about the correlation between the two levels of girders that the asymmetry extended through the whole geometry, rather than being confined to the lower level.

One of the criticisms we received after the competition scheme was made public was that the topology of the building was basically symmetrical and Beaux-Arts. It was not that we did not consider this problem during the competition stage. However, we thought it was more interesting to preserve the conflict as a generative trigger rather than impose a formal ideology – asymmetry – on to the problem. The sensitivity to the initial conditions of the brief and the reference to the local shipbuilding industry had become productive in the process of formal determination.

The other subject evolving through the development of the project has been the determination of the grid, the geometrical fabric of the project. At the competition stage, our proposal was generated by analysing the spatial locations of the different spaces of the terminal, such as the boarding decks, visitors' decks, rooftop plaza, departure and arrival hall, and traffic plaza, and linking them locally through a deformed surface. That surface was constructed through a sequence of parallel transversal sections to describe the local conditions every 15m, which were morphed along the axis of the building. The interesting question arising from the process of the evolution of the grid was its ambiguity between an organisational technique based on parallel bands and the single-surface technique that absorbed differences into singularities of a congruent space.

We were basically interested in the single surface effect, but our methods were still reliant in the techniques that we had learned at OMA, where the sequences of parallel bands developed from La Villette through Den Haag City Hall and the Grand Bibliotheque produced organisations that allowed for a maximum sectional flexibility: a kind of rotated 'plan libre'

aimed at reaching maximum programmatic freedom across levels. In so doing, though, our programmatic aims – the coherence of the circulation diagram across programs – were radically different from the programmatic incongruence and juxtaposition that originated OMA's infamous band technique.

The predominant longitudinal direction of the building and the basically symmetrical programmatic structure supported the use of this organisation, producing a conflict with our interest in programmatic continuity that would drive the evolution of the project through the Detail Design stage. The conflict between a striated organisation and a smooth congruence that we had seen between the grounding conditions and the programmatic symmetry was also present in this disparity between our intentions and the organisational requirements. A key point to stress is that despite its 'informal' appearance, our ambition for this project – and most other ones – is for a radical formal determination. The informal appearance for us is nothing but the outcome of processes of highly complex formal determination. This is the aim of integrative addition as the form of organisation of the process.

In this process of constantly refining the geometry of the project, our first step was to increase the frequency of the transversal sections from 15m to 5m, by inserting two new sections within each band. The technique we used to calculate the new intermediate sections was achieved by producing what we called 'control lines' or curves that were determined by the points of location of each element in the transversal sections – boarding and visitors' decks, parking, halls – turned into spline curves. This was the first technique where we started to establish an argument of consistency between the different sections, produced out of the determinations of successive local conditions. By cutting the 'control lines' through intermediate planes, we were able to locate the position of the different elements longitudinally.

At the same time, we dropped the originally splined geometry of the surface into a geometry of complex curves made out of a palette of seven radiuses, producing the surface out of the intersection of cylindrical or conical surfaces of regular radiuses, in order to simplify the manufacturing process. This process produced 96 transversal sections to determine the form of the building that were clearly insufficient for a detailed description of the project. So, due also to a change in the basic size of the transversal folds, we increased the resolution frequency of the grid to 3.6m, still using the 'control curves' as our technique of coherence. Soon, the 124 transversal sections we obtained doubled, as the basic scale of the transversal folds was fixed to 1.8m, which became the new spacing of the grid. The process of geometrical development became basically a problem of increasing the resolution of the grid, and every step in this process required an exponential increase in the amount of information we had to produce.

When we started the detailed design of the girders' geometry, we realised that even this amount of information was not sufficient to control the precise geometry of the project. We also noticed that by rolling parallel sections along curved control lines we would be producing irregularities in the geometry of the ramps, unless we differentiated between the transversal sections of the girders. Even worse: because of the existing geometrical definition, every face of

Above left: Port Terminal, Yokohama, folds under construction

Below: girders under construction

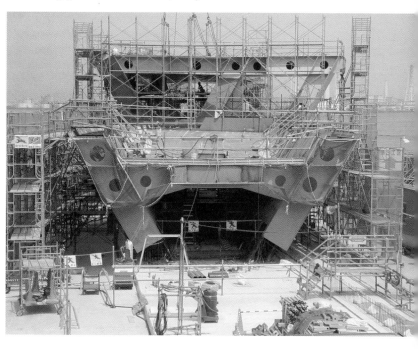

the girder would have to be triangulated, and different from each other, and every transversal fold had become a different geometry. Even if we now had control of the determination of the stiffeners that constructed the girders, we had no control over the triangulation of their faces.

One of the most important developments in the evolution of the project occurred at this point, when we started to consider the construction of the girders through the rotation of the same stiffener templates at regular intervals along the 'control lines', that also now had to be dropped into complex curves. In order to increase the regularity of the manufacturing process, we started simultaneously considering the possibility of producing local symmetry in the transversal folds by making them meet the girders at a perpendicular angle. The only way to achieve this, given the deformed geometry of the girders, was to shift from the parallel transversal grid of the competition entry to a

topological grid originated in the control lines that determined the girders' geometry. In our new topological grid, the parallel bands did not grant independence to the different parts; on the contrary, they established functions that connected them to each other, considerably diminishing the amount of information required for the determination of the form.

We had therefore moved from a 'raster' space, where each point is determined by local information, to a vectorial space, where each point is determined by differentiated global orders. Again, there was no ideological or critical statement in making this step, but rather the pragmatic resolution of technical conflicts in the process of development. These kinds of discovery are those that we think can turn processes of a purely technical nature into an architectural expression, so that the discipline emerges from the production rather than from a critical or ideological relation to its previous constitution.

The next conflict emerged between the possibility of achieving repetition in the girders' geometry or symmetry in the transversal folds. As the folds would have to link with the girders where they coincided with the stiffeners, if we wanted to achieve local symmetries to the folds, we would have to sacrifice regularity in the girders' sections, as the pitch of the stiffeners would be determined by the intersection of the folds with the girders' edge. If, conversely, we started with a regular pitch of the stiffeners in the girders, we would have to sacrifice the local symmetry of the folds. In order to set up a

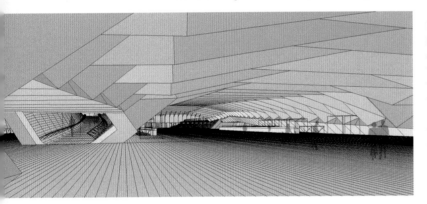

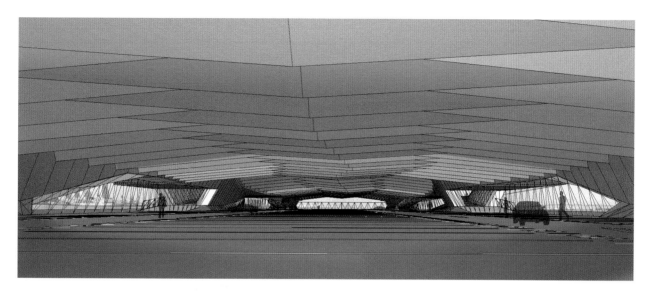

non-parallel grid to solve the problem, we gave first priority to the local symmetry of the folds, to determine the position of the stiffeners along the girders.

The position of the new gridlines was not determined geometrically, and had to be calculated numerically through a program that created iteration loops to establish the intersections of the transversal folds' local axis with the curved edges of the girders. As a program, the iteration loops had to be calculated sequentially; therefore, its results would depend on the area of the plan where we started calculating the iteration loops. However, due to the fact that after calculation, over 65 percent of the steel weight was concentrated in the girders, we decided to take a grid determined by rolling templates along the 'control lines' at regular intervals, so that the girders' construction would become as regular as possible.

In this option, the fabric of the folds had to become anti-metrical in the central folds – still identical in terms of formal determination – and symmetrical on the lateral folds, leaving only the two intermediate folds of every arch to be irregular. A third scale of folding would be produced at this stage in the process: in order to reduce the total weight of steel, we had to place small stiffeners inside the small-scale transversal folds. These were greatly increasing the manufacturing costs and, in order to avoid this increase, we decided to replace the 6mm thick plates that constituted the first proposal for the detail of the folds with a 3.2mm corrugated plate. The corrugations will provide the plates with enough strength to avoid the stiffeners.

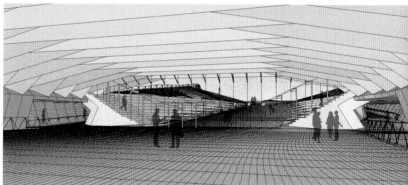

The process is not yet finished, although most of the crucial decisions have already been made. In one of the recent meetings to explain the geometry of the project and the process of setting out on site, the contractors asked us for the co-ordinates of the points of the building, as if the form was decided *a priori*, and they needed just to implement that geometry on site. To their surprise, we had to explain to them that the geometry was strictly related to the manufacturing and construction systems, and could be modified if necessary. They said that they had thought that site control was going to be the most crucial aspect in the construction process, but now they realised that the most important process was to be the manufacturing. One of them pointed out that they would have to employ the same techniques used to build rollercoasters, where the setting out utilises local references between identical templates rolled along an irregular three-dimensional geometry. 'Exactly,' we said, 'roller-coaster construction.'

This page and opposite:
Port Terminal, Yokohama, internal views

ELECTRONIC PURVEYANCE PRACTICES IN ARCHITECTURE

Marcelyn Gow

Above: Nurbline products on Nordic Net Art website

Right: Stereolithography model of Nurbia generic stack system

Electronic purveyance alters the status of objects and the protocols through which our involvements with them are staged. The venue of electronic communication is a site in which the stable identity of a spatial proposition as well as that of an author are subject to redefinition. Purveyance entails establishing menus for interaction, diverting sequences of communication in order to allow for multiple authorship and supplying a set of variables which can be adapted by a wide audience to generate variable outcomes as opposed to the production or performance of a single spatial proposition. The purveyor is an agent who packages and presents spatial propositions as transmutable material. Purveyance practices in architecture involve the integration between the academic realm, commercial manufacturing and design practice. Several case studies are presented here from the research seminar 'Machinic Processes in Architectural Design' at the ETH taught by Greg Lynn and Marcelyn Gow[1] and 'Urbantoys' a recent project from the design collaborative servo.[2] The common line of thought linking these practices is the issue

of purveyance.

The identity shift between a manufacturer, a designer and a purveyor is part of a more extensive paradigm shift implicit in design and architecture in the last 50 years. Conventional purveyance is involved with marketing strategies, packaging and delivering a product to a consumer. Architectural *purveyance* claims the territory of this interface between a spatial proposition and its audience as a site in which influences agglomerate from a number of directions to yield variable outcomes. The notion of design as a complete cycle with a specific physical instantiation as an end product has transformed into a less stable model whereby a

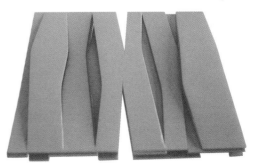

multitude of options can be handed over from one 'author' to another as potentials for producing a number of spatial realities constituted by 3D geometrical models, text, sound, image or structure. The reconfiguration of the relationship between a purveyor and a fabricator or producer involves the exchange of tools between areas of specialisation. An example of one such appropriation is that of the animation and 3D modelling software used in the film and product design industries and computer numerically controlled machinery used in the automobile and aerospace industries being adapted for architectural design. Providing an interface with a proclivity for differential and repeatable components enables options to be transferred between several authors.

Contrasting the contemporary tendency in design towards a purveyance model are a number of post-war projects like the 'Day after Tomorrow's Kitchen' which attempted to visualise a more flexible domestic future scenario although it inscribed the roles of a manufacturer as a sponsor and an architect as a commissioned designer in an extremely conventional manner. This engagement between architecture and industry resulted in the corporate sponsor commissioning an architect to fabricate an environment designed to entice consumers into buying appliances based on the marketing of an unforeseen need and the marketing of new spatial effects in the home. The kitchen was intended to simultaneously demonstrate applications of the manufacturer's product, glass, and the appropriateness of this material to realise the discourse of a more flexible environment for modern living based on effects of transparency. The architect was engaged by the manufacturer to produce an environment in which to advertise the suitability of a product. The purveyance or marketing of a new set of domestic protocols was tied to both a material and an effect, in this case glass and transparency.

Urbantoys

The conventional roles of manufacturer, architect, designer and site visitor are diffused in the *Urbantoys* online project.[3] *Urbantoys* is a set of

digitally instantiated products and instructions for their fabrication embedded in an interface intended for both viewing and extraction. Implicit in the word 'urbantoy' is a fluctuation between an architectural scale and programme and the scale of a toy or hand-held object. In the *Urbantoys* project 'toy' connotes a digitally manipulable set of geometries which are animated by the toy's user and can be assembled computationally as a three dimensional model or produced as a physical instantiation. The toy's components are set in motion as a series of spatial parcels which are activated by the user. The assembly of digital pieces is non-sequential, proliferating into a series of models. The viewer is invited to act on a supplied catalogue of materials and infiltrate the design process. The design of a product which has no inherent scale articulates the potential of a specific spatial organisation or set of instructions to exert variable influences and characteristics when applied to different media at a multitude of scales. For example, the Nurbline products can be apprehended or occupied as sets of animated geometries rendered active in the computer or the geometry can be implemented as a construction document to fabricate a physical shell from a variety of materials. The shell can be the size of a hand-held object or an envelope large enough to enclose the body. An intentional thwarting of the word 'toy' occurs as these objects are not fully operable as conventional toys yet they borrow the iconography of a toy, forcing a new reading or interpretation of toyness. The identity of the toy becomes conflated with its propensity to produce structure

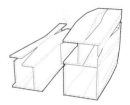

Above: Stereolithography model of Nurbia unit displayed in Cloudbox at Storefront for Art and Architecture, New York 2000

and enclosure. The Speetoy, for instance, is designed with an interchangeable set of components, incorporating a degree of formal flexibility as well as scalar flexibility.

Urbantoys are electronically purveyed spatial commodities which respond to the fact that contemporary consumers engage in a higher degree of influence on their immediate environment extending beyond appliances, vehicles and clothing into an envelope which increasingly usurps objects and architectural surroundings into the domain of personal influence. These models accelerate the effects of a tendency which sees the relationship between consumer and manufacturer becoming reconfigured by the integration of digital technologies such as rapid prototyping and e-commerce into architectural practice. This tendency enables designers to consider elastic models as products or to speculate on portable urban goods. The electronic purveyance of physical goods blurs the distinctions between a physical and an electronic product. Acknowledging that the body and its inhabitable area are conditioned by several modes of digitally manufactured and electronic environments enables a multitude of spatial products at a variety of scales to be developed from a common model. *Urbantoys* provides a venue for the design process to distribute itself to a wide audience, implicating the viewer in the role of the designer.

The *Urbantoys* site is an interface which reconfigures the relationship between a designer, a manufacturer and a client. The commerce between manufacturer and designer is radically altered by the appropriation of materials and methods, centred in the computational realm around parametric modelling techniques and rapid prototyping strategies. The site stages a scenario whereby visitors become active participants, providing the infrastructure for selecting geometries and manufacture-ready material. The project takes a proactive stance towards engaging the manufacturer by introducing a line of products for which new technologies of fabrication have been adapted for architectural applications and promoting a model in which architects collaborate with industries to enable a hybridisation of conventional construction practices with flexible manufacturing. For example, in Nurbline a main intention was to engage product design and presentation in an architectural proposal on a variety of scales. Perhaps the most critical aspect of this engagement is the interaction between a corporate domestic appliance manufacturer and a group of architects. In phase one of this project small-scale surface models of Nurbia units were fabricated using stereolithography resin prototyping normally used for testing appliances during the design development stage. The impact of this conversation is in the potential ramifications of such a collaboration to occur rather than with the artefact itself. This collaboration has the effect of bringing manufacturers into a situation in which they begin prototyping something other than the domestic appliances which they normally produce and bring architects into a design process which is influenced by contemporary modes of fabrication and the production of a new set of consumer desires.

Machinic Processes

The inherent tension between constraints in the computational realm and those in the manufacturing environment is used opportunistically to inform the design process in the research from the 'Machinic Processes' seminar. The importing of contemporary manufacturing capabilities and modelling tools currently available to industrial fabricators into stage one of an architectural design process ensures that an exchange occurs between these areas of expertise leading toward a collaborative design development. The emphasis is not on designing

Below: Fibreoptic distribution diagrams and view of Cloudbox shelving system

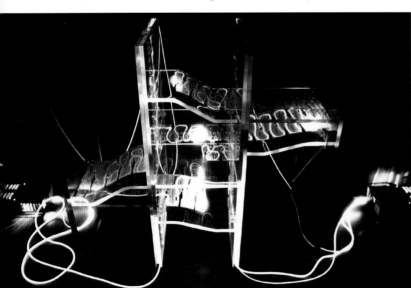

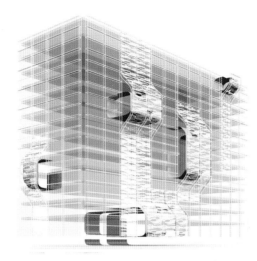

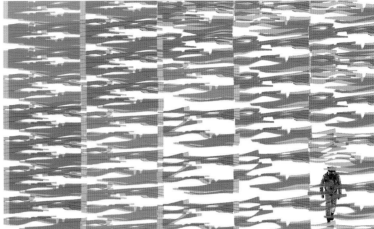

parameters to fit one particular manufacturing technique and one specific scale but rather to develop a flexible attitude toward the combination of a particular material technique and scale. The aim of the research is to develop innovative spatial and structural strategies that incorporate the embedded logics of these production techniques. The computer-numerically-controlled (CNC) milling process is the yield of positioning a set of digital instructions, the toolpath, in co-incidence with a material workpiece. The toolpath acts as a mediator between the computational and the physical realm. Simultaneously the instructions exist as a graphically presented set of u-v surfaces in the modelling environment, and as a g-code in the manufacturing environment which adheres to an x-y-z logic.

In these projects from 'Machinic Processes' a series of surfaces are broken down according to their construction lines, isoparms, into a series of differentially related members which are proposed as structural systems. In one branch of the research, the *Stripes* project, a structural system is developed which has the capacity to produce an envelope construction that ranges from solid to filigrane. This range is attained by creating continuous seams which act as regions about which the individual members can meet as sharp tangents or overlap in a gradient fashion. The seaming strategy is also designed to exploit the constraints of the manufacturing process at a specified scale, in this case a 3-axis mill with a 6 cm range in the z-axis. The *Tetris* project employs a technique of opportunistically scanning surfaces to define the most extensive areas of a given surface that can be milled as single entities. Scanning a

surface in this manner incorporates the additional constraint that the territory is inscribed by a border corresponding to the u-v isoparm logic. A number of surfaces broken down according to the 'scanner' yields a variable number of panels depending on the degree of inflection of the original surfaces. The scanning technique is consistent with the development of a product identity in that each set of panels produced is subject to a shared set of developmental parameters. The *Anamorphosis* project exploits the tension between the u-v surface logic and the x-y-z logic of the 3-axis mill by imposing the x-y-z biased toolpath onto the undulating surface in a single direction, which restricts the tool to a limited territory of influence. The result is an interface between stepped and smooth characteristics. In other work such as the *Imperfect Fit* project, a series of Boolean subtractions is carried out computationally to design apertures and surface subdivisions. The mill is also used directly as a Boolean operator by positioning the set of digital instructions onto the physical workpiece and moving the workpiece relative to the code in a non co-incident manner in order to generate moiré effects. In the *Cells* project a singular condition of poché or infill between two surfaces is set into motion via an animated sequence. This sectional poché between the surfaces is then duplicated with the interpolative effects of the transformation intact. One instance of an original surface yields a series of cellular pods which can be fabricated to stack into one another adjacently.[4]

Above: Cloudcurtain applications and moiré grooving variations

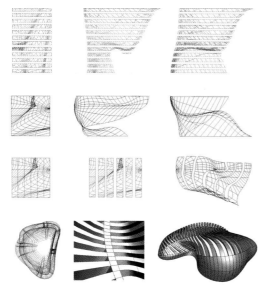

The case studies presented here are indicative of the degree to which technology-induced ambiguities between performance and production, purveyance and authorship, reconfigure not only the nature of design but of practice itself. New protocols of authorship, ownership and habitation are fostered by contemporary digital technologies which afford a high degree of variation within a given field of elements. The loss of value which is inherent in a condition of multiple authorship is replaced by a value system related to customisation and the portability of spatial experience. The loss of exclusive authorship finds its replacement in a higher degree of influence registered by multiple authors into the proliferation of spatial propositions and positions the author as a purveyor who provides menus for customisation.

Top: Anamorphosis Project showing structural surface components

Above: Stripes Project showing variable seaming strategies

Right: Tetris Project showing surface scanning panelisation ensembles

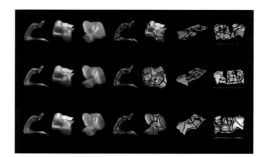

Notes
1 The 'Machinic Processes in Architectural Design' projects are available at www.arch.ethz.ch/lynn
2 Founding members of the design collaborative *servo* are David Erdman, Marcelyn Gow, Chris Perry and Ulrika Karlsson. The *servo* 'Urbantoys' project is available at www.n2art.nu
3 Collaborators on the *Urbantoys* project are: Jonas Runberger, Daniel Norell, Nina Lorber, Ulrika Wachmeister, Alice Dietsch, Johan Bohlin, Oskar Jonsson, John Stäck, Cult 3D, Prototal AB.
4 The authors of the projects from 'Machinic Processes' are:
   Stripes: Oliver Bertram, Jan Henrik Hansen, Reinhard Prikoszovich, Thomas von Pufendorf
   Tetris: Clemens Bachmann, Christopher Heinzerling, Ralf Peter, Robert Reiniger, Tobias Schaffrin
   Anamorphosis: Simon Kempf, Kevin Luginbühl, Miriam Zehnder
   Imperfect Fit: Nicola Bezzola, Juerg Ranser, Nathalie Rinne, Michaela Schulze
   Cells: Matthew Davis, Sophie Maurer, Negussu Mengstu, Odilo Schoch

wetGRID: THE SOFT MACHINE OF VISION

Lars Spuybroek (NOX)

Interviewed by Arielle Pélenc (chief-curator of *'Vision Machine'*)

When you first came to Nantes in July you where very much concerned with proprioception while discussing these experiments in perception by the artists in the show.

To explain something like proprioception, a neurological term, it might be helpful to refer to someone like Oliver Sacks, the English/American neurologist and writer. He wrote the now famous book *The Man that Mistook his Wife for a Hat*, a compilation of some 20 case studies from his practice as a neurologist working in New York. What I find so interesting about these contemporary neurologists like Sacks, is that they are the most anti-Cartesian thinkers in the world! No Ego floating above a Machine of flesh, waiting passively to be started up again and again, no mind-and-body-split, but a complex system of feedback loops, structural changes and interactions. To them consciousness is not that Holy Centre onto which the world is projected and from where it is observed. It is part of this structural relation with the world, part of the body itself and its transformations.

Now proprioception, especially to an architect, is a very interesting concept. It is the self-perception of the body, but it is both blind and unconscious. It is the internal consciousness of muscles and tendons within the whole of posture. It is completely self-referential. Actually, when you lose your sense of proprioception (and Sacks describes such a case) you can only slightly make up for it by pure, conscious attention. Instead of just picking up your cup off the table to bring it to your mouth to drink your coffee, you would have to lock in consciously on the cup with your eyes and 'send' it to your lips, without taking your eyes off it. So, proprioception is nothing but your sense of movement related to posture. An architect would say space is outside the body and there lies the possibility of movement, but movement is first and foremost part of the structure of the body. And, even more interesting, this structure of the body is plastic, capable of transforming. For instance, when you break your leg and it has to be plastered, it may happen that when the cast is taken off six weeks later, you've lost your leg. It isn't there any more! You have lost this capacity to move it, and when you have lost that capacity it is not 'yours' anymore, you are simply no longer the 'proprietor' of the leg. So movement is an abstract capacity stored in a plastic structure of the body. Merleau-Ponty (who read as much neurology as he did philosophy) refers to this as 'abstract movement', virtual movement. The body is tense, never at rest, movement is always there and has to be actualised by action, and every action again and again is written into this jelly-like soft structure of the body in order to become coherent and habituated. He also gives a beautiful example of this, in this case one of gaining movement. A woman wearing a large hat with a feather on it (this must be in the 1920s) bows her head when she walks through the door. Unconsciously she knows her head has become 50 centimetres longer, and this has become part of her actions. So, again as an architect, I have to ask myself, 'Where is space?', because obviously, as this example illustrates, space is the haptic potential, the haptic sphere of action.

Left: Digitally manipulated study for wetGRID installation

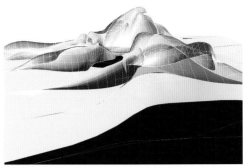

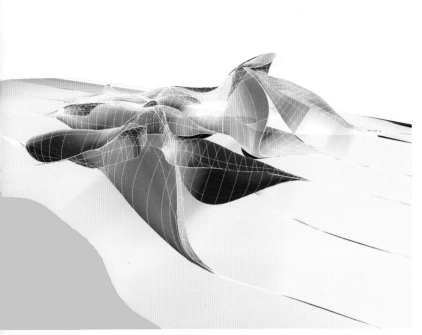

Both pages: Digitally manipulated study for wetGRID installation

What do you see as the relation between vision, body and space?

This is very much related to proprioception. Just look at what the museum generally is, as a structure, what any museum is for that matter. There is the floor, it is – as is usually the case – horizontal. All action takes place on this surface, all movement is planned (by architects) on this horizontal surface. Then there is the wall. It is vertical, perpendicular to the floor, and on it are the images, the pictures that make up the museum's exhibition. That is the surface for seeing. We should always realise that this architecture is that of the Cartesian body: the part that sees is separated from the part that walks. You either walk or see. Perception and action are completely separated. The way the bricks that make up the museum are piled on top of one another, along the vector of gravity, is exactly the posture of standing, of the standing body. It doesn't bend, twist, run, dance, jump, lie down or move about in any way – no, it is a column of flesh. So, this absolutely passive concept of the body is related to this other concept, which holds that seeing is always considered as measuring yourself against the horizon, the datum of horizontality. You see, it is completely related to not only the Cartesian split of mind and body, but also of subject and object, of

body and world. This concept still holds in cognitivist thinking, where the world is passively projected onto the mind, that after some information-processing projects its actions back onto the world.

The idea of this exhibition, the images and the architecture, is completely different. When I saw all the images, the chemical experiments of Hiller and Polke, the emergent images of Kupka and Morgner, the drug experiments of Michaux, the algorithmic hallucinations, I saw one thing only: the vortex. The vortex, the twirl, has played an enormous role in the history of art and perception. It is of course organised around a vertical axis, and when the vortex is related to perception (by Poe, by Blake, by Rimbaud) it is the axis of vertigo. And vertigo is falling within one's own body, could be heaven though, but often it is hell too. There are millions of descriptions of visions of spiraling structures of people going up or down. Just think of Huxley's *The Doors of Perception* – or all the reports of near-death-experiences, pure psychotropic trips! Always this lightening of the body is related to hyper-vision, extra-vision, the colours are a thousand times brighter, everything shines, it is pure happiness. All these visions contain radiant objects, palaces of emerald, of gold, rivers of ruby, whatever.

Anyway, this is a clear indication that the posture of 'standing up' is not the only one that enables a human body to see things, so to speak. Now in architecture in general the horizon-vision is the one of outer-orientation and vertigo-vision the one of inner-orientation. The first is the one of finding your way, the second of losing your way: the spirals of the labyrinth.

Of course I am in between, I am always in between. I agree so much with Varela that the in-between is the most radical position.

You refer to the cave image as a Vision Machine. What did the shaman see?

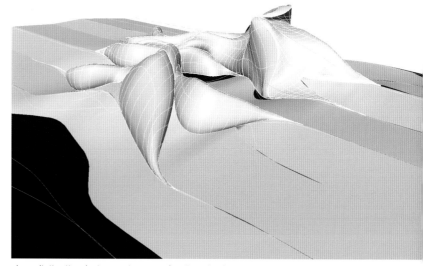

Yes, to clarify the concept of the exhibition, I have to describe two concepts of a cave. There are many more, but these two are the ones that were most on my mind while I was designing the exhibition. One is the neurological cave of two kittens, the other the cave paintings that were studied by Jean Clottes.

The first one, and I have quoted this often, is a neurological experiment with two kittens done in the 1960s by Held and Hein, and very well described by Varela in his *The Embodied Mind*. It is not a real cave, it is more of a cylinder, a circular environment of, let us say, 80 centimetres wide with a rhythmic pattern of black and white lines painted onto the inside. In the middle stands a post and, like in a fairground, there are two gondolas hanging down that do not reach the ground. They are attached to each other by a crossbeam that can rotate around the axis of the vertical pole. In each gondola is a sweet little kitten, just one week old. One kitten touches the ground with its feet, the other one does not. So, the first kitten can walk around and see, the second one is being moved around by the other one but shares the same visual experience. After two or three weeks, when all the necessary nerves in the brain have grown more into a structure both kittens are released. The first one moves around very lively and attentive, the second as if it is blind, it bumps into everything.

Now, obviously this shows just how much movement and vision are related, how much the motor and the sensory are connected. There is just no seeing without moving, no moving without seeing. *Vis à vis* the design of the exhibition this means there is no

clear distinction between inner and outer orientation, between the straight line of the horizon and the curved ones of the vortex. They are integrated into one system, which we will have to come back to later on, but I think it is not a question of either standing up straight and orienting oneself on the horizon, or falling down and seeing only visions. What interests me so much is that in everyday life we are constantly in-between, feeding back between both, not either walking straight lines or losing our way, but making curves, lines that are bent, negotiated, corrected. In fact you can only orient yourself well by making smaller or larger detours. We can only see when we act, there is no other vision.

The second study I would like to refer to is one done by Jean Clottes and David Lewis-Williams. They have studied cave paintings in the most important caves of southern France and northern Spain. For all these incredibly beautiful, horizonless paintings they have distinguished three stages of altered consciousness. The first stage is the imagery of 'scotoma', the flickering zigzags of migraine-vision, or ecstasy. Very well described by

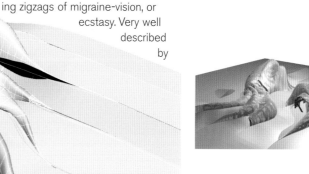

different authors – again Sacks among them – these are the images you'll see when you take LSD, or after long sensory deprivation, or in combining vigorous dancing and rhythmic sounds: the basic shamanist routines. The second stage is the 'translation', the continuation or the preservation of these images by more well-known images, for instance, a zigzag 20,000 years ago was 'translated' into the painted image of a snake. The third stage is the one Clottes and Lewis-Williams actually call the 'vortex', or the funnel. After the rite of passage, the spiraling tunnel, one enters the world where

real and unreal are no longer apart. The shaman has entered this level of transformation, of metamorphosis where he can change into a bison or a fox.

In order for this to work the cave paintings have to float on the rock, not be fixed in a frame, not be related to any 'outside' because actually the outside is in the wall, or in the body. Clottes found this fantastic feature about cave painting – which brings it extremely close to interactive electronic art – that a lot of the paintings like an antelope, or the head of a bison were only painted half. The rest of the image was the shadow thrown on the rock by the torch because of the specific topography of the rock! They 'saw' with their torch half a bison here, half an antelope there, and 'finished' it in paint! That is

exactly the relationship I would like to have between my structures and the images on them. The structure not as a means to carry and support them, but a structure that lifts the image in such a way that the body that looks at it flies in, the wall becoming a window to enter the image. To achieve that it is absolutely necessary to implode the distinction between here and there, here-eyes and there-horizon, and have the horizon be swallowed by the point were you are. As an architect you can only do that by leaving behind the distinction between floor and wall, between vertical and horizontal. That is where you enter the realm of topology, of rubber-sheet-geometry.

You call your Vision Machine a 'wet grid'. That seems like one of your oxymorons like 'deep surface'.

Yes, the grid is one of the oldest tools in architecture. If an architect wants to create order – from that perspective – he jumps into his metaphorical helicopter, flies up, and drops a grid onto the situation. It is a military action. The grid is directly connected to the top-down view itself, and to the top-down view of order and coherence at the same time. Now, the grid, the Greek grid is something completely different from what we nowadays call a network. Let us not forget both terms are diagrammatic, they are explanatory schemes, they are literally 'views', percept-schemes used as concepts. The network is of course the contemporary view of emerging order, of self-organisation, of bottom-up coherence. So, the first view is where order is forced upon matter, from above, while in the second view order emerges out of material interactions: pattern, stability, order on the edge of chaos.

The 'wet grid' is then an in-between situation, very close to 'liquid crystal', where order is neither the solid-state condition of the crystal nor the completely liquid state of 'free' movement. Actually, the liquid crystal is not a half-way form between liquid and crystal but a higher form of order. Liquid does not have enough coherence, has no holistic properties, it cannot act as a whole and on the other hand, the solid state crystal is a whole, but cannot act because it consists of only one state, so it only survives in stable unchanging conditions. The wet grid means it is neither lines nor surface, dimension 1 nor dimension 2, but strategically in-between and there it is stronger than either the one or the other. It is not neutrally half-way though, not like 1.5, as by its nature it cannot be homogeneous, it must be a heterogeneous assemblage of more dimensions. Patches of weakness and patches of strength together make up the hybrid of softness. The softness of the grid makes it transformable, it makes it stronger than a rigid grid because time is inherent in the structure, points can become little knots or springs and the springs may unfold into lines again, the lines may split up and become more structural, more like surface. But, as you see, with this interior view of the grid, the bottom-up view, the lines are suddenly not flat ink anymore, they have taken on material properties. This is no longer moulding the clay from the outside by drawing, this is building a machine of variability, one of modulations, of continuous variations.

So, I don't draw. I'm not up there in the air dropping black lines onto the world.

Wasn't the 'wet grid' also connected to the research of Frei Otto?

Yes, very much so, I referred to it in relation to his way of calculating 'optimised path systems'.

In a way the method is very close to Gaudí's suspended chain modelling technique. For Otto it is a way to calculate either the branching of columns or of roads. Taking roads as an example he has set up an experiment with woollen threads. First he maps all the possible goals in a situation as pins on a board. Then all the pins are connected by woollen threads, which means you can go from every starting point straight to every end point: a grid without any detours. But obviously this is an incorrect way to set up a road system. There is no hierarchy, there is no coherence, only the possibility of individual routings at the cost of having an enormous surplus of roads. In Frei Otto's experiment a wonderful decision is then made: all of the woollen threads are lengthened by an extra 8 to 10 percent, which indicates the average amount of detouring for all the routes. Then a little water is added to the system and this moistening of the threads makes them stick together in certain places. What actually happens is an economisation of detouring, the organisation and regrouping of the extras. When the system dries up one sees an emergent, self-organised order where the lines suddenly form a network instead of a grid, where in some instances eight lines have stuck together to form a thick line next to large open spots, and sometimes a small scale web of thin lines into what is more a surface. Suddenly there is a hierarchy in a system, like in a liquid crystal: patches of thickness, of clear singular orientations in a sea of thinner connections of multiple orientations –

This page and opposite:
wetGRID installation

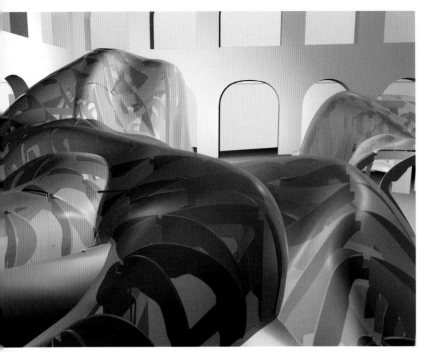

This page and opposite:
Digitally manipulated study
for wetGRID installation

attraction and rejection are simply programmatic, but also as a way to basically affirm the world as one of movements. If you study the little sketches of Finsterlin in the exhibition, which are absolutely amazing, one could speak of calligraphy, machine-states, mental machine-states drawing the lines, but it would still be very hard to circumvent subjectivism. There is no way Finsterlin could have shared his method with others, something I consider a weakness – well, at least in architecture, maybe not in art.

I analysed the existing Musée des Beaux-Arts de Nantes as typical of classicist centre-periphery relationship. The periphery is the gallery, horizontally vectorised, the centre is the atrium, basically a cupola, a dome, vertically vectorised: the eye immediately looks up towards the light. Again, the one stresses more the importance of feet, the other of the eye.

In the computer I put eight double lines on the grid of the Musée, from the entrance through the depth of the whole building – this is the general orientation of the movement. Very simple. Then I put four 'vortex-forces' in what I would call a self-choreographing machine. This machine, that looks like a hand, coordinates the movements of the vortices. Now, I should explain what this is. A vortex is a rotating force that develops itself in time according to the various parameters. They use this in Hollywood to make films on catastrophic tornadoes like *Twister* by Dutch director Jan de Bont. Very impressive software, one can have all the dirt, cars and cows flying around in the tornado. I used the vortices as movements, gestures, but the skeleton that coordinates them works interactively, it is not a marionette player's hand. It's like teaching four dancers separately a certain type of rotating movement, and then connecting them with elastic band. That changes the individual movements into a new emergent pattern – and this also happens within the structure of the eight double lines.

After we had studied the behaviour of this system, and knew what its possibilities were, we adjusted the limitations of the different bones in the skeletons until all was in accordance with our general purpose of how to read the program (I'll come back to that). What the system basically did was to have some of the lines form complex nodes while others were splitting up. Reading from the entrance of the

a heterogeneous whole of which the dimension floats between 1 and 2. Of course these are computers, Gaudí and Frei Otto have used material computers to calculate shape and structure.

So, how do you work with the computer?

The computer is the main tool to evolve from the interior of a system towards a drawing, pushing the drawing again into another system and evolving it from there towards a new level. So it alternates between emerging orders and projected orders and each time it jumps another level toward actualisation. This is different from working with the standard 'draw diagram' to 'materialise form' procedure. Architects always make conceptual diagrams, infograms, ideograms (just observe how they switch between 0.3 pencils, ink, thick blacklead and felt-tips), they sketch and sketch and work their way out of the complexity by a process of reduction, by mostly Euclidean redrawings on the sketch until it becomes a single-lined clear crystal of edges, defining where to end each architectural element. I work very differently, because in the computer this materialisation of the line, between vague and thin, can be instrumentalised, and instead of me animating the curves with *Einfühlung*, I have the software do it. This diagramming of feeling is essential to me, not only when dealing with art, where the pulses of

Musée towards the end of the atrium space, three lines formed a knot, then this knot split up into two lines moving to the left, and one to the right forming another knot on the right side of the atrium, connecting it to yet another group of lines. It is more complex than that, but it gives a general idea of the capacity of this system, namely being able to form a soft grid out of parallel lines. Normally a grid is formed by overlaying two perpendicular systems, but here it was generated by lateral movement in a longitudinal system.

I should now introduce the conceptualisation of the program into the argument. The first eight lines were placed on one level in the computer, eye-level, and when these start to twist and curve in different directions under the influence of the vortex, two things may happen. One, when a line moves down, is the tendency to become 'floor', low surface, and second, when lines split up, they have the tendency to form spaces. So structure is not around the space, but space is in the structure. All splittings of the double lines are interpreted as accessible space, the others as accessible surface, i.e. floor. This is very important in relation to the program, the paintings and images. All of them in all kinds of different ways relate to the in-between of cell and grid. Of course it is connected to vision: the cell is the monad, the pill, the helmet, the suit, the capsule, the spaceship *Enterprise* 'the vehicle to see things'. It is the 'eye of the tornado', where the

vortex gives the most vertical inclination to the system, where it opens up the most to vertiginous images of ectoplasms, drug imagery, etc. The grid is what connects, where the influence of the vortex radiates, is spread out more horizontally to another node. In this the grid and the cell are never opposites, gallery and atrium, they are states of one system, every time you see you will also walk, every time you walk you will see. The result is that no painting is 90 degrees vertical, and no floor is 90 degrees horizontal, except there where you are outside of the influence of the vortices.

How do you then translate this system into construction? You spoke about splitting of the lines like the example you gave me of the Gothic Room in the Hradshin in Prague.

To recapitulate, we have started with a system of eight double lines that can twist and bend with the forces of the vortices. These 'rubbery' lines form knots and splittings. But they have no structural capacities you can use for a built structure, they are built to absorb perception and movement, but not gravity. Now, what usually happens is putting columns under the diagrammatic lines, and then realise the result in form. That is the worst solution. If we can interpret the structural (de)formation into perception and action, then why not construction as well, to synthesize all three.

What we did came very close to Deleuze's example of sword-making. You don't cut a sword like a contour out of a metal plate. No, you have to heat it, bend it, fold it many times to make the sword supple and, in the end, you have to cool it down suddenly because this crystallisation hardens the sharp edge. All kinds of different types of action and correction are required to make the sword. It is not one homogeneous material, it has a history of different states, material states and the material itself is a movement, a structural capacity you have to negotiate with in order to tease out the best sword possible.

So when the rubber lines in the computer model were moving towards each other and at the same moment another group separated, we took a 'snapshot' – that is absolutely a top-down action – of a bunch of 16 lines with a certain pattern on a certain moment. Deleuze would call this movement-by-limits, 'the passage to the limit', very much like a gearbox: when a certain stage reaches its limit, a threshold, you must make it jump into another state. That was the moment to switch to paper modelling. We printed this snapshot of Klee-like quivering lines onto a flat sheet of paper, like a drawing, and glued it to cardboard. From thereon we introduced again 16 lines, but now made of strong thick paper, and tried to follow the twists and bends of the ink lines. But instead of trying to rebuild it as a model, we used the paper as a new way to 'calculate' the shape. In fact this stage is more like a paper computer. If two lines of ink (which is actually 'cooled down' rubber) were bending in the same direction we interpreted this as a tendency to connect, thus: we split up the paper line and had it meet the other (with a paperclip), somewhere up in the air. Now, that is a very old structural principle, a Gothic principle where the vault is nothing but a surface that emerges out of a splitting of the lines, i.e. the columns. So, we were suddenly building vaults! Vaults-helmets-cells that emerged out of a surface with zero thickness, like blisters! From then on we had a very basic structural principle that could easily be built in wood. And of course because the whole thing was done in the computer all the information of the curvature was easily translatable into a milling machine that cut all the wood for us. So, as the computer was finally twisted into a conceptual device by us, it still ended up as a very instrumental machine, which is actually the whole secret.

Project description
wetGRID (exhibition design for 'Vision Machine', Musée des Beaux Arts, Nantes, 1999–2000)

NOX
Lars Spuybroek with Joan Almekinders, Dominik Holzer, Sven Pfeiffer, Wolfgang Novak and Remco Wilcke. Project assistants: Xavier Fouquet and Sylvain Gasté

wetGRID is an installation which makes the image itself inhabitable. The exhibition 'Vision Machine' was composed of 250 paintings, drawings and installations by a mixture of artists like Pollock, Kupka, Ernst, Tanguy, Polke, Barry and architects like Parent/Virilio, Kurokawa, Hauserman, Schein, Archigram and many others. The exhibition explored the area in between the emerging view and the projected view, between subjective and objective vision. The designing method consisted of various steps, diagrammatic stages in which information is each time transposed to a new level. The first machine is one where four rotating forces interact with a linear structure derived from the structure of the existing museum. These four vortices are conceptually connected to four types of vertigo and hallucination according to the grouping of different works by curator Arielle Pélenc. This machine was transformed into a paper model, went back again into the computer, analysed again into a grid of lines, then the lines became the information of how to cut the wood (again with the computer) into all the different shapes. So, if we go from images and their groupings to a diagrammatic reading, to a machine that produces geometry of space, to space itself: then, space is the content of the images! All the works were directly hung on the complex surface, and oriented with the manifold directions of the surface... finally, when looking at the works – they sometimes hang close to the floor, or tilted, or even on the ceiling – you have to position your body according to the original forces of vertigo, and become a dancer.

SMECTIC STATE
Mark Goulthorpe (dECOi)

I've had a sense for a while now
that we're in a sort of *smectic* state

The smectic being the interstitial phase or
state-shift
between solid and fluid
as crystals begin to emerge out of their base
medium
or melt back into it

In fact, it's the prior *nematic* phase
where molecules begin to link and form chains
and the *smectic* where this stealth process
takes on geometric or directional properties
when the chains conspire into patterns and motifs

The smectic state is a *traumatic* one
trauma, unlike shock, occurring on the site of
absence
an event that somehow escapes consciousness
representative certainty dissolved in the mysterious,
osmotic emergence of form

The liquid-crystal screen, as its name suggests
born of the properties of ferro-electric smectics
whose directionality (hence colour) can be
flicked by current
pitches us into a sort of shoal-of-fish mental space

A flotation of reference
a bizarre connectivity or collective *property*
a propensity for rapid, almost convulsive fluctuation
chasing after the lure of dynamic affect
the *will to animation* as it's been called...

If one can accept that we're still essentially
iconoclasts
in despising images for their apparent degradation
of reality
then if we look into the depth of the liquid-
crystal screen
right in to a molecular level
then we're through the looking glass
image born from formal incertitude,
statelessness
an iconoclastic seizure...
I invoke this smectic state because it seems to
me that the digital revolution is a fully
technological one

not a merely technical one:
it marks a profound realignment of our base
categories of thought
our relation to memory, our *cultural* aptitude
(not just a smart new tool...)

'The Work of Art in the Age of Mechanical
Reproduction', by Walter Benjamin
evidenced a similar sentiment in light of reproductive technologies −
of cinematic and photographic logics −
his thesis being that the very conditions for the
production and reception of art
would be utterly requalified by such technological
change

the 'aura' of the work of art −
its reliance, that is, of a certain *a priori* of
representative norms
would be disenfranchised by the 'shock' of a
new art

Stoss was his word, and Heidegger's −
a slap in the face as art participated at speed in
the actuality of life

He didn't mourn this eclipse − he merely
remarked
with his usual quizzical optimism, that it was an
inevitability
a recalibration of thought and experience itself...
in light of a new technology

And, thinking back, he was objectively right...

When I speak of *trauma*, then, I do so in direct
reference to this modernist 'shock'
looking for a more ambiguous, almost interstitial
mental state
the other side of the digital revolution
that might be somehow adequate to account for

Below: Aegis project

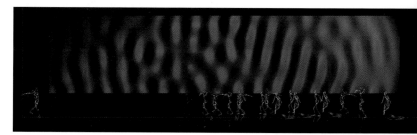

the cultural – rather than technical –
smectic state that we seem suspended within

Trauma being that state of heightened bodily
awareness
engendered by an absence of memory
a vertiginous compulsion chasing after a disappearing referent
an event that has escaped assimilation
which seems to me where cultural imagination
is suspended
in an open-ended and evolutive digital
environment…

I'm going to show two projects which follow this
drift
speculating on the shift from *autoplastic* to
alloplastic space
terms used by Sandor Ferenczi in his studies of
trauma
where he broadens the notion to that of an
almost generalised condition
Autoplastic presupposes a determinate and
fixed relation between the self and the
environment
one designs, graphically, almost bodily…
whereas *alloplastic* describes a malleable and

reciprocal relationship
an essentially smectic indeterminacy, or flux

These terms I use not so much literally, to
describe a (possibly) malleable architecture
(although we'll come to that)
but as a means of describing an entirely
reconfigured creative and receptive context

My experience of working in a digital
environment
suggesting that we're leaving *determinate*
modes of operation, ideologies
in favour of an open-ended sampling of the
greatly-enhanced generative capacity
of software systems
a sort of *precise-indeterminacy…*
which is a smectic state…

Exploring what I believe are the two essentially
new possibilities offered by computers –
programmatic and *parametric* generative
processes
I realise that we're creating not so much
architecture
as the *possibility* of an architecture
which is born as a potentiality at the intersection
of a matrix of variables

The *Paramorph* project and the *Aegis* project
which I'll show here
are parametrically and programmatically
conceived, respectively
Which allows them to escape my volition, somehow
are no longer 'designed' as such
with scientific-rational certitude
but open to a much looser formal potential
nonetheless uncannily precise…

Even the names seem to anticipate this flotation
a 'paramorph' being a body that can change its
form whilst maintaining its properties
this descriptive of the parametric generative
process
which allows an 'elastic' relation in its base
geometric description
And Aegis being the supple and ambiguous
cloak of the Greeks
adopted by Athena as a beguiling
passive/aggressive shield
into which she would weave trophies of her
conquests

a subtle surface of reciprocity, a soft yet deadly
mirror of events
a masculine/feminine alterity…

And my suggestion in presenting these projects
is that such disfocused generative processes
which sample and edit a fickle infinity
carried over into their receptive register
somehow *actualise the virtual* of a new medium
in offering a similarly open-ended, restless,
almost *bodily* engagement
of the alloplastic digital imagination

Paramorph
This, then, the Paramorph
our competition-entry for a Gateway to the
South Bank here in London
the start of the South-Bank pedestrian route at
Waterloo
which developed as an open ended digital
process…

The idea of a cultural front door in London
seemed anathema
given that it's a city that wears its culture in the
streets
suspicious as it is of any 'high' art
and I was intrigued to think how one might
instead create a sort of reciprocal event-space

The site was intriguing in that it was already a
zone in depth –
a pedestrian tunnel beneath a railway viaduct –
and where the physical environment, albeit
imposing
seemed less important than the movements and
sounds
in and around the site
which give the space its actual character

I also thought of Virilio's comment
that the last Gateway to the city
is the scanning device at airports
but where this suddenly extends in depth
throughout the city
as a vast network of electronic receptors that
modulate
implicitly or explicitly our behaviour

And I wondered if, almost by an overdeployment
of such technology
one couldn't begin to create a sort of liberal chaos

This page ad opposite:
Pistons, Aegis project

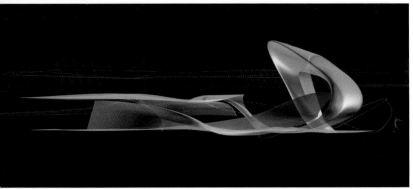

This page ad opposite:
Paramorph project

like that wonderful restaurant scene in Jacques Tati's *Playtime*
when the breakdown of the over-wrought technology
creates a pure human pantomime…

Tati, of course, continually teasing Big Brother…

So we set about working with the ephemeral traces of movement and site-sound
able to begin to register fluidity in a digital medium
pouring fluid through the site to generate
a sort of envelope of tendency, of impulsion
an invisible second-site

This we began distorting through sound-modelling (entirely inexpertly)
but giving birth to series and series of shell-forms
which we began immediately to imagine as a sort of giant aural canal
a listening device
receptive to the passage of people
and host to endlessly evolving sound-sculpture
created by bodies in transit
floated through the echoic space

The forms that began to emerge
were born digitally
were not *designed*
but emerged from an open-ended evolutive process
that is neither legitimate nor illegitimate
in its contextual *implication*

Literally that – this weaving together of different strains
sound and movement condensing somehow into aural vessel…

At a certain point we'd derived a series of quite compelling forms
a 'slow' entrance to the quite static space of the

plaza in front of Waterloo
and a more high-speed exit to the slip-road at the rear of the Festival Hall
a morphing series of shell-forms in between

All modelled parametrically to allow a rapid and controlled reconfiguration of their fluid forms

But at a certain point we realised that we were back to the entrance/exit routine
that we were looking to avoid
so after several weeks of modelling we just dumped the lot
and I sent everyone home to sleep, somewhat dismayed

And the very next day,
with a sort of proprioceptive sense of the thing
we simply sketched it in 3-dimensions

Perfectly improvisational
although, like any decent improvisation
drawing from the body of knowledge acquired in the process

Curiously, I remember Bill Forsythe e-mailing me to say
'I want you to tell me that this took hours and hours of back-breaking, agonising work
or else the cat sat on the keyboard and this popped out'
and I wrote back and said it wasn't the cat
although by the end it was kind of effortless, understood for what it was

All the processural meanders folded deftly into these four surfaces
which we imagined as a double skin of tessellated aluminium
drawing light into the tunnel as a sort of *optikinetic* effect
and allowing sound to drift through the deep surface texture

The electronics we imagined calibrated to respond not simply to movement
but to *change of movement*
encouraging an active participation and constant invention
normalcy not registering as such
so a sort of Ministry of Silly Walks for the pinstriped commuters

And which I reckoned probably would serve as
a somewhat appropriate introduction
to British culture

And as it turned out we seem to have indeed
traumatised the 'expert' jury
since we didn't win
but we did then win the popular vote of the
commuters who use the space
so Tati smiles

I referred to it as *parametric*
and in fact it was developed doubly with Mark
Burry's postgraduate team at Deakin University
developing a smart-sculpting machine, if one
can call it that
which draws from his 20 years of research into
Gaudi's *Sagrada Familia*
which turns out to be derived entirely from
hyperbolic surfaces
or highly constrained straight-line geometries

Here, realising the budget was highly constrained,
we set out to model the form
such that it could be constructed from straight
sections of aluminium
and derived a parametric model –
a reiterable elastic geometric model that
describes relations (parameters)
that are readily reconfigured

Such that we went to the jury with a contractor
who pledged to fabricate it within budget
fully appreciating the strict and reiterable basis
of the project

So *alloplastic* in both its generative process
and its ambiguous and contingent destination…
a *paramorph*, as I've said
whose form may change whilst its essential
properties remain…

Aegis
The *Aegis* project also suggests an alloplastic
genesis
but sustains this into its very physicality
which becomes indeterminate

It began as a proposition for an interactive artwork
for the cantilevered 'prow' of the Birmingham
Hippodrome Theatre
which, penetrating from outside to inside,

offered opportunity to create an *animate*
architectural surface
responsive to events in and around it
and to the theatre itself

We imagined it as a mute planar surface of
bipolar metallic facets
but which harbours a dynamic potential
in that it is driven by a matrix of actuators
that allow displacement of the surface 'real-time'

The proposition being to take the calculating
speed of the computer
out into 3-dimensional space
to create a dynamic surface or 3-dimensional
screen
responsive to real-time events

An architecture of *reciprocity*, as it were

At the time of the competition, even,
we were working with mathematicians and
programmers
realising that to create co-ordinated effects at
high speed
would require a precise interface

Yet the very specialism and overlap
provided all sorts of areas of looseness and
creative overspill
such that we came to think of it as *precisely
indeterminate*

As we developed the project through a series of
working prototypes
such interdisciplinarity has become embedded
as the essential characteristic
the sheer flow of information required
to activate up to 10,000 pistons every hundredth
of a second
demanding quite specialised mechatronics
engineering
keyed in to streamlined mathematical programming

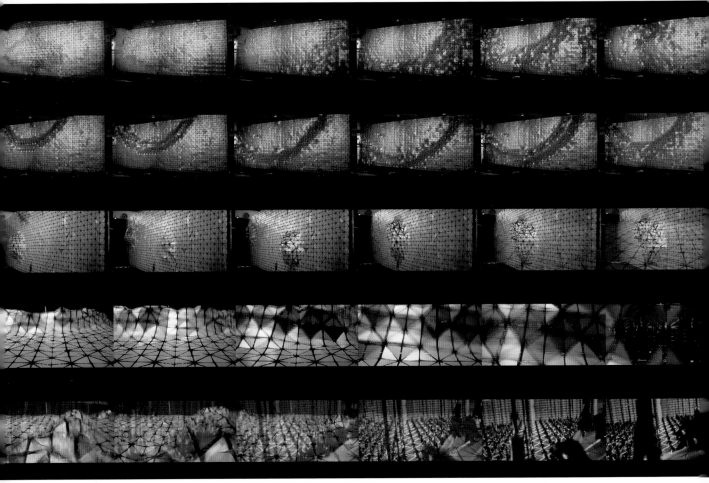

The resulting system, still here in early stages of development,
has proved highly performative
sound and movement being translated instantly by the
dynamically reconfigurable surface

Currently we're deploying about 1000 pneumatic actuators
every 0.01 sec
wavefronts propagating at speeds of up to about 60kmh
and displacing the surface some 500mm two to three times per second

The control computer has been specially fabricated to allow such high rates of information flow coupled to a parallel-processing computer which calculates real-time

in response to sound or movement

Aegis, then, a literally-animate architecture announcing, in its effortless co-ordination of many thousands of mechanical devices,
the birth of nano-technology –
of the intersection of information and form
where electronic stimuli deform matter

And hence new genres of alloplasticity
here not just as a psychological interactivity
but as the literal formal malleability of architecture itself
reconfiguring continually in response to an ambient reciprocity

Now, my interest here is not overtly technical despite the evident fascination of the mergence of different specialist fields

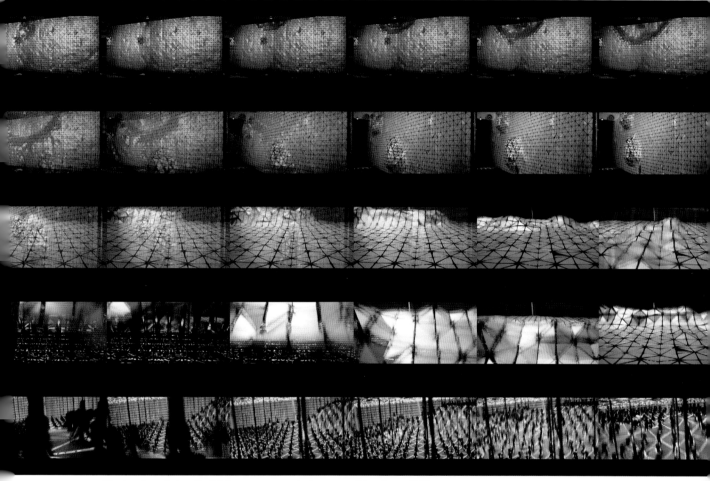

Above: Aegis project

my sense of technology being that it is essentially nothing
other than the recalibration of desire
released in the attainment of new technical capacity

A monkey wriggling ants out of an anthill with
a stick
consumed not with a fascination for sticks
but with a new-found *desire for ants*

My therefore *cultural* interest being, once again,
to determine new modes of creative and
receptive possibility
released in the interstices of digital *praxis*

The creative process here
based on the implication of technical specialism –
no longer 'designed' as such
as a determinate singularity –

but as a *matrix of possibility*
a sort of silhouette of potential

Hypo designating a subliminal, almost unconscious happening
resulting from an open mathematical triggering
that conjours an endlessly disappearing
physical 'event'

My suggestion being that
as we pass from autoplastic to alloplastic
cultural space
that such works raise the spectre of *trauma* as
the apposite category
of an emergent digital medium
which needs to be thought as such

The Work of Art in the Age of Electronic
Hyperproduction…

ROBOTIC FIELDS: SPATIALISING THE DYNAMICS OF CORPORATE ORGANISATION

Patrik Schumacher

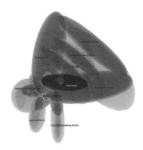

'Robotic fields' is a chapter within a three-year design research effort, 'Corporate Fields', conducted at the AA Design Research Laboratory.[1] This research experiments with architectural responses to emergent forms of corporate organisation.

With respect to recent patterns of corporate management a number of related tendencies stand out that concern our attempt to offer architectural translations:

1 The enormous increase in communication density translates into an insatiable need for spatial connectivity and points toward deep, porous spaces.

2 A momentous acceleration of organisational restructuring translates into an insatiable request for flexibility with respect to the spatial distribution of domains and activities, pointing towards kinetic systems.

3 The tendency to move from management by means of command and control to strategies of self-organisation implies an open, underdetermined environment that allows for an ongoing allegorical play of interpretation and appropriation.

4 A new level of organisational complexity calls for strategies of super-position, hybridisation and multiple affiliation.

Architectural solutions to these challenges might be enhanced by robotic capabilities. The possibility of augmenting architecture by means of electronic intelligence has been investigated in the context of the overall expansion of spatial repertoires that emerged from the discourses of *deconstruction* and *folding* in architecture. For example: an underdetermined and formally excessive 'space of becoming'[2] might be further 'virtualised'[3] by means of augmenting various

architectural elements with an electronically engineered kinetic spontaneity which allows the variously activated spatial features to participate in the aleatoric play of (re)appropriation. One of the three projects to be introduced below – 'Learning Environments' – has been exploring this possibility of mutual play and learning between users and kinetic architectural elements. Another project – 'Intelligent Fields' – took on the quest for self-organisation to establish a level of organisational complexity that might not be achievable on the basis of human concepts of order. Complex patterns of flocking/clustering are computed on the basis of profiles administering multiple project affiliations. A third project – 'Office Life Game' – has been steering emergent organisational patterns on the basis of local rules of association.

Before elaborating these projects a few general remarks outline the socio-economic setting and the overall intentions that have been guiding the research.

Identifying an Emancipatory Project: Non-hierarchical Work Patterns

We live in a period of reactionary politics. The political arena has been eroded by the frustration of national politics in a globalised world. The 1980s suffered the 'neo-liberal' reversal of earlier social reform programmes. This continued in the 1990s, combined with a further erosion of civil democracy. The co-optation and disintegration of any organised left-wing opposition implies that an architectural commitment to progress and emancipation can no longer be guided by a straightforward political agenda.[4]

But while politics proper stagnates, one can identify progressive tendencies within the process of corporate restructuring. The modern strategy of rationalisation based on the rigid segmentation and routinised specialisation of work within clear-cut functional hierarchies is failing today in respect to the complexity and dynamism of the overall socio-economic process. New ways of organising the labour process are emerging in organisation theory.

A glance at the booming literature in management theory will suffice to capture the

Above: Layers of transience: field of light, Sandmeier/Simon

Below: Diagramme to space2 Ryu/Lei/Ko

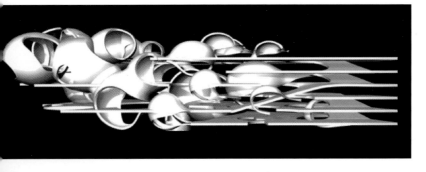

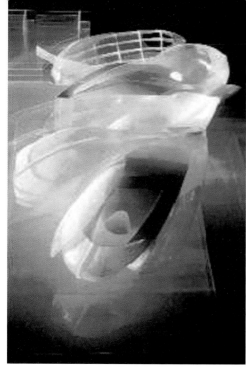

ongoing frenzy of restructuring: *Welcome to the Revolution, The New Paradigm for Business, Liberation Management – Necessary Disorganisation for Nanosecond Nineties, The Postmodern Organisation, Deconstructing Organisations, Catching the Wave, The One Minute Manager, Thriving on Chaos, The Complexity Advantage, Competing on the Edge – Strategy as Structured Chaos*, etc.[5]

Although the word 'democratisation' is not among the slogans circulating around the management 'revolution', democratisation seems the repressed logic of recent (and future) productivity gains, a necessity for the corporation to be able to cope with permanent reorientation and innovation. The renunciation of command and control is forced upon the capitalist enterprise by the new degree of complexity and flexibility of the total production process within which it has to function. The more information-based, the more dependent upon research and development production becomes, the less can it proceed autocratically. These hard facts of production – more than ever – seem to confirm left intuitions about the effectiveness of radically democratic, participatory relations on an advanced level of socio-economic complexity.

The left wing organisational paradigms (e.g. the rhizome), which Deleuze and Guattari elaborated in the late 1970s, in dialogue with the new left forms of revolutionary struggle and organisation,[6] seem to become the very paradigms of corporate restructuring: Deleuzian *de-territorialisation*[7] is dissolving the rigid departmentalisation of competencies and the *aborescent* pyramid of classical corporate

organisation is mutating towards the rhizomatic plateau upon which the leadership is distributed within a permanently shifting multiplicity of latent centres.

Today there is no better site for a progressive project than the most competitive contemporary business.[8]

Spatialising Organisational Knowledge

Contemporary business processes are more about the generation of knowledge than about producing immediate material values. More and more work takes place in the realm of ideas and information rather than immediate physical production. Thus the structure and pattern of economic activity in general are assimilated to the processes of science. This is the hallmark of the new economy as *knowledge economy*.[9]

As an organisation shifts from being a straightforward manufacturer or provider of a standard service to become a creative innovator, it no longer just utilises a given knowledge, but needs to operate as an original producer of knowledge. The new discipline of knowledge management takes account of this situation. Management theory offers concepts like 'the learning organisation'[10] or 'the intelligent enterprise'.[11] Here learning, knowledge and intelligence are attributed to organisations rather than to individuals. For us this is just the first step towards the further expansion of the notion of organisational intelligence to include the various spatial systems that structure and sfacilitate the vital communication processes within the business.

Knowledge becomes the most precious resource within the organisation. But this resource can not be bought in from outside like energy or labour. It can not be acquired ready-made. Knowledge involves much more than information: it is the right information employed at the right time and place, evaluated and adapted within a complex praxis. *Organisational knowledge*, furthermore, goes beyond individual knowledge. Organisational knowledge resides within the organisational pattern itself, in the corporate system of communication and collaboration, i.e. in the distribution and dynamic

Above left: Deep/porous space2, Blum/Lin/Ritter

Above: Deep/porous space1, Videcnik/Oman

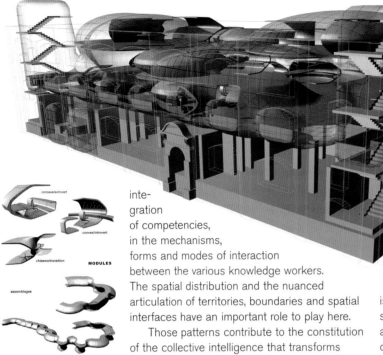

Top: DEGW office headquaters, Office Life Game

Above: Modules and assemblages, Office Life Game

Below right: Plan View, Office Life Game

integration of competencies, in the mechanisms, forms and modes of interaction between the various knowledge workers. The spatial distribution and the nuanced articulation of territories, boundaries and spatial interfaces have an important role to play here.

Those patterns contribute to the constitution of the collective intelligence that transforms information into vital operative knowledge.

One might ascribe intelligence/knowledge to every organisation that integrates a series of individual intelligent agents/knowledges into a larger, more complex intelligence/knowledge. Within a bureaucratic hierarchy all organisational knowledge is condensed and fixed within the proper procedures to be followed at every specific position within the administrative machine. Here learning can only take place at the top in the form of adjusting and rewriting sthe system of rules. Within a non-hierarchical network organisation the system of rules can evolve only if the organisation is at the same time based on self-organisation rather than a fixed constitution. The organising and orienting spatial structures, i.e. team spaces, have to coevolve alongside the determination of the social system of collaboration, its temporary division of labour, its groupings and channels of communication. The potential advantages of kinetic systems and the attendant possibilities of utilising artificial intelligence – in the form of life-game rules or flocking scripts etc. – are to be investigated with respect to specific corporate scenarios.

In contrast to the hype about the supposed collapse of space and the end of architecture in an age of telecommunication, our working hypothesis is that the desired production of operative knowledge can be catalysed and sustained by built architectures which remain the indispensable spatial substratum of organisational life.[12] Architecture increases its impact as the content of corporate production undergoes a process of progressive dematerialisation. This hypothesis does not deny the increase of telecommunication. Rather, it assumes that this increased capacity of communication is swamped by an exponential demand for sbusiness communication that can only be addressed by means of new levels of spatial complexity and connectivity – further augmented by kinetics and electronic intelligence embedded within the spatial organisation.

From (Animated) Diagram to (Animated) Space

The translation of organisational patterns into space utilises the organigramme as a spatial (2D) medium of articulation that architecture shares with organisation theory and the practice of management consultancy. The graphic repertoire employed determines the scope of organisational patterns that the consultancy business is able to work with. This repertoire is currently limited to 2D Venn diagrams operating with boxes within boxes and network diagrams operating with lines connecting nodes. The combination of the two formalisms is the most complex that has been achieved within the domain of corporate organisation design.

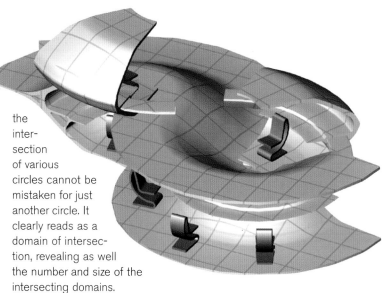

Above: 3D Team Cluster,
Office Life Game

Therefore graphic representation does not really play an innovative role within this discourse.

In contrast, the expansion of graphic diagramming repertoires has been a key aspect of our research. This includes the systematic incorporation of layering, the articulation of gradients, the employment of morphing to produce morphological series and matrices of similitude, the move to complex 3D diagrams and the computer animation of 4D time-figures. These time-figures are geared to capture, model and manipulate the dynamics of organisational life on various time scales: the daily patterns of movement and communication within the company, the formation and reformation of team structures across the cycle of a project, as well as more long-term corporate growth/ restructuring scenarios.

Each design language is dependent on a given or chosen *formal a priori*, i.e. graphic language or 'design world':[13] a certain set of graphic primitives and attendant rules of aggregation and transformation. While the computer expands available repertoires it nevertheless represents a strictly bound design world, further constrained by the choice of tools and specific ways of building up the formal structures in each project. While this reduction of complexity is unavoidable, it is all the more important to choose on the basis of comparative experimentation with various formal systems and to be aware of the contingency of any argument/result upon the initial formal choices. For example, when it comes to articulating an organisation in terms of the grouping of individuals, various formalisms might be considered. One might start with rectangles next to/within rectangles to express relations of division and subsumption. Alternatively, one might operate with circles next to/within circles. At first sight these two formalisms might seem functionally equivalent. But the formalism on the basis of circles has a number of important iconographic advantages: the circular system allows the hierarchical level of a domain to be read off locally from its radius and the distinction between inside and outside can be read off the difference between concave and convex while the orthogonal system remains mute in these respects. In the case of overlapping domains the orthogonal intersection between two rectangles might be read as just another rectangle, while the intersection of various circles cannot be mistaken for just another circle. It clearly reads as a domain of intersection, revealing as well the number and size of the intersecting domains.

The move from 2D to 3D, from intersecting circles to interpenetrating spheres, has the further advantage of allowing for the articulation of a more complex pattern of overlap than can be managed within a 2D plane. At an even higher level of complexity the diagram might have to resort to deformed 3D blobs to avoid accidental intersections.

This comparative evaluation demonstrates how formal decisions might be rationalised within a functional context that poses the semantic dimension of architecture, i.e. *orientation through articulation*, to be crucial. This also shows why − once an articulate level of the visualisation/spatialisation of organisational relations has been achieved within the diagram − the directive for the translation of the diagram into an architectural space can only be *as literal as possible* − in order to maintain the orienting features of the formalism.

If this slogan is applied to the animated time-diagrams that claim to model and articulate the temporalisation of organisational complexity as an essential component of the organisational system, then the literal translation of the respective time-figures into robotic fields is called for. The hypothesis is that animated, kinetic spaces will have a critical advantage with respect to facilitating and orienting the dynamic life of the organisation.

Layers of Transience: Furnishing the Dynamic of Social Communication

The first step in making this vision of an animated architecture tangible is the recognition of the total mass of furnishings − fixed as well as mobile – as the crucial space-making substance rather than regarding it as an accidental filling of an already constituted space. The dichotomy of space versus furniture is dissolved into *layers of transience* that start with the most ephemeral flux of light or images on computer screens, the movement of people and paper across the space of the office, files, mobile chairs, trolleys and the semimobile swarm of light fixtures, the more stable tables, shelves and cabinets, the semifixed partition walls, etc. all the way to the supposedly permanent structural shell and external envelope. The tendency of our design research has been to blur these typologies and to aim for an overall increase and acceleration of transience and mobility within all of these strata (including structure). On the other hand the attempt is made to increase the space-defining power of each system with the result of dynamising what is phenomenologically recognised as *the space*.

Once the substance of spatial articulation is thus put in motion the electronic augmentation and steering of the behaviour of these substances can be elaborated. The invention/refinement of behavioural patterns and their dynamic spatial co-ordination is the challenge of this new paradigm of animated design. The consideration moves from mere form to morphology in relation to behaviour: types of movement, modes of transformation, and the agglomeration into collective organisms.

The organisational function of corporate headquarters depends heavily on interior furnishings, both in terms of the diversity of types as well as with respect to the coherent inter-relatedness of the various typologies. A closed semantic universe is constituted subject to a complex matrix of differentiations: formal – informal, fixed – flexible, individual – collective, demarcating – connecting, etc.

There is an immediate configurational as well as material engagement with the human body and its close-range activities, both individually and with respect to the formation of groups and patterns of collaboration. In the final analysis it is the speculation about new social configurations and patterns of communication that we are concerned with.

Three Projects

The following projects are embedded in the general research agenda of corporate restructuring within the emerging knowledge economy. Each successive year one project was marked out to investigate the incorporation of robotic capabilities into the spatial construct. In this sense the following examples of 'robotic fields' are special cases of the 'corporate fields' explored within the AADRL.

Each project team was working with a quasi-client: DEGW, Ove Arup, Razorfish – companies that exemplify the general tendencies

Bottom right: Urban Contest, Learning Environments

Below: Workspace, Learning Environments

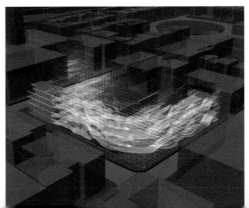

of corporate development discussed above. These companies and their organisational strategies served as a concrete point of departure for the development of experimental spatial scenarios resulting in proposals for the respective London headquarters of these enterprises. On a more general level these scenarios attempt to translate key concepts and stratagems proposed within recent management theory.

Office Life Game – DEGW
AADRL 1997/98: Kevin Cespedes, Chin Jung Lin

DEGW[14] is an internationally operating space planning firm, integrated into a larger management consultancy business. Its expertise coincides with our overall research agenda: spatial organisation as tool of corporate restructuring. DEGW has used its own corporate space for a radical demonstration of the organisational potential of a system of multiple depersonalised work settings, regulated by occupation protocols. The DRL project radicalises this approach through the idea of space-making protocols conceived in analogy to life-games producing emergent global patterns from local rules. Such an indirect quasi-control leaves each individual move indeterminate.

A number of entangled ambitions have been pursued and balanced:

First ambition: the creation of a feasible kinetic system with a sufficiently large universe of possibility/difference.

Second ambition: the search for temporary protocols that restrain and order this universe in harmony with certain social activities.

Third ambition: the rules should nevertheless leave a large margin of free choice for the users, i.e. the social order is perceived to emerge on the basis of freedom.

Here the solution is a system of circular intersecting tracks that allow the movement and

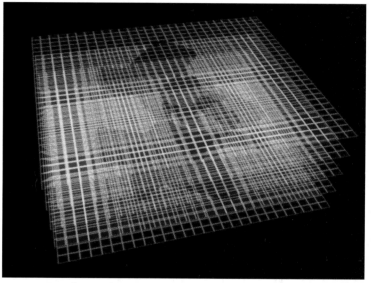

aggregation of a small number of modules (concave/extrovert, convex/introvert, chiasma/transition) into a suprisingly rich diversity of configurations. A series of dramatic transformations of the global space is possible: from a nearly isotropic distribution of individual fragments, to a number of strongly articulated, separate circular domains, to a single large congregation for special occasions that involve the whole firm.

Social and spatial oscillations are investigated in exploring the idea of a corporate office landscape that re-emerges every time according to the geometrically installed rules of a space-making game. It is an attempt to create a spatial life-game through latent territorialisation and moveable space-fragments that would temporarily capture and fix a distinct spatial order out of the fluidity of potential collaborative relations. The moving pieces are semi-enclosing furniture units which also engage in multiple sectional relations and share their essential formal features with the fixed spatial envelope in order to allow the more transient layers to appear quite substantial in each of their temporary states. The mobile elements in effect extend and transform the otherwise fixed conditions.

Learning Environments – Ove Arup Partnership AADRL 1998/99: Theo Lorenz and Anna Sutor

Artificial life elaborates the concept, geometry and aesthetics for a new computer-based form of spatial malleability. The aim is the formulation of a generalised logic widely applicable to any working environment requiring dynamic social patterns of collaborative grouping and regrouping in space.

The point of departure for this research project is the modelling of the spatio-temporal rhythms of team working scenarios within the

able to a computer user. Embedded touch-screens would become the interface to lead operations and changes not only on the screens but also within the physical space surrounding the employee, letting his/her environment be transformed and modelled like objects in a CAD program.

The integrated family of transformable elements populates a space-frame, which in turn displaces its structural members and thus constantly redistributes the structural voids that are possible within the system.

The system of furnishings generates dynamic configurations constantly subject to further transformations through the individual's intervention. The overall environment will thus be subject to cumulative changes generated by multiple local interventions. The environment

Right: Technoscape, Intelligent Fields

Below: Flocking Chairs, Intelligent Fields

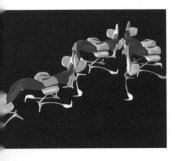

Ove Arup Partnership via animated time-figures. These time-figures find their translation on a number of different scales from the overall spaceframe that operates without any fixed members through to shifting and folding floor surfaces and a series of robotic, self-deforming furniture elements.

The building is conceived as an interactive territory almost as flexible as the interface avail-

operates symbiotically with the users coproducing an artificial intelligence where users and robotic elements engage in a mutual process of collective learning. The furniture pieces produce spontaneous, randomised self-deformations which act as suggestions to the users who might either pick up on those suggestions – thus learning new uses and reward the element – or otherwise intervene and remodel the piece as well as the local configuration between pieces. The pieces will 'remember' the respective correlation of movements by adjusting the statistical likelihood of the respective correlations for their future suggestive behaviour. Strict determinations are excluded and a measure of random mutations remains at play for further evolution. New social tropes and communicative situations emerge through the aleatoric play and mutual learning between furniture and employees.

Intelligent Fields – Razorfish
AADRL 1999/2000: Marcel Ortmans, Markus Ruuskanen, Ivan Subanovic, I Yu

In contrast to the universal formalism of the animated folds of the previous project this project operates by way of articulating discrete and diverse creatures with distinct behavioural capacities. However, these discrete creatures are nevertheless derived from a number of base modules and tectonic/kinetic principles and exhibit certain genealogical similarities.

The project investigates the thesis of structured self-organisation by means of computer programming robots within an overall techno-ecology. The fluid and complex patterns of project and skill affiliation that should determine the distribution and grouping of people (i.e. individual workstations) and resources (e.g. meeting rooms) are tackled by means of the robotic mobilisation of all workstations and facilities. Each element is scripted with respect to its temporary project assignments which in turn are programmed as fields of attraction engendering the repositioning of individual elements. The various workstations are differentiated according to skill category and developed as distinct species in terms of morphology and behavioural pattern: Moth, Walker, Stalker, Silverfish, Whale etc. – the beginnings of a veritable techno-diversity. The temporary script or profile of the robotic species establishes its

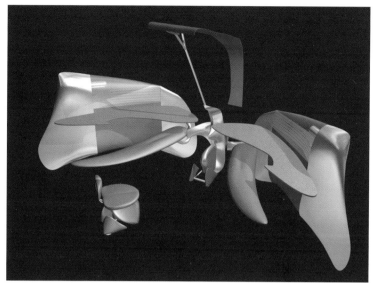

weighted sensitivity to the various fields competing for resources. Fields are either fixed around project foci (static fields) or emerge from the mutual attraction of affiliated individuals (dynamic fields). The human agents are guided by the intelligent flocking patterns of their robotic chairs, worktops, meeting tables etc. while maintaining the power to override, redirect and even 'enslave' or chain their robotic resources to their own movement. Individualised elements have the potential to couple, embrace and cluster into larger assemblages and collective organisms – all the way to camouflaging and blending into the overall living structure.

The space populated by the robots is conceived as a differentiated landscape that produces its own peculiar biases: stepped versus ramped sections, bottlenecks versus wide access, and so on. In relation to the various creatures and their capabilities – rolling, walking, gliding, hanging – these biases and their dynamic manipulation (tightening of bottlenecks, flattening of ramps etc.) act as functional equivalents (material computing) to the eclectronic scripting of attractions/repulsions.

Outlook
The technique of scripting allows one to define temporalised functions between the properties (position, movement, deformation, transparency etc.) of any set of objects. This opens up a new paradigm of design speculation: each architecture creates its own dynamic universe, complete with its own ontology and quasi laws of nature.

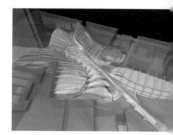

Top: Embracing Furniture, Intelligent Fields

Above: Urban Setting, Intelligent Fields

Below: Unfolding Furniture, Intelligent Fields

folding

Notes

1 The DRL is the March course at the Architectural Association School of Architecture, London. For a summary of the research agenda *Corporate Fields* see: Patrik Schumacher, 'Business – Research – Architecture'. In *Daidalos* 69/70, *The Need of Research*, December 1998/January 1999.

2 Peter Eisenman. 'Processes of the Interstitial'. In *El Croquis* 83, Peter Eisenman, Madrid 1997.

3 Brian Massumi, 'Sensing the Virtual, Building the Insensible'. In *Architectural Design: Hypersurface Architecture*, London 1998. John Rajchman, 'The Virtual House'. *Any Magazine* No. 19/20, 1997.

4 The current wave of anti-capitalist protests – gathering momentum around occasions like the G8 summits or the annual meetings of the World Bank – is united only on the basis of a diffuse rejection of the status quo without yet achieving sufficient levels of programmatic resolution to orient a progressive research effort.

5 T Cannon, *Welcome to the Revolution – Managing Paradox in the 21st Century*. London 1996; M Ray and A Rinzler, *The New Paradigm for Business*. Los Angeles, CA 1993; T Peters, *Thriving on Chaos*. New York 1987; T Peters, *Liberation Management – Necessary Disorganisation for Nanosecond Nineties*. New York 1993; W Bergquist, *The Postmodern Organisation – Mastering the Art of Irreversible Change*. New York 1993; M Kilduff, *Deconstructing Organisations*. Academy of Management review 18; K Blanchard and S Johnson, *The One Minute Manager*. New York 1982; J L Bower, *Disruptive Technologies – Catching the Wave*. Harvard Business Review, Jan/Feb 1995; S Kelly and M A Allison, *The Complexity Advantage*. New York 1998; SL Brown and KM Eisenhardt, *Competing on the Edge – Strategy as Structured Chaos*, Boston, MA 1998.

6 Deleuze and Guattari's philosophy relates to the radical Italian 'autonomia' movement. See: *Italy: Autonomia* – Post-political Politics, Semio-text(e), NYC 1980. This discourse entered architecture in the form of the philosophical abstractions propagated by Deleuze and Guattari's *Thousand Plateaus*, the main source of inspiration for the formal strategies of 'Folding'.

7 Departmentalisation/sub-departmentalisation as the structural principle of the bureaucratic mode of organisation is a perfect instance of Deleuze and Guattari's concept of 'territorialisation'.

8 This serves here as a hypothesis, even if one has to acknowledge that the corporate reality remains suspended within the contradiction of participatory production and divisive distribution and the promised 'liberation management' remains constrained by the strictures of class-society.

9 A number of fundamental economic laws have to be rewritten as the logic of knowledge production/consumption increases its weight with respect to the determination of economic rationality. In contrast to material production the cost of reproducing and disseminating a knowledge product is negligible in comparison to its research and development component. In contrast to material capital like raw materials or machinery knowledge resources appreciate rather than depreciate with employment. Utilisation gathers rather than consumes value – here in the form of contextualising information products. See: Helmut Wilke, *Systemisches Wissensmanagement*. Stuttgart 1998; Thomas Steward, *Intellectual Capital. The new wealth of organisations*. New York 1997.

10 Peter Senge, *The Fifth Discipline*. New York 1990.

11 James Quinn, *Intelligent Enterprise. A knowledge and service based paradigm for industry*. New York 1992.

12 The ongoing tendency of spatial concentration in places such as Wall Street and the City of London seems to confirm this thesis. See: Saskia Sassen.

13 William Mitchell, *The Logic of Architecture*. Cambridge, MA 1990.

14 DEGW: Duffy, Eley, Giffone, Worthington.

DELEUZE AND THE USE OF THE GENETIC ALGORITHM IN ARCHITECTURE

Manuel DeLanda

The computer simulation of evolutionary processes is already a well-established technique for the study of biological dynamics. One can unleash within a digital environment a population of virtual plants or animals and keep track of the way in which these creatures change as they mate and pass their virtual genetic materials to their offspring. The hard work goes into defining the relation between the virtual genes and the virtual bodily traits that they generate; everything else – keeping track of who mated with whom, assigning fitness values to each new form, determining how a gene spreads through a population over many generations – is a task performed automatically by certain computer programs known collectively as 'genetic algorithms'. The study of the formal and functional properties of this type of software has now become a field in itself, quite separate from the applications in biological research which these simulations may have. In this chapter I will deal neither with the computer science aspects of genetic algorithms (as a special case of 'search algorithms') nor with their use in biology, but focus instead on the applications that these techniques may have as aids in artistic design.

In a sense evolutionary simulations *replace design*, since artists can use this software to *breed new forms* rather than specifically design them. This is basically correct but, as I argue below, there is a part of the process in which deliberate design is still a crucial component. Although the software itself is relatively well known and easily available, so that users may get the impression that breeding new forms has become a matter of routine, the *space of possible designs* that the algorithm searches needs to be sufficiently rich for the evolutionary results to be truly surprising. As an aid in design these techniques would be quite useless if the designer could easily foresee what forms will be bred. Only if virtual evolution can be used to explore a space rich enough so that all the possibilities cannot be considered in advance by the designer, only if what results shocks or at least surprises, can genetic algorithms be considered

useful visualisation tools. And in the task of designing rich search spaces certain philosophical ideas, which may be traced to the work of Gilles Deleuze, play a very important role. I will argue that the productive use of genetic algorithms implies the deployment of three forms of philosophical thinking (populational, intensive and topological thinking) which were not invented by Deleuze but which he has brought together for the first time and made the basis for a brand-new conception of the genesis of form.

To be able to apply the genetic algorithm at all, a particular field of art needs first to solve the problem of how to represent the final product (a painting, a song, a building) *in terms of the process that generated it*, and then, how to represent this process itself as a well-defined sequence of operations. It is this sequence or, rather, the computer code that specifies it, that becomes the 'genetic material' of the painting, song or building in question. In the case of architects using computer-aided design (CAD) this problem becomes greatly simplified given that a CAD model of an architectural structure is already given by a series of operations. A round column, for example, is produced by a series such as this: 1) draw a line defining the profile of the column; 2) rotate this line to yield a surface of revolution; 3) perform a few 'Boolean subtractions' to carve out some detail in the body of the column. Some software packages store this sequence and may even make available the actual computer code corresponding to it, so that this code now becomes the 'virtual DNA' of the column. A similar procedure is followed to create each of the other structural and ornamental elements of a building.

At this point we need to bring in one of the philosophical resources I mentioned earlier to understand what happens next: population thinking. This style of reasoning was created in the 1930s by the biologists who brought together Darwin's and Mendel's theories and synthesised the modern version of evolutionary theory. In a nutshell, what characterises this style may be phrased as 'never think in terms of Adam and Eve but always in terms of larger reproductive communities'. More technically, the idea is that despite the fact that at any one time an evolved form is realised in individual organisms, the population, not the individual, is the matrix for the production of form. A given animal or plant architecture evolves slowly as genes propagate in a population, at different rates and at different times, so that the new form is slowly synthesised within the larger reproductive community.[1] The lesson for computer design is simply that once the relationship between the virtual genes and the virtual bodily traits of a CAD building has been worked out, as I just described, an entire population of such buildings needs to be unleashed within the computer, not just a couple of them. To the CAD sequence of operations the architect must add points at which spontaneous mutations may occur (in the column example: the relative proportions of the initial line; the centre of rotation; the shape with which the Boolean subtraction is performed) and then let these mutant instructions propagate and interact in a collectivity over many generations.

To population thinking Deleuze adds another cognitive style which in its present form is derived from thermodynamics but which, as he realises, has roots as far back as late medieval philosophy: intensive thinking. The modern definition of an *intensive quantity* is given by contrast with its opposite, an *extensive quantity*. The latter refers to the magnitudes with which architects are most familiar: lengths, areas, volumes. These are defined as magnitudes which can be *spatially subdivided*: if one takes a volume of water, for example, and divides it in two halves, one ends up with two half volumes. The term 'intensive', on the other hand, refers to quantities such temperature, pressure or speed, which cannot be so subdivided: if a volume of water at 90 degrees of temperature is divided in half, one does not end up with two half volumes at 45 degrees but with two halves at the original 90 degrees. Although for Deleuze this lack of divisibility is important, he also stresses another feature of intensive quantities: a *difference of intensity* spontaneously tends to cancel itself out and, in the process, it drives fluxes of matter and energy. In other words, differences of intensity are *productive differences* since they drive processes in which the diversity of actual forms is produced.[2] For example, the process of embryogenesis, which produces a human body

out of a fertilised egg, is a process driven by differences of intensity (differences of chemical concentration, of density, of surface tension).

What does this mean for the architect? That unless one brings into a CAD model the intensive elements of structural engineering – basically, *distributions of stress* – a virtual building will not evolve *as a building*. In other words, if the column I described above is not linked to the rest of the building as a *load-bearing* element, by the third or fourth generation this column may be placed in such a way that it can no longer perform its function of carrying loads in compression. The only way of making sure that structural elements do not lose their function, and hence that the overall building does not lose *viability as a stable structure*, is to somehow represent the distribution of stresses, as well as what type of concentrations of stress endanger a structure's integrity, as part of the process that translates virtual genes into bodies. In the case of real organisms, if a developing embryo becomes structurally unviable it won't even get to reproductive age to be sorted out by natural selection. It gets selected out prior to that. A similar process would have to be simulated in the computer to make sure that the products of virtual evolution are viable in terms of structural engineering prior to being selected by the designer in terms of their 'aesthetic fitness'.

Now, let's assume that these requirements have indeed been met, perhaps by an architect-hacker who takes existing software (a CAD package and a structural engineering package) and writes some code to bring the two together. If he or she now sets out to use virtual evolution as a design tool, it may be disappointing to realise the fact that the only role left for a human is to be the judge of aesthetic fitness in every generation (that is, to let buildings die that do not look aesthetically promising and let those that do mate). The role of design has now been transformed into (some would say degraded down to) the equivalent of a prize-dog or a race-horse breeder. There clearly is an aesthetic component in the latter two activities – one is, in a way, 'sculpting' dogs or horses – but hardly the kind of creativity that one identifies with the development of a personal artistic style. Although today slogans about the 'death of the author' and attitudes against the 'romantic view of the genius' are in vogue, I expect this to be a fad and questions of personal style to return to the spotlight. Will these future authors be satisfied with the role of breeders of virtual forms? Not that the process so far is routine in any sense. After all, the original CAD model must be endowed with mutation points at just the right places (and this involves design decisions) and much creativity will need to be exercised to link ornamental and structural elements in just the right way. But still this seems a far cry from a design process where one can develop a unique style.

There is, however, another part of the process where stylistic questions are still crucial, although in a different sense than in ordinary design. Explaining this involves bringing in the third element in Deleuze's philosophy of the genesis of form: topological thinking. One way to introduce this other style of thinking is by contrasting those results which artists have so far obtained with the genetic algorithm and those achieved by biological evolution. When one looks at current artistic results the most striking fact is that, once a few interesting forms have been generated, the evolutionary process seems to run out of possibilities. New forms do continue to emerge but they seem too close to the original ones, as if the space of possible designs which the process explores had been exhausted.[3] This is in sharp contrast with the incredible *combinatorial productivity* of natural forms, like the thousands of original architectural 'designs' exhibited by vertebrate or insect bodies. Although biologists do not have a full explanation of this fact, one possible way of approaching the question is through the notion of a 'body plan'.

As vertebrates, the architecture of our bodies (which combines bones bearing loads in compression and muscles bearing them in tension) makes us part of the phylum 'chordata'. The term 'phylum' refers to a branch in the evolutionary tree (the first bifurcation after animal and plant 'kingdoms') but it also carries the idea of a shared body plan, a kind of 'abstract vertebrate' which, if folded and curled in particular sequences during embryogenesis, yields an elephant, twisted and stretched in another sequence yields a giraffe, and in yet other sequences of intensive operations yields snakes, eagles, sharks and humans. To put this

differently, there are 'abstract vertebrate' design elements, such as the tetrapod limb, which may be realised in structures as different as the single digit limb of a horse, the wing of a bird, or the hand with opposing thumb of a human. Given that the proportions of each of these limbs, as well as the number and shape of digits, is variable, their common body plan cannot include any of these details. In other words, while the form of the final product (an actual horse, bird or human) does have specific lengths, areas and volumes, the body plan cannot possibly be defined in these terms but must be abstract enough to be compatible with a myriad combination of these extensive quantities. Deleuze uses the term 'abstract diagram' (or 'virtual multiplicity') to refer to entities like the vertebrate body plan, but his concept also includes the 'body plans' of non-organic entities like clouds or mountains.[4]

What kind of theoretical resources do we need to think about these abstract diagrams? In mathematics the kind of spaces in which terms like 'length' or 'area' are fundamental notions are called 'metric spaces', the familiar Euclidean geometry being one example of this class. (Non-Euclidean geometries, using curved instead of flat spaces, are also metric.) On the other hand, there are geometries where these notions are not basic, since these geometries possess operations which do not preserve lengths or areas unchanged. Architects are familiar with at least one of these geometries: projective geometry (as in perspective projections). In this case the operation 'to project' may lengthen or shrink lengths and areas so these cannot be basic notions. In turn, those properties that do remain fixed under projections may not be preserved under yet other forms of geometry, such as differential geometry or topology. The operations allowed in the latter, such as stretching without tearing and folding without gluing, preserve only a set of very abstract properties invariant. These topological invariants (such as the dimensionality of a space, or its connectivity) are precisely the elements we need to think about body plans (or more generally, abstract diagrams.) It is clear that the kind of spatial structure defining a body plan cannot be metric since embryological operations can produce a large variety of finished bodies, each with a different metric structure. Therefore body plans must be topological.

To return to the genetic algorithm, if evolved architectural structures are to enjoy the same degree of combinatorial productivity as biological ones they must also begin with an adequate diagram, an 'abstract building' corresponding to the 'abstract vertebrate'. And it is at this point that design goes beyond mere breeding, with different artists designing different topological diagrams bearing their signature. The design process, however, will be quite different from the traditional one which operates within metric spaces. It is indeed too early to say just what kind of design methodologies will be necessary when one cannot use fixed lengths or even fixed proportions as aesthetic elements and must instead rely on pure connectivities (and other topological invariants). But what is clear is that, without this, the space of possibilities which virtual evolution blindly searches will be too impoverished to be of any use. Thus, architects wishing to use this new tool must not only become hackers (so that they can create the code needed to bring extensive and intensive aspects together) but also be able 'to hack' biology, thermodynamics, mathematics, and other areas of science to tap into the necessary resources. As fascinating as the idea of breeding buildings inside a computer may be, it is clear that mere digital technology without populational, intensive and topological thinking will never be enough.

Notes

1 'First…the forms do not pre-exist the population, they are more like statistical results. The more a population assumes divergent forms, the more its multiplicity divides into multiplicities of a different nature…the more efficiently it distributes itself in the milieu, or divides up the milieu…. Second, simultaneously and under the same conditions…degrees are no longer measured in terms of increasing perfection…but in terms of differential relations and coefficients such as selection pressure, catalytic action, speed of propagation, rate of growth, evolution, mutation…. Darwinism's two fundamental contributions move in the direction of a science of multiplicities: the substitution of populations for types, and the substitution of rates or differential relations for degrees.' Gilles Deleuze and Félix Guattari, *A Thousand Plateaus*. Minneapolis: University of Minnesota Press, 1987, p. 48.

2 'Difference is not diversity. Diversity is given, but difference is that by which the given is given…Difference is not phenomenon but the nuomenon closest to the phenomenon. …Every phenomenon refers to an inequality by which it is conditioned. …Everything which happens and everything which appears is correlated with orders of differences: differences of level, temperature, pressure, tension, potential, difference of intensity'. Gilles Deleuze, *Difference and Repetition*. New York: Columbia University Press, 1994, p. 222.

3 See for example, Stephen Todd and William Latham, *Evolutionary Art and Computers*. New York, Academic Press, 1992.

4 'An abstract machine in itself is not physical or corporeal, any more than it is semiotic; it is diagrammatic (it knows nothing of the distinctions between the artificial and the natural either). It operates by matter, not by substance; by function, not by form…. The abstract machine is pure Matter-Function – a diagram independent of the forms and substances, expressions and contents it will distribute.' Gilles Deleuze and Félix Guattari, *A Thousand Plateaus*. Minneapolis: University of Minnesota Press, 1987, p. 141.

DIGITAL REALITIES

FROM VIRTUAL REALITY TO THE VIRTUALISATION OF REALITY

Slavoj Žižek

How are we to approach 'virtual reality' from the psychoanalytical perspective? Let us take as our starting point Freud's most famous dream, that of Irma's injection.[1] The first part of the dream – Freud's dialogue with Irma, this exemplary case of a dual, specular relationship – culminates in a look into her open mouth:

> There's a horrendous discovery here, that of the flesh one never sees, the foundation of things, the other side of the head, of the face, the secretory glands *par excellence*, the flesh from which everything exudes, at the very heart of the mystery, the flesh in as much as it is suffering, is formless, in as much as its form in itself is something which provokes anxiety. Spectre of anxiety, identification of anxiety, the final revelation of you is this – You are this, which is so far from you, this which is the ultimate formlessness.[2]

Suddenly, this horror changes miraculously into 'a sort of ataraxia' defined by Lacan precisely as 'the coming into operation of the symbolic function'[3] exemplified by the production of the formula of trimethylamin, the subject floats freely in symbolic bliss. The trap to be avoided here, of course, is to contrast this symbolic bliss with 'hard reality'. The fundamental thesis of Lacanian psychoanalysis is, on the contrary, that what we call 'reality' constitutes itself against the background of such a 'bliss'; i.e. of such an exclusion of some traumatic Real (epitomised here by a woman's throat). This is precisely what Lacan has in mind when he says that fantasy is the ultimate support of reality: 'reality' stabilises itself when some fantasy-frame of a 'symbolic bliss' forecloses the view into the abyss of the Real. Far from being a kind of fragment of our dreams that prevents us from 'seeing reality as it effectively is', fantasy is constitutive of what we call reality: the most common bodily 'reality' is constituted via a detour through the maze of imagination. In other words, the price we pay for our access to 'reality' is that something – the reality of the trauma – must be 'repressed'.

What strikes one here is the parallel between the dream of Irma's injection and another famous Freudian dream: that of the dead son who appeared to his father and addressed him with the reproach, 'Father, can't you see that I'm burning?' In his interpretation of the dream of Irma's injection, Lacan draws our attention to the appropriate remark by Eric Ericson that, after the look into Irma's throat, after his encounter of the Real, *Freud should have awakened* as did the person who dreamed of the burning boy who woke up when he encountered this horrifying apparition: when confronted with the Real in all its unbearable horror, the dreamer wakes up; i.e. escapes into 'reality'. One has to draw a radical conclusion from this parallel between the two dreams: what we call 'reality' is constituted exactly upon the model of the asinine 'symbolic bliss' that enables Freud to continue to sleep after the horrifying look into Irma's throat. The anonymous dreamer who awakens into reality in order to avoid the traumatic Real of the burning son's reproach proceeds the same way as Freud who, after the look into Irma's throat, 'changes the register'; i.e. escapes into fantasy which veils the Real.

What has this to do with the computer? As early as 1954 Lacan pointed out that, in today's world, the world of the machine proper, the paradigmatic case for 'symbolic bliss' is the computer,[4] as one can ascertain when one enacts a kind of phenomenological investigation, leaving aside (technological) questions of how the computer works, and confining oneself to its symbolic impact, to how the computer inscribes itself into our symbolic universe.

In other words, one must conceive the computer as a *machine à penser* (a thinking machine) in the sense that Levi-Strauss talks about food as an *objet à penser* (to think about) and not just an *objet à manger* (to eat); because of its 'incomprehensibility' , its almost uncanny nature, the computer is an 'evocatory object,'[5] an object which, beyond its instrumental function, raises a whole series of basic questions about the specificity of human thought, about the differences between animate and inanimate, etc. – no wonder that the computer metaphor is reproduced in miscellaneous fields and achieves universal range (we 'program' our activities; we do away with a deadlock via 'debugging', etc.). The computer is the third, new stage in Marx's scheme of development, which goes from tool (an extension of the human body) to machine (which works automatically and imposes its rhythm on man). On the one hand, it is closer to a tool in that it does not work automatically, man provides the rhythm; on the other hand, it is more independently active as a machine, since it works as a partner in a dialogue in which it raises questions itself. In contrast to a mechanical machine, its internal action is 'nontransparent', *stricto sensu* unrepresentable (we can 'illustrate' its workings, as with a clutch or a gear box), and it operates on the basis of a dialogue with the user; for that reason, it triggers in the subject-user a split of the type 'I know, but nevertheless…' Of course, we know that it is 'inanimate', that it is only a machine; nevertheless, in practice we act toward it as if it were living and thinking…

How, then, does one 'think with a computer' beyond its instrumental use? A computer is not unequivocal in its socio-symbolic effect but operates as some kind of 'projective test', a fantasy screen on which is projected the field of miscellaneous social reactions. Two of the main reactions are 'Orwellian' (the computer as an incarnation of Big Brother, an example of centralised totalitarian control) and 'anarchistic', which in contrast sees in the computer the possibility for a new self-managing society, 'a co-operative of knowledge' which will enable anyone to control 'from below', and thus make social life transparent and controllable. The common axis of this contrast is the computer as a means of control and mastery, except that in one case it is control 'from above' and in the other 'from below'; on the level of individual impact, this experience of the computer as a medium of mastery and control (the computer universe as a transparent, organised and controlled universe in contrast to 'irrational'

social life) is countered by wonderment and magic: when we successfully produce an intricate effect by means of a simple program, this creates in the observer – who of course in the final analysis is identical to the user himself – the impression that the achieved effect is out of proportion to the modest means, the impression of a hiatus between means and effect. It is of particular interest how, on the level of programming itself, this opposition repeats the male–female difference in the form of the difference between 'hard' (obsessional) and 'soft' (hysterical) programming – the first aims at complete control and mastery, transparency, analytical dismemberment of the whole into parts; the second proceeds intuitively: it improvises, it works by trial and thus uncovers the new, it leaves the result itself 'to amaze', its relations to the object are more of 'dialogue'.

The computer works most effectively of course as an 'evocatory object' in the question of 'artificial intelligence' – here, an inversion has already taken place which is the fate of every successful metaphor: one first tries to simulate human thought as far as possible with the computer, bringing the model as close as possible to the human 'original', until at a certain point matters reverse and it raises the questions: *what if this 'model' is already a model of the 'original' itself, what if human intelligence itself operates like a computer, is 'programmed'*, etc.? The computer raises in pure form the question of semblance, a discourse which would not be a simulacrum: it is clear that the computer in some sense only 'simulates' thought; *yet how does the total simulation of thought differ from 'real' thought?* No wonder, then, that the spectre of artificial intelligence summons the paradoxes of the prohibition of incest – 'artificial intelligence' appears as an entity which is simultaneously prohibited and considered impossible: one asserts that it is not possible for a machine to think, at the same time being occupied in prohibiting research in these directions, on the grounds that it is dangerous, ethically dubious, and so on.

The usual objection to 'artificial intelligence' is that in the final analysis, the computer is only 'programmed', that it cannot in a real sense 'understand', while man's activities are spontaneous and creative. The first answer of the advocates of 'artificial intelligence' is: are not man's creativity, 'spontaneity', 'unpredictability', etc., an appearance which is created by the simultaneous activity of a number of programs? So the path towards 'artificial intelligence' leads via the construction of a system with multiple processors…. But the main answer of advocates of 'artificial intelligence' is above all that the computer is far from obeying a simple linear–mechanical logic: its logic follows Gödel's, the logic of self-reference, recursive functions, paradoxes, where the whole is its own part, self-applicable. The idea of a computer as a closed, consistent, linear machine is a mechanical, precomputer age concept: the computer is an inconsistent machine which, caught in a snare of self-reference, can never be totalised. Here the proponents of the computer culture seek the link between science and art: in the principled, not just empirical, nontonality, and inconsistency of the computer — is not such self-reflective activity of the computer homologous to a Bach fugue which constantly takes up the same theme?[6]

These ideas form the basis of the hacker subculture. Hackers operate as a circle of initiates who exclude themselves from everyday 'normality' in order to devote themselves to programming as an end in itself. Their enemy is the 'normal', bureaucratic, instrumental, consistent, totalising use of the computer, which does not take into account its 'aesthetic dimension'. Their 'master-signifier', their manna, the aim, trick, of the hack is when one succeeds in beating the system (for example, when one breaks into a protected, closed circuit of information). The hacker consequently attacks the system at the point of its inconsistency — to perform a hack means to know how to exploit the fault, the symptom of the system. The universalised metaphorical range of the hack corresponds exactly to this dimension: so, for example, in the subculture of the hacker, Gödel's theorem is understood as 'Gödel's hack', that subverted the totalitarian logic of the Russel-Whitehead system….

Yet in contrast to this search for the point of inconsistency of the system, the hacker's aesthetic is the aesthetic of a 'regulated universe'. It is a universe that excludes intersubjectivity, a relation to the other *qua* subject: notwithstanding all the danger, tension, amazement which we experience when immersed in a video game, there is a basic difference between that tension and the tension in our relation to the 'real world' — a difference which is not that the computer-generated video world is 'just a game', a simulation; the point is rather that in such games, even if the computer cheats, it cheats consistently — the problem is only a matter of cracking the rules which govern its activities. So, for the hackers, the struggle with the computer is 'straightforward': the attack is clean, the rules are laid down, although it is necessary to discover them, nothing inconsistent can interfere with them as in 'real life'.

Therein consists the link of the computer world with the universe of science fiction: we conceive of a world in which all is possible, we can arrange the rules arbitrarily, the only predetermined thing is that these rules must then apply; i.e. that world must be consistent in itself. Or, as Sherry Turkle puts it: all is possible, yet nothing is contingent — what is thereby excluded is precisely the real. Impossible *qua* contingent encounter…. This reality, the reality of the other which is excluded here, is, of course, woman: the inconsistent other *par excellence*. The computer as partner is the means by which we evade the impossibility of the sexual relationship: a relationship with the computer is possible. *Das Unheimliche* (the eeriness) of the computer is exactly in that it is a machine, a consistent other, stepping into the structural position of intersubjective partner, the computer is an 'inhuman partner' (as Lacan says of the lady in courtly love).[7] One can also explain from this the feeling of something unnatural, obscene, almost terrible when we see children talking with a computer and obsessed with the game, oblivious of everything around them: with the computer, childhood loses the last appearance of innocence.

How, then, to resolve the discrepancy between the computer universe as a consistent 'regulated universe' and the fact that the hacker tries to catch the system precisely at the point of its inconsistency? The solution is elementary, almost self-evident. We simply have to distinguish between two levels, two modes of inconsistency or self-reference: the hacker's finding of the point of inconsistency, the point at which the system is caught in the trap of its own self-referentiality and starts to turn in a circle, always leaves untouched some basic consistency of the 'regulated universe' − the self-reference at which the hacker arrives is, if we can out it thus, a consistent self-reference. The difference between the two levels of self-reference with which we are concerned is contained in Hegel's distinction between 'bad' and 'proper' infinity − the computer's self-referentiality remains on the level of 'bad infinity'. We can clarify this distinction with two different paradoxes of self-reference which were both developed along the same subject, a map of England.

First, there was an accurate map of England, on which were marked all the objects in England, including the map itself, in diminished scale, on which they again had to mark the map, etc., in bad infinity. This type of self-reference (which is today mainly familiar in the form of television pictures which are reflected by television) is an example of Hegel's bad infinity; the giddiness triggered by this vicious circle is far removed from 'proper' infinity which is only approached by the other version of the paradox, which we encounter − where else − in Lewis Carroll: the English decided to make an exact map of their country, but they were never completely successful in this endeavour. The map grew ever more enlarged and complicated, until someone proposed that England itself could be used as its own map − and it still serves this purpose well today…. This is Hegel's 'proper' infinity: the land itself is its own map, its own other − the flight into bad infinity does not come to an end when we reach the unattainable final link in the chain but when we recognise instead that the first link is its own other. From there we can also derive the position of the subject (in the sense of the subject of the signifier): if the land is its own map, if the original is its own model, if the thing is its own sign, then there is no positive, actual difference between them, though there must be some blank space which distinguishes the thing from itself as its own sign, some nonentity, which produces from the thing its sign − that 'nonentity', that 'pure' difference, is the subject…. Here we have the difference between the order of sign and the

order of signifier: from the sign we may obtain the signifier by including in the chain of signs 'at least one' sign which is not simply removed from the designated thing, but marks the point at which the designated thing becomes its own sign. The computer's self-referentiality remains on the level of bad infinity in that it cannot reach any position of turn-around where it begins to change into its own other. And perhaps we could find in this − beyond any kind of obscurantism − the argument for the claim that 'the computer doesn't think'.

The reason why the computer 'doesn't think' thus keeps to the above mentioned logic of the reverse metaphor where, instead of the computer as a model for the human brain, we conceive of the brain itself as a 'computer made of flesh and blood'; where instead of defining the robot as the artificial man, we conceive of man 'proper' as a 'natural robot', a reversal that could be further exemplified in a crucial case-in-point from the domain of sexuality. One usually considers masturbation an imaginary sexual act, i.e. an act where bodily contact with a partner is only imagined; would it not be possible to reverse the terms and to think of the sexual act proper, the act with an actual partner, as a kind of 'masturbation with a real (instead of only imagined) partner'? The whole point of Lacan's insistence on the 'impossibility of a sexual relationship' is that this, precisely, is what the 'actual' sexual act is (let us just recall his definition of phallic enjoyment as essentially masturbatory)! And, as we have already seen, this reference to sexuality is far from being a simple analogy: the Real whose exclusion is constitutive of what we call 'reality', virtual or not, is ultimately that of woman. Our point is thus a very elementary one: true, the computer-generated 'virtual reality' is a semblance; it does foreclose the Real in precisely the same way that, in the dream of Irma's injection, the Real is excluded by the dreamer's entry into the symbolic bliss − yet what we experience as the 'true, hard, external reality' is based upon exactly the same exclusion. The ultimate lesson of virtual reality is the virtualisation of the very true reality. By the mirage of 'virtual reality', the 'true' reality itself is posited as a semblance of itself, as a pure symbolic construct. The fact that 'the computer doesn't think' means that the price for our access to 'reality' is also that something must remain unthought.

Notes

1 See Sigmund Freud, *Interpretation of Dreams*, Chapter II. Harmondsworth: Penguin Books, 1977.

2 'The Seminar of Jacques Lacan', *Book 11: The Ego in Freud's Theory and in the Technique of Psychoanalysis*. Cambridge: Cambridge University Press, 1988, pp. 154–155.

3 Ibid., p. 168.

4 Ibid., Chapter XXIII.

5 See Sherry Turkle, *The Second Self: Computers and the Human Spirit*. New York: Simon & Schuster, 1984.

6 See Douglas R. Hofstadter's cult book *Gödel, Esher, Bach: An Eternal Golden Braid*. New York: Basic Books, 1978.

7 Turkle offers here a rather naïve psychological interpretation: the subculture of the hacker is a culture of male adolescents who are running away from sexual tension into a world of formalised 'adventure', in order to avoid 'burning their fingers' with a real woman. Their attitude is inconsistent: they fear loneliness, at the same time being afraid of the approach of the other, woman, who because of her inconsistency is undependable; she can cheat, betray trust. The computer is a salvation from this dilemma: it is a partner; we are no longer alone, and at the same time it is not threatening, it is dependable and consistent.

THE UNCONSCIOUS DESTINY OF CAPITAL
(ARCHITECTURE IN VITRO/MACHINIC IN VIVO)

Karl S Chu *(Metaxy)*

The world in all the plurality of its parts and forms is the phenomenon, the objectivity, of the one will to life.[1]
Schopenhauer

Architecture, one of the last surviving remnants of classical thought, has finally arrived at the scene of bifurcation. No longer is it simply a question of extending the infinite linear time of modernity, the degraded culture of equivalence according to Nietzsche, into the distributive networks of global capitalism. Instead, this bifurcation, which is a consequence of the convergence of numerous developments in science, technology, politics, economy and globalisation in the last century, signifies an historical phenomenon in the making: the sublimation, if not the culmination, of the dialectics of the Enlightenment. The complex web of arguments and counterarguments concerning reason, history, tradition, faith, freedom and revolution promulgated by the discourse on Enlightenment will now move on to another plane of reference instantiating a whole new set of questions stemming from and extending beyond the construction of artificial life and abstract beings. In other words, we are in the midst of a paradigm shift and there is no name for it as yet. However, as a first approximation, I have elsewhere referred to this new condition as the Hyperzoic Paradigm since it entails the development of a neo-biological civilisation. From all indications, it will most likely lead to the transubstantiation and transmutation of everything within the orbit of the cultural universe of humanity into a living, organic, albeit machinic, body that is monadic in scope and in function. With the advent of the Universal Turing Machine, we have now begun to transform matter and energy into a new form of organic substance derived from bits by unraveling the Promethean fire locked within the creative matrix of physical reality, which so far has remained elusive and opaque if not wholly inaccessible. As a consequence, we are now entering into a completely artificial space, a parallel universe engendered by the dream of instrumental reason, which will appear, *prima facie,* to be entirely alienated from nature and human history. However, this new terrain may prove, paradoxically, in the final analysis, to be the most internal and intrinsic to nature itself. The assimilation of these developments into the cultural world has so far remained relatively impervious to the transformative power inherent within such an epigenetic propulsion: a truly radical intervention into the deep structure of modal space by bootstrapping the universe of architecture and launching it into the multiverse of possible worlds via genetic computation.

The internal logic of the Hyperzoic Paradigm responsible for such a propulsion is based on the productive synthesis of computation and biogenetics, both of which are now being hijacked by the capitalist system of axiomatisation. It provides the key that unlocks and points to the development of a parallel universe with profound ramifications unlike anything we have seen in the history of planetary evolution. This is a second order phase transition signified by the emergence of a new ontological realm of simulation, or virtual reality. As a consequence, it introduces a new plane of immanence transposed onto the cultural universe of humanity founded upon the terrestrial surface of Earth. Architecture has always been a theory of the surface of Earth. As such, it is a form of machinic *in vivo*, a mechanism for territorialisation and colonisation that alters the biography of the surface culture of Earth enveloped by the biosphere. In contrast, architecture in the sphere of simulation can be effectively thought of as architecture *in vitro,* i.e. inside the simulated glass of cyberspace or virtual reality even though it is sustained by hardware, at least at this stage, embedded within the physical architecture of machinic *in vivo*. Since it is theoretically possible to build computational devices at the atomic level, these nanomachines will eventually displace cumbersome hardware machinery. It would eventually give rise to intensive fields comprised of microcomputational monads endowed with both genetic and dynamical properties. At these scales, computational monads can and will, on the one hand, infiltrate into the human body to augment its internal system of information processing much like pharmaceutical pills invade and alter the molecular chemistry of the body. On the other hand, these monads can dynamically cluster themselves into swarms capable of transfiguring the spatio-dynamical aspects of reality including architecture. Such forms of computational monads will come into existence and transform the configuration space of both domains: architecture *in vitro* and architecture as machinic *in vivo*. These two spheres of fertilisation, which interact and exchange information, together form a single bionomic ecology, a mechanosphere engendered by and incorporated into the capitalist system of axiomatisation.

Capitalism, after having gone through various stages of development, is the only economy that has managed to become global. According to Ernest Mandel, the economist of scientific socialism, there have been three fundamental moments in capitalism, each one transforming the previous stage through dialectical expansion: market capitalism, monopoly capitalism, and the current phase, late capitalism. The stage that is about to come will transform and sublate its present form far more radically than ever into a neo-biological system of exchange: demiurgic capitalism. Whereas Mandel's formulation sees history driven by scientifically predictable laws of motion toward a socialist destination, demiurgic capitalism, on the contrary, even though influenced and enabled by scientific developments, is not pre-ordained to arrive at any specific form of socio-political organisation. The virtual economy of cyberspace, as the new arena of the global market place is now called, has already begun to revolutionise the mechanism of communication, exchange and production and will do so even more radically once capitalism saturates itself with the logic of genetic processes into its system.

The fundamental premise of capitalist axiomatisation, above and beyond the systemic regulation of an economic system, is the quest for Information Capital at all cost. Information is the currency of life. Even though information is integral to every paradigm, it is only now that information has acquired a biological orientation and is emerging as the new modus operandi. Some of the preliminary contours implicit within salient tendencies that have begun to emerge suggest the potential existence of a teleological function latent within capitalism, one that is neither based on theological foundations nor on the injunction of a manifest destiny. It nonetheless points to the presence of an inherent tendency toward self-organisation that could potentially lead toward some form of organic morphology, a capitalist macrocosm at the global level. Any system with an ecumenic ambition such as capitalism, although its excuse is merely economic and monetary, is not devoid of fundamental issues that are universal and existential in nature. It is only from the standpoint of its metaphysics that some of these issues, which are concealed within the dynamics of its configuration space, become apparent. Along this line, we can excavate two fundamental repressions of the first order, related to the quest for Information Capital, implicit within capitalism. The first is linked to the exchange value of abstract labour, or instrumental procedures, and the second is predicated on the range and intensity of use value derived from surplus enjoyment.

First and foremost, with the shift into the Hyperzoic Paradigm, one of the latent ambitions of capitalism has finally crystallised into the foreground: the transvaluation of all values into the surplus value of life. Through coding, decoding and recoding of genetic information, and subsequent appropriation of value on abstract labour or process required in the artificial production of life, especially in relation to the complexity and difficulty that it entails, and, subsequently, on the artificial life of architecture, be it that of *in vitro* fertilisation or genetic simulation via computation, the future of capitalism will be involved in the generative condensation and fabrication of artificial life forms at all scale within the fabric of the mechanosphere. This endeavour is based on the underlying premise of Artificial Life, which, according to Christopher Langhton[2], the founder of ALife, states that the origin of life is inherent within the structure of formal principles and not in carbon-based materials. Matter therefore is a simulacrum from such a formulation. Genetic computation, in its generality, does not rely explicitly on any pregiven model of representation even though the existence of abstract objects is tacitly affirmed. Its programmatic agenda is to systematically explore the space of permutations in order to arrive at self-organisation and, subsequently, the development and proliferation of artificial species. Three principles pertain to such a development: the Principle of Generative Condensation, the Principle of Combinatorial Expansion, and the Principle of the Conservation of Information. Let it suffice for the moment to say that a whole host of ethical issues will be raised by this and not the least of which is the master/slave relationship that Hegel along with numerous others have brought to light, both in philosophy and in commerce.

Beyond the production of artificial life and the constellation of problems that accompany such a grand enterprise, there is as yet a still deeper stratum of obscure intentions that lies hidden within capitalism: its metaphysical and theological aspirations which, with the rise of globalisation during the latter part of the twentieth century, has remained forgotten, if not construed as being irrelevant, and lay buried in the midst of massive proliferation and commodification of life world relations. Any system that relies on and taps into the deep reservoir of creative potential latent within the universe, at such a grand scale, in order to generate, sustain and expand its monadic ecology will eventually come to face questions of ontology pertaining to such a system within the larger context of the metaphysics of Being.

The consequence of these metaphysical ambitions, along with the transvaluation of artificial life and their ultimate realisation through recursive sublimation of Information Capital, will alter the functional matrix of normative capitalism into a demiurgic economy: an emergent phenomenon that will be a manifestation of the Unconscious Destiny of Capital. It signals the becoming alive of Capital, of embodying artificial life and intelligence within its infrastructure to become fully organic within the larger context of the cosmos. In other words, a cosmocapital organism. This is a phenomenon that is nothing less than a phenomenology of the spirit of universal information processing exploring through the labyrinthine universe of possible worlds, most of which are and will prove to be epistemically and ethically unfathomable to earthbound *homo sapiens* such as us. Such a transmutation of monadic agents and agencies within modal space will inevitably lead to the transubstantiation of the very spirit of human existence into a phenomenology of the artificial life of spirit: a machinic alchemy that is none other than universal simulation of symbiosis within the

Cosmocapital Organism. Correspondingly, the concrescence of this organon will signify the emergence of a new plane of immanence transposed onto the terrestrial surface of Earth: the eruption of the Turing Dimension within the ontological abyss of reality.

Having thus re-oriented and grounded in systems that are information-theoretic in origin, not to mention the fact that archiving and accounting technics are internal to computation, the quest for Information Capital will be informed and inspired by theoretical implications derived from computation itself: the insatiable need for ever more and more powerful algorithmic programs that could engender a maximum of possible effects and, by extension, possible worlds with the least number of bits. Less is more is a minimalist manifesto that is also the unspoken assumption of all algorithmic programming. One conclusion that could be drawn from this is the resulting quest for the Universal Code, a metacode that would entail the resurrection and modification of Leibniz's Principle of

This and following four pages: *X_Phylum,* © *Metaxy* (Karl S Chu)

Sufficient Reason[3] to encompass a theory of everything. Even though such an effort has been unequivocally proven to be futile by Gregory Chaitin with his Algorithmic Information Theory[4] – which also proved the random nature of mathematics, the demiurgic system of Capital, a mechanosphere composed of a machinic phylum of universal computing systems, will most likely persist, as unreasonable as it may seem, in the quest for the code without ever coming to a halt for reasons that are both theoretical and metaphysical. The so-called Halting Problem as discovered by Alan Turing states that it is not possible to know ahead of time whether a given program for computation will ever come to a halt or will continue forever. The only recourse is to let the system run and see what the ensuing output is at the end if there is one. Given such an undecidable and uncertain proposition, the search for the Universal Code – a metaphysical desire guided by faith in the possible existence of such a code – would be the equivalent of finding a software program having the power and function to generate a maximum of possible affects. Such an endeavour could be interpreted as a computational version of an allegorical performance, even though it may not be entirely motivated as such, that is at once emblematic of the metaphysical desire for the *Word* of God. This is especially true in the face of Kurt Gödel's Theory of Incompleteness and Undecidability which has once and for all shattered all notions of ontological sufficiency and completeness of Being.

Notwithstanding the profound gap that exist between the dream for hyper-compression of reality and ontological incommensurability derived from the limits of computation, the phenomenon of computation can still be effectively thought of as an engine of creation, one of the instrumental functions of Being *par excellence.* Given such a powerful mechanosphere, a capitalist monadology of computing systems, the quest for the Code, will prevail in one capacity sor the other. In the process, it will discover and archive a universe of nested codes, both cohesive and fragmentary, that will have the efficacy for the production of new forms of desire, and subsequent fulfilment of these desires in terms of communal ecstasy. Once these endeavours reached a level of self-organized criticality, the dynamic impulse within the cosmocapital organism will not cease its internal quest for the Code that would be responsible for the attainment of immortality. As unreasonable as it may seem, these aspirations are no longer considered to be far fetched since they are now within the speculative province of modern science. Capitalism, as a system that is predicated on the fulfilment of manufactured needs and desire, will not be immune to the metaphysics of desires. Therefore, the Will to Capital will be coextensive with the will to bring these aspirations and their subsequent achievements under the auspices of capitalist interest. More likely than not, capitalism will make sure that the value of abstract interest accrued is based on the use value derived from the kernel of surplus-enjoyment that is deeply buried within the medium of ecstasy, and, above all, the placement of abstract universal value on the production and maintenance of immortal life, be it that of human life or otherwise.

From the standpoint of this perspective, whose vanishing point is neither immanent nor transcendent – and this is yet another indication of the transgression beyond the discursive arena defined by the Enlightenment and modernity – the project of architecture, if we can call it such, is inextricably linked with the unconscious latent within Capital. With the emergence of this parallel universe, the conception of architecture has fundamentally changed. More than ever, it is now being perceived, along with the rest of reality, as the realm of virtual affects engendered by the universal abstract machine of Capital. As such, the realm of architecture is a simulacrum endowed with the latent capacity to simulate its own *in vitro* fertilisation within the universal model of computing systems. These are monadic singularities whose emissions are woven into the invaginated surface of the universe of the larger set that forms an incomplete totality. In other words, the world of architecture is part of the internal organ of the mechanosphere that functions as a machinic *in vivo* at the global level of the macrocosm. The internal reality within the kernels of this cosmocapital organism is constituted by the sum total of the superposition of all computational bandwidths, each of which oscillates, interferes, and comingles with adjacent frequencies in order to engender dynamic condensation of spectral layers composed of *infrareals*: combinatorial clusters of random codes that are pure virtualities latent with the capacity to evolve into genetic seeds or codes. As an organic entity, it will find itself perpetually engaged in the exfoliation of its potentiality from within itself as part of the metempsychosis of possible worlds, with its entire vicissitudes and, thus, pointing to a monadology of the absolute experience of reality. Within such an organon, micrological productions of architecture will be analogous to specific tunings into existence of microcosms out of the computational bandwidths of Being.

Reality therefore has become a form of machinic alchemy. Simulation of reality can now be understood as forming part of the search for theory concerning the Real. The experience of reality is the experience of simulation. The effects of simulation, in turn, are the experience and embodiment of theory: *in vivo* cultivation of the code within the body of architecture. Even though there is a degree of consonance with Jean Baudrillard's description of simulation as *'that of which it is possible to give an equivalent reproduction...,'*[5] the reality of simulation that is being discussed here is modal and infinitely more intense and variable than Baudrillard's exposition. Simulation, in its purest form, is a metronomic secretion from within the metaphysical black box of reality. Computation is a machinic incarnation of this black box. Therefore, it is not unlike *in vitro* fertilisation with in-put and out-put mechanisms, which establishes conditions of possibility for the biogenetic transmutation and incarnation of affects. Both theoretically and physically, the efficacy of computation relies on the efficacy of the Turing Principle[6], a reformulation of the Church/Turing Thesis by

David Deutsch, one of the physicists who opened the way for quantum computation. The Principle essentially states that there exists a universal model of computing system whose repertoire includes every physically possible environment. This is a delimitation of the Church/Turing Thesis which defines effective computability based solely on recursively enumerable systems without taking into consideration the physical limits of computation. The Turing Principle therefore is an astounding proposition that gives a certain degree of ontological sustenance to the reality of simulation based on the laws of physics. The concept of buildability, be it that of architecture or otherwise, is an extension of the logic of constructability, which is now reformulated as a function of computability. It can therefore be surmised that the universe of composability is infinitely larger than the universe of constructability defined by conventional notions of buildability, as it has been predominantly the case with architecture since time immemorial.

Notwithstanding the limits of computation, which have profound philosophical ramifications within the metaphysics of modality, the Turing Principle provides theoretical basis for the construction and composability of architecture. No longer is architecture to be construed as simply the art of putting two bricks together, as Mies van de Rohe once suggested; instead, it has become the art of arranging two bits, or qubits (quantum bits), together. Whereas all forms of modelling, including computer modelling, rely on the principle of entailment which makes reference back to a transcendent origin or the natural world, the process of simulation, contrary to its conventional understanding as a derivative form of imitation, does not rely on or entail any referential origin other than its internal system of monadic encoding, which is purely abstract. In other words, it is its own reality. It is free to explore combinatorial space of possibilities to engender various forms of self-organisation and does not merely function as a representation of nature. With evolutionary computation, whose realisation is immanent in the near future, these bits will recursively replicate, mutate and evolve to engender new forms of architectural species beyond our current capacity to imagine them. The universe, or rather, the multiverse of architecture as an expression of the Turing

Principle, therefore contains an infinity of schizo-phrenic cosmologies that have yet to come into existence. The conceptual seed for architecture, however, is already inherent within the episte-mological and, by extension, autoscopic definition of architecture: the conjoining of two Greek terms, archē (pertaining to underlying principles) and technē (technology, method, craft, etc.), refers implicitly to the metaphysics of world making or universal simulation potentially beyond mimetic conceptions of reality. As such, architecture has now begun to enter into a new ontological domain: the realm of universal simu-lation without the necessity to prove itself as buildable or to be subordinated to conventional notions of building. This is a consequence of the bifurcation of architecture that will once and for all radically transform our perception of world making into a modal conception of reality.

In summary, it can be said that the limits of Capital are coextensive with the limits of computation. Universal capitalism, in addition to being a neo-biological organism, is the attempt to search for and ultimately embody, through generative condensation of its internal economy, the demiurgic code of the universe. As such, the ghosts of Parmenides, Plato and Leibniz are still present within the cosmology of Capital. Ultimately, the Will to Ethics implicit within deconstruction must come to augment the Will to Power inherent within Capital in order to determine, by intervening into the deep struc-tures of capitalist axiomatisation, whether it evolves and develops into a demiurgic or a demagogic capitalism. Once again, the ghost of Marxian insight into the instrumental rationality of domination therefore will have to be kept alive within such a cosmocapital organism in order to allow for the currency of life to flow freely within its metabolic pathways. Either way, the emergence of Universal Capital will signify the formation of a new species in this remote corner of the Milky Way, which is but a miniscule spiralling organ, a machinic *in vivo* catalysed by capitalist enzymes from within the body of the physical universe.

Notes

1 Arthur Schopenhauer, *The World As Will And Idea* (The Everyman Library, The Guernsey Press Co, Ltd.), p.216.

2 Christopher G. Langton, 'Artificial Life' in *Artifical Life* (Santa Fe Institute Studies in the Sciences of Complexity, Addison-Wesley Publishing Co). According to Langton, biology concerned itself with the material basis of life, whereas, Artificial Life is concerned with the formal basis of life.

3 G. W. Leibniz, *Monadology* (tr. By Nicholas Rescher, Pittsburgh University Press, 1991). See Sections 32-37. Leibniz posits two kinds of truths, the truths of reason and the truths of fact. The analysis of necessary truths (of reason) is finite whereas the analysis of a sufficient reason for truths of fact is of unending complexity. Therefore, the final reason, according to Leibniz, must lie outside of the sequence of contingencies. Since computation is a physical activity, the search for the metacode would be akin to finding a sufficient reason for the truths of fact.

4 Gregory J. Chaitin, *The Limits of Mathematics* (Springer-Verlag, 1998), p. 18.

5 Jean Baudrillard, *Simulation* (Semiotext(e) Inc., 1983), p. 146.

6 David Deutsch, 'Quantum Theory, the Church-Turing Principle and the Universal Quantum Computer,' *Proc. R. Soc.* Lond. A400), p. 97-117 (1985).

ARCHITECTURE = SPACE = INTERFACE
Hani Rashid (Asymptote)

This page: New York Stock Exchange, digital model

For Asymptote the art and science of architecture are being radically influenced and inflected by new and uncharted concepts. In particular the advent of digital interfaces and the new spatial models that they are inspiring and spawning are forging new territories for architectural research and theory. The intersection of first reality (physical space) and virtual reality (digitally produced environments) has afforded Asymptote the opportunity to operate in areas that have traditionally excluded architects or within situations that have not necessarily engaged the discipline of architecture. These new areas include information-data environments, Web-based spatial experiences and 'real-time' technologically enriched environments.

Data, Information and Pixel Real-estate

In 1998 the New York Stock Exchange approached Asymptote with an intriguing problem. The NYSE had been developing a strategy for dealing with the ever-increasing complexity of managing data and information, and with that in mind they approached Asymptote with the task of developing a virtual reality environment that would facilitate the reading, correlating and quantifying of massive amounts of information. The NYSE determined that the complexity of the information that they contend with on a daily basis needed an innovative solution, one predicated on three-dimensional 'visualisation'.

This prompted the commission to design a robust computer simulated environment. As the project proceeded it became apparent that there were a number of architectural issues to deal with. First, one had to consider how to navigate through data, and that instigated an approach where the information would be a terrain or landscape. With that in mind form, iconography, composition and even memory became important protagonists and dictates for the architectural assemblies and entities that were developed. The design of the Virtual Trading Floor essentially began as a re-interpretation of the existing physical trading environment and through that exercise the floor was idealised and refined for virtual deployment. This was accomplished by developing a 'wireframe' model that actually corresponded to the 'real' trading floor in terms of its geographic constituent elements and particular attention was paid to accurate placement and location. The wireframe idealisation needed to provide absolute flexibility, particularly for the data feeds that would eventually be fed into it. The initial modelling also needed to permit constant shifts in scale, the insertion of numerous other kinetic models and objects and a number of other criteria related to real-time data inputs. The strategy to reconfigure the actual floor was necessary because of the technological demands placed on the model to function in real time, and the extremely large amount of

data to be revealed. Second, the project posed an interesting opportunity to reconsider the floor's 'reality'. The Asymptote version of the trading floor, although virtual and not intended to be constructed outside of a computer environment, is effectively a direction for a possible future trading environment where data exist in surfaces and the technology is merged into the architectural environment. The Virtual Trading Floor as designed by Asymptote is both a reflection of the existing trading environment as well as a 'desired' provocation for a new physical architecture. The scope of objects and assemblies that make up the virtual trading floor includes two facilities of computer servers and networks, as well as news and data feeds, and countless data mining capabilities. All of the information that is relevant to the NYSE and its daily activity of trades and transactions is mapped into this fully-navigable multi-dimensional environment. Although the VR environment was initially designed for the operation needs of the NYSE, the project has evolved to cater to other usages, including brokerage houses and, most recently, is being developed into a large scale internet initiative and a television broadcasting environment. These mutations and elaborations of the project have further architectural implications as the virtual realm slowly usurps the real trading floor as a 'place'. The fact that the general public will soon be able to navigate a virtual trading floor, check stocks news and valuations, make trades and meander about at will is unprecedented and begs the question as to what actually constitutes an architectural experience and presence? And further to that for those who do inhabit and 'know' the real floor, what new intimacy with the environment will be attained and how will that alter their understanding of what constitutes the architecture itself?

An Internet Museum

As part of the Guggenheim's architectural initiatives, Asymptote was commissioned in 1999 to design a new museum. What was completely unprecedented about the prestigious commission was that the site for the implementation of the new museum would not be a city but rather the

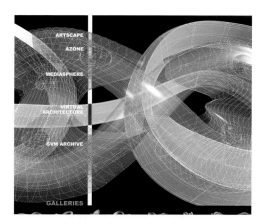

internet. Also the programme brief was completely new: a museum dedicated to digitally produced and archived art. Designing such a 'structure' posed a number of intriguing problems, particularly of what constitutes an event in such a place and what indeed would be an architectural experience and entity within the confines of cyberspace. The visual language, for example, although borrowed from architecture in respect to tectonics and form, needed to be more attentive to time-based experience and the prospects of mutation and transformation. This approach, although theoretically possible in actual building design, had far more potential in a terrain constituted of pixels and binary code. The possibility that such a museum could be visited by anyone, anywhere and at anytime was an exciting and provocative one, and this presented an interesting opportunity to develop a new type of interface and event for the internet and for architecture.

This page: Guggenheim Virtual Museum

The Guggenheim Virtual Museum (GVM) is essentially designed as an architectural entity to be primarily delivered over the internet. The 'museum body' itself is thought of as a mnemonic vessel; a catalogue which contains and provides access to information stored within it. Moving, or more appropriately navigating, through this museum was conceived in terms of a meander over a territory as opposed to either a room to room scenario or any sort of click-through model which is normally the case with Web environments. In opposition to such 'page-based' environments, an architectural experience is predicated on the notion that arbitrary discovery is as important as arriving and this served as the model which the virtual museum adhered to. Moving about these 'spaces' involves certain aspects of actual architectural experience that frame the experience, such as delay, path and other time-based experiences, while also drawing on filmic experiences such as jump cuts, fades, morphs and so on. The fusion of these 'spatial' paradigms allowed for the GVM to evolve as something closer to a landscape than an object or even place. This rethinking of movement and time, together with other unconventional approaches to programming, brought about another reading, that of the museum as evolving and fluid. The galleries, archives, public areas and even 'external landmarks' are all derived from and readings of 'first reality' situations and artefacts. However, their usage and occupancy are unlike that of any building experience. One can wander through a hall, then visit a gallery or watch a media event at the Mediasphere simultaneously and 'switch' instantaneously from one experience to another. The 'halls', for example, are fluid and morphing and their morphology and physical state are based upon the visitor's

various decisions in regard to certain preferences and decisions. The exhibition spaces themselves are not rooms *per se*, but rather evolving entities that continually reconfigure according to certain criteria regarding the contained artist's works. The Mediasphere, for example, is an elusive, ever-changing entity that orbits throughout the virtual museum and constantly inhabits some other region or precinct arbitrarily. This museum is an architecture where the parameters of the internet and its implicit digital flux are tempered by new potentials of occupying a landscape of space-time and transforming events.

The FLUXSPACE Projects

Recently Asymptote completed two FluxSpace installations in San Francisco (CCAC residency) and Venice, Italy (Venice Biennale 2000). The two projects were full-scale built works utilising digital technologies in both their design and manifestation. The aim of FluxSpace is to blur the distinction between actual and digitally augmented architectural constructs. FluxSpace 1.0 is about mid size somewhere between that of a large model or small building, and was modelled in the computer and constructed using full-size computer-generated templates. The computer model's accuracy to exacting specifications afforded us the opportunity to augment the 'architectural reality' of the project by manipulating the wireframe assemblies and projecting these transformations of the constructed objects into the gallery. This created the effect of a structure under a constant state of mutation and distortion in real-time and real-space. One could approach the free form object and, by passing a hand over its surface in certain locations, it would immediately respond by means of its electronic

This page: Guggenheim Virtual Museum

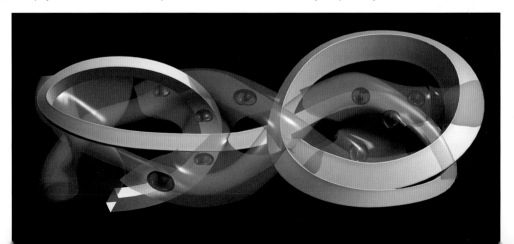

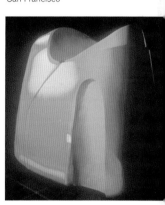

counterpart. An audio soundtrack that evolved accompanied each response from the same algorithmic structures that were being deployed to change the form's physical state. The thesis that architecture could respond to physical presence, by registering chance operations tied to a computer data feed, was implemented and tested in FluxSpace 1.0.

FluxSpace 2.0 sought to move the experiment into another direction, that of architecture as intermediary to an online or Web-based spatial experience. The project was somewhat larger than the San Francisco project, measuring 100ft in length and standing over two storeys high on the grounds of the Venice Biennale in the Giardini. The work utilised pneumatics to achieve its formal presence and a steel frame structure to define its free-form interior. The air-filled envelope sat upon a computer-modelled framework that dictated the morphology of the interior cavity. In the interior two large rotating discs, fabricated with one-way mirrors and measuring about 8ft in diameter, were located at two 'focal' points at opposite ends of the interior space. The semi-reflective, semi-transparent mirrors were able to fully pivot in place and housed at their centre two 360-degree cameras. These cameras recorded the ever-changing interior space and relayed that information to the internet. What was seen on the Web was an evolving architectural project in a constant state of flux. These cameras were able to record the interior condition of Flux2.0 at 30-second intervals for the duration of the five-month installation in Venice. FluxSpace 2.0 therefore generated 1.6 million different images of the interior condition and in this way the project was able to be virtually occupied. The project allowed us to develop a new comprehension and understanding of an architecture's virtual state, especially in terms of its geometry, spatiality, form and, above all, its constant state of augmentation.

Summary

Virtual architectural environments therefore hold the possibility of both augmenting real experience of physical spaces and environments while gaining a new-found autonomy and actually offering unique spatial experiences in and of themselves. The evolution of these soft architectures will be interesting to watch as we become increasingly involved in such endeavours. The ways architects choose to deal with such spatial, informational, formal and aesthetic concerns will be critical to the future design, implementation and significance of these types of project. It goes without saying that there is incredible potential here to develop and achieve new types of architecture, and redefine what actually constitutes space, architecture and event.

PLAN FOR NOW
Jeffrey Inaba (AMO)

The future is suspect. Forecasts promoting new technologies, changes to the profession, and lifestyle transformations require us to put faith in what has little weight. Inspired by fantasy, these claims about our 'e-destiny' feel overwrought with hearsay. Who can be so certain about the future in the midst of volatile and unpredictable change? Moreover, meditating on tomorrow turns attention away from the significance of uncertainties today. Instead of imagining future realities, AMO has chosen to explore current unknowns. AMO is obsessed with the present.

For us, the greatest dilemma to understanding the contemporary condition is the surplus of information. With more data, less is sure. The tremendous amount of available output cannot be translated into easy conclusions

Right: Culture: All Union Exhibition of Achievements of the National Economy, Moscow.

Below: Shopping: Display, Los Angeles.

since the methods, assumptions and reliability of material on any given topic vary widely. As a result, we at AMO are ill-suited to configure large scales of downloadable air into solid facts. This operation is further cursed by our interest in examining the present across a broad spectrum of phenomena. We are committed not only to investigating culture, but also areas of equal if not greater influence, such as shopping, the unofficial and business. The breadth and inconsistency of today's information, the non-correspondence of data among inherently different fields, combined with the rate of development of emerging social patterns, have necessitated that AMO internally rethink the nature of research. Meticulous, comprehensive data analysis cannot in itself establish an adequate account of what is here and now.

Out of urgency and necessity, AMO has adopted 'Tourism' as a means of inquiry. To complement our investigation of 'hard' facts, AMO has turned to intensive observation. Despite criticism that it is subjective and circumstantial, observation in the form of 'Tourism' is an invaluable vehicle to take in otherwise unattainable information from real world events. In this respect, we are willing to compromise critical detachment in exchange for the benefits of immediacy, objectivity for acute insight, and competency for acquired expertise. The concept of Tourism concedes that superficiality and adulteration are inevitable. At the same time, it announces that contamination is welcome. AMO is eager to take stock of mock realities. The more simulated the better.

Until recently, research has been regarded as the backwater of architecture. It has lagged behind design and theory in influence, having little direct impact on the field's direction. Today, turning the discipline's hierarchy on its head may aid in its revitalisation. An inversion of roles is starting to occur. Research rather than theory is being applied to assess the discipline's current state. Tasks previously used to examine the past are now adopted to formulate recommendations for the present: the historian's function of collecting, evaluating and

contextualising information is put in service to reanimate the creative mission of the designer. And knowledge generated from this undervalued specialty is one aspect of the discipline of increasing interest to an external audience.

AMO's project is to articulate the contemporary moment through analysis. It has extracted latent procedures of the profession, learned from working alliances, and retooled its own operations while knowing that the plan is entirely provisional. It is in this sense that AMO's plan for now is to simultaneously attend to the present and to remain open to contingency in forming its own approach. With each new realisation of the present, AMO redefines its agenda, organisation and methods of production.

Above: The Unofficial: Advertisement, Los Angeles.

Below: Business: Focus Group, Atlanta.

SKIM.COM
Ben van Berkel and Caroline Bos (UN Studio)

The concept proposal for Skim.com shop design strategy is based on the following principles:
• The offline/online interaction is central to the shop concept.
• Each shop is a recognisable Skim.com outlet but, unlike a chain, takes up local difference and leaves room for the individual identity of the shop's owner.
• The Skim.com shop is more than a shop; it is a lively and stimulating environment in which followers encounter a variety of cultural expressions compatible with their lifestyle,
such as fashion, music, art and entertainment. Thus the shop is also a gallery, it offers free internet access, at night turns into a lounge, and hosts facilities for playing music, to name but a few possibilities. This is a new step in retailing. The shop of the future articulates a more hybrid approach than ever before and, very importantly, both through its concept and design, signals its integrity to an increasingly sophisticated audience.

Analysis of Time-differentiated Global Network of Online/Offline Shops
The architectural research was premised on the notion that the Skim.com concept is in fact a 24-hour concept. Either online or offline Skim.com is always open and accessible – if not in New York, then in Matsuyama. To fully exploit this concept, there have to be Skim.com shops in different time zones. The shop strategy therefore points to a network of shops looped around the globe.

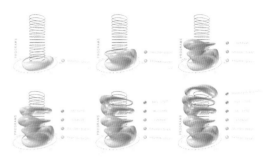

Definition of the Skim.com Platform: Local Differentiation within the Global Network
Making maximum use of the network of shops within the 24-hour concept implies promoting virtual and real circulation between the shops. Therefore differentiation between the various shops can be advantageous. In our vision there are seven categories of products and services that relate to the Skim.com concept and lifestyle, which can be disseminated through the shops. We propose that the local Skim.com outlets aim to specialise to some extent, to make the nodes in the network complementary to each other and thus promote customer movement (both real and virtual) from one shop to another. Only together the shops offer the full spectrum of products and services (global comprehensiveness). Individually their attractiveness resides in their special focus (local difference).

Categorisation of Retail Outlets on Three Scale-levels, Dependent upon Size and Extent of Hybridity
The scale levels refer to pre-set packages that are offered to potential retailers. Size plays a role in the choice of package, but also the vision of the individual retailer and the specific market in which the shop is positioned.

Online Presence
In order to emphasise the online presence the architectural concept entails large screens, not monitors. We recommend the webcam installations to be ceiling-mounted.

Articulation of Architectural Concept in Prototypical Shop Design
The shop concept is a mixture of fixed and free arrangements. The underlying thought is that

Top right: Programmatic Studies

Below: Furniture Studies

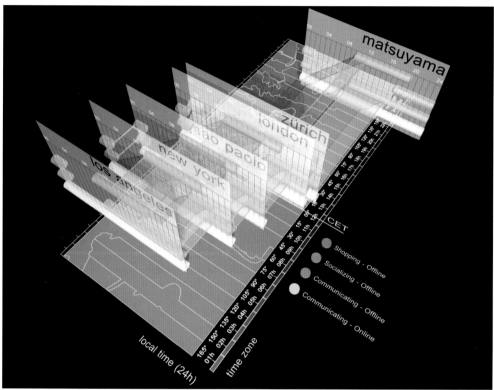

Left: Programmatic Studies
Below: Furniture Studies
Bottom: Layout

the concept should be easily adaptable in different circumstances. The architectural concept must accommodate various sizes, geographies, cobranded packages and atmospheres. There should be an element of recognisability, but also of difference and individuality. The elements that make up the architectural concept are:
• Technological equipment and its methods of storage/fixation: to be prescribed centrally and offered by Skim.com to retailers as a package.
• Background (i.e. wall and floor coverings): guidelines to be given, but essentially filled in locally.
• Furniture: specific pieces related to Skim.com concept such as cash deck/turntable, scales, dispatch unit are standardised and custom-built locally according to centrally distributed specifications. Again, local difference with respect to materials or size could be considered.
• Lighting fixtures: filled in locally with certain guidelines.
• Plug-in modules.

Plug-in Modules
The plug-in modules are furniture elements that are standardised in structure but which can be customised with regard to material. In this way, the appearance of the shops may be drastically different by applying a different type of front

panel to a standard unit. These pieces include the counter, display cabinets and changing rooms. All these elements are backless, so that when the shop changes function at night they can be shifted around and serve as storage units. The pieces may be mass-produced and could themselves be articles for sale, as might the specially designed toilet unit.

Chair
A signature piece of furniture designed by UN Studio is put in all the shops to function as the recognition factor. This is a flexible seating element that can be combined in different ways to accommodate the use of the space during shop and leisure hours.

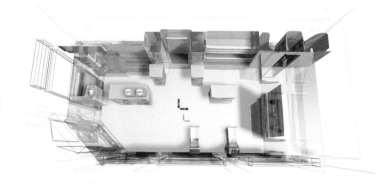

Contributor Profiles

David Turnbull

Christian Huebler

Andrew Gillespie

Neal Leach

Sadie Plant

Mark Goulthorpe

Richard Coyne

Sarah Chaplin is an architect and Senior Lecturer in Visual Culture and Media at Middlesex University where she set up the MA in Digital Architecture in 1998. She is also a Director of the design consultancy evolver. She is the co-author with John A Walker of *Visual Culture, an Introduction* (1997), and co-editor with Eric Holding of *Consuming Architecture* (1998).

Karl S Chu is an architectural theorist and an experimental practitioner. He teaches at both SCI Arc and Columbia University, and is Principal of the architectural studio *Metaxy*. His work is published in numerous architectural magazines worldwide, and he has taught and lectured extensively. He is currently involved in the research and development of a new meta-physics of architecture based on generative systems, which he refers to as the Hyperzoic Paradigm.

Richard Coyne is Head of the Department of Architecture at the University of Edinburgh. His recent publications include *Designing Information Technology in the Postmodern Age* (1995) and *Technoromanticism* (2001). He focuses on how the invention and usage of computers are woven into the fabric of human practices, and the theoretical and philosophical sources that support and attempt to counter the imperatives of praxis.

Mark Goulthorpe created the dECOi atelier in 1991 as a forward-looking architectural practice, whose design calibre was quickly established through winning entries in several international competitions, and with awards from cultural institutions around the world. This has been reinforced by numerous publications, international lectures and conferences, and frequent guest-professorships, including a design unit at the Architectural Association in London and the Ecole Spéciale in Paris.

Manuel DeLanda teaches at the Graduate School of Architecture at Columbia University, New York. He is the author of three philosophy books – *War in the Age of Intelligent Machines* (1991), *A Thousand Years of Nonlinear History* (1997), and *Intensive Science and Virtual Philosophy* (due 2002) – as well as of many philosophical essays published in various journals and collections.

Andrew Gillespie is Executive Director of the Centre for Urban and Regional Development Studies and Professor of Communications Geography at the University of Newcastle. His research interests focus on the implications of information and communications technologies for the development of cities, regions and rural areas.

Marcelyn Gow currently teaches a design research seminar with Greg Lynn on CNC fabrication at the ETH in Zürich. She is a member and co-founder of the research and design collaborative servo, and has exhibited and lectured in Berlin, London, Stockholm and New York.

Jeffrey Inaba is a principal of AMO, an architecture-based research office dedicated to conceptualising opportunities in contemporary culture. He also

Patrik Schumacher

William J Mitchell

Sarah Chaplin

teaches at Harvard University's Graduate School of Design and is writing on 1960s institutional environments by architects Gordon Bunshaft and Kevin Roche for a forthcoming book.

Knowbotic Research (KR+cF) is a media art group established by Yvonne Wilhelm, Alexander Tuchacek and Christian Huebler in 1991. Together they teach New Media at the University of Art and Design, Zurich, and experiment with formations of information, interface and networked agency. They have received several major international awards. They have published a CD ROM of the *IO_dencies* project, and their work has been featured in many publications.

Neil Leach teaches at the Architectural Association and the University of Bath, where he is

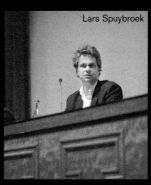
Lars Spuybroek

Professor of Architectural Theory. He is the author of *The Anaesthetics of Architecture* (1999) and *Millennium Culture* (1999); editor of *Rethinking Architecture* (1997), *Architecture and Revolution* (1999), and *The Hieroglyphics of Space* (2001); and co-translator of L B Alberti, *On the Art of Building in Ten Books* (1988).

William J Mitchell is Professor of Architecture and Media Arts and Sciences, and Dean of the School of Architecture and Planning at MIT. His publications include *E-topia* (1999), and *City of Bits* (1995).

Sadie Plant is a writer. She has held academic posts at the Universities of Birmingham and Warwick, and has published four books: *The Most Radical Gesture* (1992), *The Situationist International in the Postmodern World* (1992), *Zeros and Ones: Digital Women and the New Technoculture* (1998), and *Writing on Drugs* (1999).

Alejandro Zaera Polo and **Farshid Moussavi** established Foreign Office Architects in 1993. They have taught for many years at the Architectural Association, and have held numerous visiting appointments elsewhere. Their designs have been exhibited throughout the world, and their writings published in *Quaderns*, *El Croquis* and *Architectural Design*. A monograph on their work was published by Editorial Gustavo Gili in 2000.

Hani Rashid is, along with Lise Anne Couture, a founding partner of New York firm Asymptote.

Hani Rashid

The practice is involved in architectural design at all scales, including furniture, interior, building and urban design, but also extends into the realms of digital environments and installations. Rashid is an Adjunct Associate Professor of Architecture at Columbia University, New York. He was one of two US representatives who exhibited in the American Pavilion during the Venice Biennale 2000.

Douglas Rushkoff is the author of eight best-selling books about media, technology and society, including *Cyberia* (1994), *Media Virus* (1996), *Children of Chaos* (1997), *Coercion* (2000) and the novels *Ecstasy Club* (1997) and *Bull* (2001). His works have been translated into 15 languages. He is a regular

Douglas Rushkoff

Manuel DeLanda

Farshid Moussavi

Karl S Chu

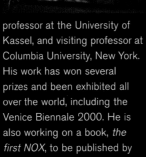

Marcelyn Gow

commentator on National Public Radio, an internationally syndicated columnist, and a Professor at New York University.

Patrik Schumacher is co-director of the Design Research Laboratory at the Architectural Association School of Architecture in London. Since 1988 he has been working with Zaha Hadid in London. His writings have appeared in various European journals, including *AA Files*, *ARCH+* and *Daidalos*.

Lars Spuybroek is principal of NOX, an architectural practice based in Rotterdam. He is a

professor at the University of Kassel, and visiting professor at Columbia University, New York. His work has won several prizes and been exhibited all over the world, including the Venice Biennale 2000. He is also working on a book, *the first NOX*, to be published by Thames and Hudson.

Sherry Turkle is Abby Rockefeller Mauz Professor in Science, Technology, and Society at MIT. She is the author of *Psychoanalytic Politics* (1978), *The Second Self* (1984) and *Life on the Screen* (1995). Dr Turkle's current research is about the psychological impact of computational objects, from 'affective computers' to robotic dolls and pets.

David Turnbull is a director of ATOPIA and Professor of Architecture at the University of Bath. He has also been visiting professor at Yale University and the University of Toronto. He is particularly interested in changing lifestyles and the way that individual buildings and new patterns of development respond to the impact of telecommunications and digital media.

Ben van Berkel and **Caroline Bos** set up Van Berkel & Bos Architectuurbureau in 1988. Ten years later they established a new firm, UN Studio (United Net), which presents itself as a network of specialists in architecture, urban development and

infrastructure. They have taught at many architecture schools around the world. Central to their teaching is the inclusive approach of architectural works integrating virtual and material organisation and engineering constructions.

Slavoj Žižek is a Professor at the Institute for Sociology, University of Ljubljana. Politically active in the alternative movement in Slovenia during the 1980s, he was a candidate the presidency of the Republic of Slovenia in the first multiparty elections in 1990, and was Ambassador of Science there in 1991. His writings have been published widely twelve languages. Recent books include *The Ticklish Subject* (2000), *On Belief* (2001), *The Fragile Absolute* (2001) and *Did Somebody Say Totalitarianism?* (2001).